A DICTIONARY OF
LINGUISTICS

A

DICTIONARY

OF

LINGUISTICS

MARIO A. PEI
Columbia University

AND

FRANK GAYNOR
Contributing Editor, *Britannica World Language Dictionary*

PHILOSOPHICAL LIBRARY
New York

GIFT OF NATHAN LYONS
2017

Preface

Grammatical terminology, based upon the prescriptive principles of Classical grammarians and the well-defined structure of the Indo-European languages, has been traditional since the days of ancient Greece.

The largely historical linguistic discipline evolved in the course of the 19th century led to the creation of a considerable body of terms used to describe changes of a diachronic nature.

It remained for the 20th century, with its emphasis upon synchronic, descriptive and structural linguistics, to evolve another, abundant terminology which is, even at the present moment, in a state of flux, with new terms being created and existing terms being either discarded or redefined and reinterpreted.

There is obvious need for a work of reference that will present, with simplified definitions, at least the more commonly used and accessible terms in vogue among those who devote themselves to linguistic pursuits.

Accordingly, the editors have endeavored to compile a dictionary that will include:

a) the general run of traditional grammatical terms, even though they already appear in standard dictionaries and works of reference;

b) the more frequently used terminology of the field of historical linguistics, as it is used in the manuals of the last century and a half;

c) that portion of the terminology of modern descriptive linguistics concerning which there is some measure of agreement among its users;

d) the names, affiliations, and very brief descriptions of the major languages and dialects of the world, both past and present.

This work makes no pretense whatsoever of being either definitive or exhaustive. The field of linguistic terminology changes from day to day, and new terms are continually being coined and introduced. The definitions themselves are far from exhaustive, since the ramifications of many terms would call for treatment in an encyclopedia rather than a dictionary of linguistics. It is expected that numerous revisions will be in order from time to time; therefore the editors earnestly request that reviewers and users of this volume will call to their attention omissions and inaccuracies, and voice suggestions for desiderata and addenda.

At the same time, it is expected that this work will serve a very useful practical purpose. Being, for the present, the only one of its kind in the English language, it will be a handy work of reference for students and workers in the allied fields of grammar and language study, philology and historical linguistics, phonetics, phonemics and structural linguistics. Here, for the first time, gathered in one handy volume, will be found definitions of terms which have heretofore appeared in scattered books and in the pages of many different linguistic periodicals.

The teacher of modern or Classical languages who has been puzzled by the use of certain terms occasionally appearing in the writings of the specialists will find here at least a partial interpretation of those terms. The philologist whose terminology was derived mainly from Leskien, Brugmann, Hirt, Meillet and Meyer-Lübke will be able to trace some of the usages of his descriptive colleagues, while the latter, who in their enthusiasm for a newly developed field have largely neglected the older works, will be able to refresh their memories. All will be aided by finding in a single volume brief scientific descriptions of little-known languages whose names keep appearing in the literature of the linguistic field.

The editors wish to express their heartfelt appreciation to all those who have aided them in their work, and in particular to Professor Urban T. Holmes, Jr., of the University of North Carolina, who went over the entire manuscript in proof and offered many valuable comments and suggestions, and to Dr. Eugene Dorfman of the Department of General and Comparative Linguistics of Columbia University, who contributed the major portion of the entries dealing with the recent terminological innovations of the descriptive-structuralist school of linguistics.

References

(*Unless otherwise indicated, when the names of the following authors are mentioned in the Dictionary, they constitute references, respectively, to the books listed below.*)

Bally, Ch.: Linguistique Générale et Linguistique Française. (A. Francke, S. A., Berne, 1950.)

Bloomfield, L.: Language. (Henry Holt & Co., New York, 1933.)

Bodmer, F. and *Hogben, L.* (ed.): The Loom of Language. (W. W. Norton & Co., Inc., New York, 1944.)

Diringer, D.: The Alphabet—A Key to the History of Mankind. (Philosophical Library, New York, 1948.)

Gelb, I. J.: A Study of Writing. (University of Chicago Press, Chicago, 1952.)

Graff, W. L.: Language and Languages. (D. Appleton & Co., New York and London, 1932.)

Gray, L. H.: Foundations of Language. (The Macmillan Co., New York, second printing, 1950.)

Harris, Z. S.: Methods in Structural Linguistics. (University of Chicago Press, Chicago, 1951.)

Jespersen, O.: Language, Its Nature and Development. (George Allen & Unwin, Ltd., London, 9th impression, 1950.)

Marouzeau, J.: Lexique de la Terminologie Linguistique—Français, Allemand, Anglais, Italien. (Librairie Orientaliste Paul Geuthner, Paris, 1951.)

Meillet, A.: Les Dialectes Indo-européens. (Librairie Ancienne Edouard Champion, Paris, 1950.)

Pei, M. A.: The World's Chief Languages. (S. F. Vanni, New York, 1946.)

de Saussure, F.: Cours de Linguistique Générale. (Payot, Paris, 1949.)

Swan's: Swan's Anglo-American Dictionary (Scott, G. R., ed.). (Library Publishers, New York, 1952.)

Sweet, H.: A New English Grammar. (The Clarendon Press, Oxford, 1900.)

Weseen, M. H.: Cowell's Dictionary of English Grammar and Handbook of American Usage. (Thomas Y. Crowell Co., New York, 1928.)

A DICTIONARY OF
LINGUISTICS

A

Abakan: An Asiatic language; a member of the Eastern Turkic group of the Altaic sub-family of the Ural-Altaic family of languages.

abbreviation: (1) A short written symbol for a full word or expression (*etc.* for *et cetera; e.g.* for *exempli gratia*, meaning *for example*).—(2) A synonym for *shortening* (q.v.).

aberrant: Deviating from the normal or average.

abessive: A Finno-Ugric declensional case, having the same connotation as the English preposition *without*.

Abkaz: A language (also referred to as *Abkhasian*) spoken in the Caucasus; a member of the Western branch of the North Caucasian family of languages.

Abkhasian: See *Abkaz*.

ablative: That case of a noun, adjective, pronoun or numeral denoting the source, agent or means, occasionally also time or place, of an act or occurrence. (In Latin, also used after certain prepositions.)

ablative absolute: A Latin grammatical construction, consisting of the ablative case of a noun or nouns or pronoun or pronouns and an adjective or participle which have no grammatical connection with the rest of the sentence in which the expression as a unit constitutes an interpolated entity.

ablaut: A vowel gradation (q.v.), characteristic of Indo-European languages, denoting distinctions in meaning (e.g., different tenses of a verb).—Also called *apophony*.

abnormal vowel: A designation applied in English phonetical terminology to a vowel representing an intermediate sound between a front and a back vowel. (E.g., the German *ö* [ø], the

3

French *u* [y], the vowel sound in the English word *but* [ʌ], etc.)

abridged clause: A clause without a finite verb form, such as an infinitive or participial clause.

Abruzzese-Neapolitan: A generic term for a group of south Italian dialects spoken in southern Latium, Abruzzi, Campania, Lucania and Puglia, and generally characterized by loss of clarity of the final vowels and umlaut distinctions in the root vowels.

absolute: Considered in and for itself (e.g., *absolute form*), or constituting a self-sufficient entity (e.g., *absolute ablative*).

absolute ablative: See *ablative absolute*.

absolute adjective: An adjective used as a substantive. (E.g., "The *meek* shall inherit the earth.")

absolute case: The case in which a noun is said to be when it is the subject of a sentence but is grammatically isolated from the other sentence-elements. (E.g., in Japanese, this case is usually formed by placing the particle *wa* after the noun.)

absolute construction: A construction no element or part of which is linked grammatically to the rest of the sentence. (E.g., *absolute ablative.*)

absolute form: The basic, uninflected, phonetically and morphologically unchanged form of a word as it appears when detached from context, i.e., when spoken alone. (Cf. *sandhi-form.*)

absolute position: In phonetics, the position had by a word, phrase or another linguistic form (q.v.) when it constitutes a sentence without being a part of a larger linguistic form.

absolute superlative: A superlative used to denote a high degree of a quality, without indicating or implying comparison.

absorption: The suppression of a sound or its incorporation into an immediately following or preceding sound.

abstract noun: A noun denoting a quality or characteristic in general.

abstract term: In general, any term, word or expression which denotes a notion, concept, idea, in contradistinction to a *concrete term* (q.v.).

accent: (1) The *stress* (q.v.) with which a certain syllable of a given word is pronounced, in comparison with the other syllables of the same word.—(2) Short for *accent mark* or *written accent* (see *diacritic mark*).—(3) Cf. *pitch*.

accentuation: The laying of vocal stress on certain parts of a word or phrase. Graff calls it "accent as a flowing feature of speech."

accidence: (1) The inflectional changes of words, to denote various cases, tenses, numbers, etc. of the same word. —(2) That branch of grammar which treats of these changes.

accommodation: The partial assimilation (q.v.) of a phoneme, in which the assimilated phoneme takes over just one of the characteristics of the assimilatory phoneme.

accommodative aspect: See *benefactive aspect*.

accusative: In Indo-European languages, that case of a noun, adjective, pronoun or numeral denoting that the word in question is the object of the sentence. (Also used after certain prepositions.)

Achaean: One of the western dialects of ancient Greek.

acoustic: Relating to sound and sound perception.

acoustic features: The features of sound in any given utterance, as they are or may be recorded experimentally. (Also called *gross acoustic features*.) These features may have a bearing on meaning and thus be essential to communication by speech (*distinctive* acoustic features) or have no bearing on meaning and clarity of communication (*non-distinctive*).

acoustic phonetics: The study of the sound-waves produced when sounds are uttered. A branch of *experimental* or *laboratory phonetics*.

acrophonetic writing: A method of writing, employing signs which were originally *ideographs* (q.v.) but have come to be phonetic signs, representing the initial sound of the object which they depict.

acrophony: The employment of the pictorial representation of an object as the phonetic sign of the initial sound or syllable of the name of that object.

action noun: Any noun naming an action.

active case: See *ergative case.*

active verb: (1) A transitive verb (q.v.).—(2) A verb used in the active voice (q.v.).

active voice: The conjugational form denoting that the grammatical subject of the sentence is the performer of the action expressed by the verb.

actor-action-goal: The sequence of forms in languages like English where word order normally indicates or marks grammatical relationships; compare 'The man bit the dog' and 'The dog bit the man', where the action remains the same, though the meaning is reversed, since actors and goals have changed position.

actualization: The perceptible result of the articulation of the phonemic variants or of the *archiphoneme* (q.v.). Also called *realization.*

acute accent: The diacritic mark ['], placed over a vowel to indicate the correct sound in pronunciation; occasionally used (e.g., in Spanish) as a mere orthographic mark, without affecting the pronunciation, or to indicate the accented syllable.

adaptation theory: The theory that flexional endings originally were stem formatives. (*Ludwig*)

additive clause: A clause which adds something to the main clause, without modifying or restricting the idea expressed in the latter.

adessive: A Finno-Ugric declensional case, having the same denotation as the English preposition *at* or *near.*

adherent adjective: Attributive adjective (q.v.).

aditive case: In Basque, a declensional case, having the same denotation as the English preposition *toward.*

adjectival clause, etc.: See *adjective clause*, etc.

adjective: A word used to describe, qualify or modify a substantive.

adjective clause: A clause that is used, in the same manner as an adjective, to modify a substantive.

adjective numeral: A numeral used as an adjective.

adjunct word: A modifier.

adnominal: Relating or belonging to a noun.

adstratum: A term used occasionally, especially in Romance linguistics, as a synonym of *superstratum* (q.v.).

adverb: A word which modifies a verb or adjective or another adverb.

adverbial: Having the nature or function of an adverb.

adverbial clause: A clause that is used, in the same manner as an adverb, to modify a verb, adjective or adverb.

adverbial expression: Two or more words which, as a unit, have the function of an adverb.

adverbial modifier: Any word, group of words, or sentence, which modifies a verb, an adjective or an adverb.

adversative conjunction: A dissociative conjunction (q.v.) serving to express a contrast. (E.g., *but*.)

Adyghe: A language-group of the Western Caucasian branch of the North Caucasian family of languages; it comprises Circassian (or Cherkess) and Qabardi.

Aequian: One of the extinct dialects of the Sabellian branch of the Italic group of the Indo-European family of languages.

affinity: With reference to language, structural similarities or analogies which converge from different origins. The term has been used also to mean "common origin."

affirmative conjunction: A conjunction (q.v.) serving to introduce a word or word-group or clause which adds to or confirms the meaning of a previous word or word-group or clause.

affix: A collective term for *prefixes, suffixes* and *infixes* (q.v.).

affricate: In phonetical terminology, a sound articulated as a *stop* (q.v.) with a sharp homorganic fricative release. (Also called *semi-plosive*.)

Afghan: An alternative name of the *Pushtu* (q.v.) language.

Afghan Mongol: A near-extinct member of the Mongol branch of the Altaic sub-family of the Ural-Altaic family of languages.

African: A collective designation of the three families of languages spoken in Africa: Sudanese-Guinean, Bantu, Hottentot-Bush-man.

Afrikaans: A Dutch dialect, characterized by great simplicity of grammatical forms, spoken in the Union of South Africa.

age and area theory: A theory propounded by Bartoli in 1928, setting forth and explaining the influence and effects of sub-merged linguistic substrata and of the speech habits of neigh-boring, co-existent language areas and speech communities on a given language.

agent: The doer of an action; the person or thing performing or responsible for the performance of the action expressed by the given verb.

agent-noun; agential noun: Any noun that names the agent of an action.

agglutination: In general, the addition to a word or root of suf-fixes for the purpose of expressing grammatical categories and relationships, syntactical function, etc., and resulting in an easy-to-analyze organic unit. (Cf. *agglutinative language.*)

agglutinative language: A language which combines into a single word various linguistic elements, each of which has a distinct, fixed connotation and a separate existence. (E.g., the Finno-Ugric languages, Turkish, etc.)

Aghul: A language spoken in the Caucasus; a member of the Samurian branch of the Eastern group of the North Caucasian family of languages.

Agnean: See *Tokharian.*

agreement: See *grammatical agreement.*

Ahom: An extinct Siamese (*Shan*) dialect, surviving to a certain extent as the sacred language of a very small group.

Ainu: A language spoken by about 20,000 persons in Japan. While considered linguistically unrelated to any other known lan-guage, it is classified as a member of the *Hyperborean* or *Palaeo-Asiatic* group of languages (a geographical rather than a linguistic classification).

Akkadian: An extinct Semitic language, the only known repre-sentative of the Eastern branch of the Semitic group of languages, known to have been spoken in Mesopotamia from 2800 B.C. to the first century B.C. *Old Akkadian*, 2800-650 B.C., is called *Assyrian; New Akkadian*, after 650 B.C., is referred to as *Babylonian*. (*Assyro-Babylonian* is a term formerly generally used instead of *Akkadian*.)

Albanese: See *Albanian*.

Albanian: A member of the Indo-European family of languages, the native tongue of approximately 1,500,000 persons in Albania. Its two principal dialects are: *Gheg* and *Tosk*.

Alemannic: A Germanic dialect which became extinct about 1000 A.D., and which, with Bavarian and Lombard, developed into *High German* (q.v.).

Aleut: See *Eskimo-Aleut*.

Algonkin: See *Algonquian*.

Algonquian: A family of North American Indian languages, also called *Algonkin* or *Algonquin*, consisting of six surviving groups: *Eastern* (Central and Eastern Canada), *Central* (the Great Lakes region), *Californian* or *Ritwan*, *Blackfoot* (Alberta, Canada), *Cheyenne* (Montana) and *Arapaho* (Montana, Wyoming and Oklahoma).

aljimiado: Cf. *Mozarabic*.

allative: A declensional case used in various languages (e.g., Finnish, Eskimo, etc.), having the same denotation as the English preposition *toward*.

alliteration: The recurrence of the same initial sound or letter (or group of sounds or letters) in succeeding words.

allogram: A term used by I. J. Gelb, to designate "logographic, syllabic, or alphabetic signs or spellings of one writing when used as word signs or even phrase signs in a borrowed writing."

allomorph: A positional variant of a morpheme occurring in a specific environment. (E.g., *am* is an allomorph of *be*, occurring in the environment of *I*.)

allophones: The several variants of speech sounds, which constitute a phoneme (q.v.).

alogisms: Harold E. Palmer's term for the linguistic devices or *markers* (q.v.), such as word order, intonation, affixation (qq.v.) which may be used to indicate the concepts of time, number, relation, etc.

alphabet: The written characters of a language, in their conventional order, each representing a sound or combination of sounds, exclusive of ideograms or logograms and syllable-signs.

alphabetic writing: The act or method of representing, or the representation itself, of ideas, words and spoken language by signs, each of which normally represents isolated and individual sounds or phonemes or certain groups of sounds or phonemes, although occasionally also digraphs or trigraphs (qq.v.) are used.

Altai: A language spoken in Western Asia; a member of the Eastern Turkic group of the Altaic sub-family of the Ural-Altaic family of languages.

Altaic: (1) A sub-family (also called Turco-Tartaric or Turkish) of the Ural-Altaic family of languages. It consists of three main branches: Turkic, Mongol and Manchu or Tungus. The linguistic characteristics of the languages of this sub-family are: very high degree of agglutination and synthetic construction, and vowel harmony (q.v.). Some linguists consider Mongol and Manchu distinct sub-families of the Ural-Altaic family, and consider only the members of the Turkic group as the true Altaic languages; hence the alternative designation *Turkish* for the Altaic sub-family.—(2) An alternative designation of the Eastern group of the Turkic branch of this sub-family.

alternants: The modified forms in which *markers* (q.v.) of the same grammatical category may appear; as in the differing articulation of "hat-*s*", "cad-*s*", "fish-*es*", where they are phonetic, *regular* and automatic; in "die, dice", "child-ren", "oxen", where they are *irregular;* in "sheep-", "deer-", where they are *zero alternants;* and in languages like Latin and German, where they are not *phonetic,* but *grammatical.*

alveolar: In phonetical terminology, a consonant pronounced with the tongue touching the gum above the upper teeth. (E.g., [s], [z].) Also called *post-dental.*

alveolo-palatal: In phonetical terminology, a consonant pronounced with the tongue held between the ridge behind the upper teeth and the front part of the hard palate.

amalgamating language: A flexional language in which the affixes are intimately fused with the roots of the words and do not possess or retain independent identity.

ambiguous: Indefinite; capable of being understood in more than one way.

amelioration: The gradual betterment in the meaning of a word; e.g., "knight", which originally meant "youth", "servant", or "man-at-arms", has come to mean a person of a certain rank conferred by royalty.

American English: The variety of English spoken in the United States of America, extending into Canada. It is subdivided generally into three main dialects: Eastern, Southern, and Midwestern or General American.

American Indian languages: The indigenous languages of the Western hemisphere, many of which became extinct during the past two or three centuries. The number of their speakers is estimated to total about 16,000,000, of which about 250,000 live in the United States and Canada. These languages have different structures (although a great many of them are polysynthetic [q.v.]), so that the affinity among many of the language-groups or families is questionable. Many of them are insufficiently known, so that a precise classification is impossible. Rivet (*Les langues du monde*, 1924, pp. 597-712) lists 25 language-families with 351 languages for North America, 20 families with 96 languages for Mexico and Central America, and 77 families with 783 languages for South America and the Caribbean. Other authors (e.g., Kieckers, in *Die Sprachstämme der Erde*, 1931, pp. 169-230) mention widely divergent numbers of languages and families. The most important recognized language-families are: (*1*) *United States, Canada and Mexico*: Algonkin or Algonquian, Athapascan (which according to Rivet is the member of a greater unit, the Na-Dene group, including Haida and Tlingit), Iroquoian or Iroquois, Mushkogee or Mushkogean, Siouan or Sioux, and Uto-Aztecan (which, according to Rivet, includes the Nahuatlan group, a member of which, Aztec or Nahuatl, was the language of an ancient civilization); (2) *Central America*: Mayan (a member of which, Maya, was the language of another ancient culture), and Zapotec; *(3) South America and the Caribbean:* Araucan, Aymará, Arawak, Carib, Quechua or Kechua (the language of the Inca empire), and Tupi-Guaraní.

Americanism: A word, expression or grammatical or syntactical form or construction which is peculiar to or characteristic of English as spoken in the U.S.A., or which is not in current use outside of the U.S.A.

Amharic: A language belonging to the Ethiopic sub-group of the Southern West Semitic languages, the daily vernacular of approximately 3,000,000 persons in Ethiopia.

Amina: See *Twi*.

amplificative: See *augmentative*.

anacolouthon: The interruption and new beginning in the middle of an utterance. (E.g., "I suppose you—anyway, it's no use.")

anagram: A word, name or phrase formed by transposition of the letters of another.

analogical creation: The derivation of words or word-forms on the analogy of a number of existing similar words or word-forms.

analogical extension: The modification of the form (cf. *morphological extension*) or meaning (see *semantic extension*) of a word on the basis of analogy with or imitation of existing or widely used patterns.

analogical form: A form or construction made on the pattern of several others, according to a determined rule or law.

analogue: A word in a language which corresponds to a word in another language is said to be the analogue of the latter.

analogy: The tendency or process of modifying or creating words on existing patterns.

Analphabetic Notation: Jespersen's system of phonetic transcription, using Greek letters and Arabic numerals, with Latin letters as exponents.

analysis: The act or process of splitting something into its component parts. Specifically, the use of separate words or particles to replace inflectional endings. (E.g., the use of *habeo* in Vulgar Latin *amare habeo,* to replace the classical Latin *amabo.*)

analytic, analytical: Pertaining to or constituting an *analysis* (q.v.).

analytic language: A language in which auxiliary words are the chief or sole means of expressing grammatical relationships of words, to the total or partial elimination of inflection.

anaphoric word: Jespersen's term for a word which refers to a word already said or written. (The word *one* in the phrase "I have a green hat, he has a black *one*" is a typical example.)

anaptyctic vowel: A vowel interpolated in a word for euphony or to facilitate pronunciation. (E.g., the interpolation of the *i* in the Italian *lanzichenecco,* which is a borrowed form of the German *Landsknecht.*)

anaptyxis: The development of an interpolated vowel (vocal glide) in a word, for euphony or to facilitate pronunciation.

Anatolian: A dialect of the Southern Turkic group of the Altaic sub-family of the Ural-Altaic family of languages.

Andalusian: The dialect of southern Spain (Andalusia), an outgrowth of Castilian.

Andamanese: A family of languages, without demonstrable affinities to other language groups or families, spoken in the Andaman Islands (in the Bay of Bengal). It is divided into *Great Andamanese* (consisting of Ba, Chari, Kora, Yeru, Juwoi, Kede, Kol and Puchikvar, forming the northern subgroup, and Bale and Bea, which form the southern subgroup), and *Little Andamanese* (Önge and Yärava). These languages are characterized phonologically by the absence of *s* and all fricatives, grammatically by a very intricate system of prefixes and suffixes, an animate and an inanimate gender and a very elaborate class-system. They have separate numerals only for *one* and *two;* counting from three to ten can be done only by showing the required number of fingers, and no counting above ten is possible.

Andi: A language spoken in the Caucasus; a member of the Avaro-Andi branch of the Eastern Caucasian group of the North Caucasian family of languages.

Anglian: A collective term for the Northumbrian and Mercian dialects of Anglo-Saxon (Old English).

Anglic: An international auxiliary language proposed by Zachrisson in the early part of the 20th century, based largely on phonetically spelled English.

Anglo-American: The designation preferred by many modern linguists and authors to the term *English* when referring to the modern form of English as a world-wide unit.

Anglo-Frisian. A sub-division of the West Germanic branch of the Germanic group of languages; it consists of Anglo-Saxon, with its modern descendant, English, and Frisian. (The original Anglo-Frisian speech area is usually referred to as *Ingweonic.*)

Anglo-Indian: A vernacular developed by British soldiers, officials and civilians stationed or residing in India. (Also called *Hobson-Jobson.*)

Anglo-Norman: The Norman dialect of Old French as used in England from the time of the Norman conquest to the end of the 13th century. Many of the greatest works of Old French literature were written in this dialect.

Anglo-Saxon: The parent of modern English (450-1100 A.D.), also called *Old English,* a member of the West Germanic branch of the Germanic group of the Indo-European family of languages.

Annamese: (1) A language spoken, with its numerous related dialects, in Annam, a member of the Annamese-Muong branch of the Austro-Asiatic family of languages. Also called *Vietnamese.* —(2) Often used as the designation of the entire *Annamese-Muong* branch of the Austro-Asiatic family.

Annamese-Muong: A branch of the Austro-Asiatic family of languages, spoken in and around Annam; it consists of Annamese (or Vietnamese) and Muong, each with a number of dialects.

anomaly: Deviation from the norm; irregularity.

antecedent: Grammatically, in general, any word to which a word occurring later in the sentence refers; specifically, a substantive to which a pronoun, occurring later in the discourse, refers is said to be the antecedent of that pronoun. (E.g., in the phrase "The man who came," *man* is the antecedent of *who*.)

antepenult: The third syllable from the end of a word, i.e., the syllable immediately before the *penult*.

anticipation: (1) In phonetics, the effect of a phoneme on a preceding phoneme, in that the vocal organs prepare for pronouncing the second phoneme even while uttering the first one.—(2) See *prolepsis*.

antonomasia: The substitution of a generic term or class designation, or of an adjective of quality, for a proper name; also the use of a proper name as a generic term.

antonym: A word which means the opposite of another.

anvil: See *hammer and anvil*.

Anzanite: See *Elamite*.

aorist: A term, borrowed from Greek grammar, denoting a tense which expresses action, usually past, where the time is indefinite or unimportant.

aoristic: Having the characteristics or connotations of the aorist (q.v.). The expressions *aoristic aspect* and *aoristic verb* are often used as synonyms for *perfective aspect* and *perfective verb* (qq.v.) respectively.

Apabhramsa: A name applied to the old vernaculars of India which were derived from the Prakrits (q.v.). The Apabhramsas are the direct linguistic ancestors of the modern Indic vernaculars.

Apache: A member of the southern branch of the Athapascan family of North American Indian languages.

aperture: The degree of opening in the speech organs which is needed for the production of the continuing stream of air in all non-stop sounds, as in fricatives, semi-vowels, vowels, etc.

aphasia: A broad term, subsuming various losses of speech functions due to cerebral lesions or injuries to other nerve centers.

apheresis: The dropping of the initial vowel of a word, often under the influence of the final vowel of a preceding article; e.g., Latin *illa ecclesia* > Italian *la chiesa*.

apical articulation: In phonetical terminology, the formation of a sound with the tip of the tongue making contact with some part of the oral cavity.

apocope: The loss or deliberate omission of the last letter, syllable or part of a word.

apodosis: See *consequence clause*.

apophony: Ablaut (q.v.).

aposiopesis: The interruption or breaking off in the middle of an utterance. (E.g., "I suppose you—")

apostrophe: (1) The rhetorical figure consisting in addressing in the second person somebody or something not present.—(2) The punctuation mark ['], used to indicate the omission of a sound or syllable.

apparitional aspect. A verbal aspect expressing that the action or state denoted by the verb seems to be performed or to exist.

appellative: (1) An obsolescent synonym for *common noun*. (2) Currently used (cf. Troubetzkoy, etc.) as the second of the three important aspects of language, viz.: *expressive*, characterizing the speaker; *appellative*, characterizing the hearer, and *representational*, denoting the subject of discourse.

application: The extensional meaning (q.v.) of a word or term.

applicative aspect. See *benefactive aspect*.

apposition: The use of paratactically (q.v.) joined linguistic forms which have the same grammatical form or function but not the same meaning or semantic content.

Aquitanian: According to some linguists, an extinct dialect of Iberian, the language spoken in the Iberian peninsula in pre-Roman times; unknown and unrecorded except for about two hundred proper names (places and deities). These linguists assume that Aquitanian was the parent of modern Basque. Other linguists consider *Aquitanian* a general term for the pre-Roman vernaculars, not necessarily interrelated, of Iberia, one of which was Basque.

Arabic: See *North Arabic, South Arabic*.

Aragonese: One of the great medieval dialects of Spain, spoken in the east central portion of the Iberian Peninsula. Only traces of it survive today.

Arakan-Burmese: A branch of the Tibeto-Burmese sub-family of the Sino-Tibetan family of languages, consisting of Arakanese, Burmese (or *Maghi*), the Kuki-Chin group and Old Kuki.

Arakanese: A Tibeto-Burmese dialect.

Aramaic: A subdivision of the Northern West Semitic branch of the Semitic group of the Semito-Hamitic family of languages. Divided into Western Aramaic and Eastern Aramaic (qq.v.).

Arapaho: A North American Indian language, member of the Algonquian family; surviving in Oklahoma, Wyoming and Montana.

Araucan: A family of South American Indian languages spoken in and around Chile; its surviving members are: Huiliche (or Kunko), Leuvuche, Mapuche, Pehuenche, Rankel, and Taluche (or Taluhet).

Arawak: A family of South American Indian languages, in ancient times spoken in South America and in the Caribbean, but superseded shortly before the Spanish conquest by the languages of the victorious Caribs. According to the classification of Rivet, the Arawak family consists of seven branches, with a combined total of 101 surviving and 29 extinct languages.

archaic: Old-fashioned, no longer in general use, obsolescent.

archaism: An archaic word, expression, grammatical form, idiom, etc.

archiphoneme: The sum total of the relevant features common to two mutually neutralizable phonemes. (Cf. *neutralization*.)

areal linguistics: See *linguistic geography*.

Argobba: An Ethiopic dialect.

argot: A class jargon, unintelligible to uninitiated listeners.

Armenian: A member of the Indo-European family of languages, spoken in Asia Minor by about 3-4,000,000 native speakers. The classical form of the language, still used as the learned and liturgical language, is called *Grabar;* the modern form, in use since the 16th century A.D., and in use as a vernacular and as the language of modern literature, is termed *Ashksarhik* or *Ashksarhabar*.

article: The designation of auxiliary words, used in many languages as a particle inserted before or prefixed to the noun (in certain languages added to the noun as a suffix) to define, limit or modify its use. Articles are classified mainly as *definite*, *indefinite*, and *partitive* (q.v.); grammars of certain languages list other types of articles, too.

articulate sentence: Jespersen's term for a sentence which contains all the essential grammatical parts.

articulate speech: Speech consisting of a systematic and organical combination of meaningful elements.

articulation: The formation of sounds by the vocal organs; the totality of the movements of the organs of speech required for pronouncing distinct sounds. (Cf. *levels of articulation.*)

articulator: A movable speech-organ, such as the tongue or the lips.

artificial language: A language created for international communication, for use by a group or class, etc.

Artshi: A language spoken in the Caucasus; a member of the Eastern group of the North Caucasian family of languages.

Aryan languages: In general, an alternative term for the Indo-European family of languages. Specifically, the languages of India and Iran.

Asante: See *Twi*.

Ashanti: See *Twi*.

Ashkenazic: (1) The language used by the Ashkenazim, or northern European Jews (see *Yiddish*); (2) the system of pronunciation of the Hebrew vowels used by the Ashkenazim, in contrast with the Sephardic pronunciation.

Ashksarhik: Modern Armenian (q.v.), in use since the 16th century A.D., currently used as the Armenian vernacular and modern literary language; also called *Ashksarhabar*. (Cf. *Grabar*.)

Asianic: The designation of a group of extinct languages, spoken or originated in remote antiquity in and around Mesopotamia and Asia Minor. This designation is geographical rather than linguistic, for these languages have no proven or even demonstrable linguistic affinity to one another or to any other known language. They are, in alphabetical order: Bithynian, Cappadocian, Carian, Cilician, Cossaean (or Kassite), Cretan (or Epicretan), Cypriote (or Epicyprian), Elamite (or Susian, Anzanite or Hozi), Etruscan, Gergito-Solymian, Isaurian, Khattian, Lycian (or Trmmli or Trknmli), Lydian, Mariandynian, Mysian, Palwa (or Palaian or Balaian), Pamphylian, Paphlagonian, Pisidian, Pontic, Subaraean (including Mitannian and Hurrian), Sumerian, and Vannic (or Khaldic or Urartaean) (qq.v.).

aspect: With reference to verbs, a category indicating whether the action or state denoted by the verb is viewed as completed or in progress, as instantaneous or enduring, as momentary or habitual, etc. Aspects of a verb are variously formed in the various languages, by prefixes, suffixes, infixes, by phonetical changes of the root, by the use of auxiliaries, etc.

aspirate: In phonetical terminology, (1) the sound [*h*] and its cognates; (2) in general, a sound the pronunciation of which involves an intensity in the expulsion of air from the oral cavity.

aspirated: In phonetical terminology, said of a consonant pronounced followed immediately by a puff of breath.

aspiration: (1) The puff of breath which accompanies the articulation of certain phonemes.—(2) The pronunciation of a consonant as an *aspirate* (q.v.—2).

Assamese: (1) An Indic language, related to Bihari and Bengali. —(2) A designation, geographical rather than linguistic, of a number of languages classified as constituting a branch of the Tibeto-Burmese sub-family of the Sino-Tibetan family of languages, divided, according to this system of nomenclature, into the *North Assamese* and *Middle and South Assamese* (q.v.) groups. However, these designations are misleading, because they may lead to confusion with the Indic language properly called *Assamese* (see above), and therefore the name

Lo-lo-Mo-so group and *Bodo-Naga-Kachin group* are prefer-able to *North Assamese* and *Middle and South Assamese*, re-spectively.

assibilation: In phonetical terminology, the process of assimilation (q.v.) by which a non-sibilant consonant becomes a sibilant. (E.g., Latin *vitium* > Italian *vezzo*.)

assimilated phoneme: That phoneme which is caused to undergo an *assimilation* (q.v.) by another phoneme.

assimilation: A phonetical process, in which two phonemes, ad-jacent (*contiguous assimilation*) or very near to each other (*in-contiguous assimilation*) acquire common characteristics or be-come identical. When the phoneme which produces this phe-nomenon (the *assimilatory phoneme*) precedes the *assimilated phoneme*, the assimilation is said to be *progressive* (e.g., Latin *hominem* > *om'ne* > French *homme*); when the assimilatory phoneme follows the assimilated one, the assimilation is called *regressive* (e.g., Latin *domina* > *dom'na* > Italian *donna*). When both phonemes affect each other, the assimilation is designated as *reciprocal* (e.g., Latin *rapidum* > *rap'du* > Italian *ratto*, with unvoicing of *d* from *p*, and dentalizing of *p* from *d*). (Cf. *morphological assimilation*.)

assimilatory phoneme: A phoneme which causes the *assimilation* (q.v.) of another phoneme.

association group: Words which are associated by form and/or meaning.

associational word: In semantics, a word denoting a thing or concept with which the speaker has no direct, first-hand per-sonal experience.

assonance: The repetition of a sound or sounds, particularly of vowel sounds, but not of consonants.

Assyrian: Old Akkadian, i.e., the Akkadian language from 2800 to 650 B.C.

Assyro-Babylonian: Akkadian (q.v.).

asterisk: The sign [*] prefixed to words in philological texts to indicate that the word or word-form to which it is affixed (*"starred form"*) does not actually occur in the language, but is assumed to have existed or is a hypothetical form, reconstructed on the basis of known data and linguistic laws.

Asturian: A Spanish dialect spoken in the Asturias, along the northern coast of Spain.

asyllabic: A phoneme incapable of forming a syllable by itself or of serving as the nucleus of a syllable. (Cf. *non-syllabic*.)

asyndetic: Formed by simple juxtaposition, without the use of any conjunction or other distinct connecting particle.

asyndetism: The absence of distinct connecting words between parts of a phrase or sentence.

asyndeton: A construction or phrase characterized by *asyndetism* (q.v.).

asyntactic compound: A compound word, the component members of which show a relationship to each other which according to the syntactic rules of the language in question they could not have if they were used as independent words in a sentence.

atelic aspect: Synonymous with *imperfective aspect* (q.v.); a form of the verb used when the action is viewed as incomplete in itself. (*L. H. Gray*.)

Athapascan: A family of North American Indian languages, consisting of three groups: *Dene* (northwestern Canada), *Hupa-Matole* (California), and *Apache-Navajo* (southern United States). According to Rivet, the Athapascan family is a member of a greater linguistic unit, the *Na-Dene* family.

athematic: Not relating to, not connected with or not constituting a *stem*.

athematic formation: A flexional form in which the suffix or prefix is added to the root without a thematic (q.v.) morpheme.

atomic language: The French designation (*langue atomique*) of a *radical language* (q.v.)

atomistic approach: That approach to language which considers every phoneme as an individual, isolated unit, in contrast to the structural approach.

atonic: Without stress or vocal pitch.

attested form: A word or word-form which has been recorded as actually in use at some time. (Cf. *starred form*.)

Attic: The major literary dialect of ancient Greek, spoken in Athens.

attraction: (1) The tendency toward a morphological change in a word under the influence of an adjacent word or words. This change, which may be termed a *morphological assimilation*, may be one of gender, case, tense, mood, etc.—(2) In phonemics, the attempted integration and stabilization of a phonemic pattern, usually manifested by filling "*holes in the pattern*" (q.v.).

attribute: A word or group of words which denotes a quality or characteristic of a substantive.

attributive adjective: A descriptive adjective (q.v.) which modifies a noun or noun-equivalent directly (e.g., the *white* house), in contradistinction to *predicate adjectives* (q.v.).

auditory language: Speech, in contradistinction to written, sign or gesture language.

augment: A prefixed element (e.g., as used in classical Greek).

augmentative: A word derived from another by the addition of an *augmentative suffix* (q.v.).

augmentative suffix: A suffix added to a word, particularly a noun, to convey the idea of bigness.

Australian: A collective designation of the languages of the aborigines of Australia. These languages, numbering over one hundred, are divided into a *Northern Australian group* and a *Southern Australian* group. The classification of these two groups into a general Australian family or group is geographic rather than linguistic, for no linguistic affinity has been proven between these two groups; in fact, the linguistic interrelationship among the languages of the Northern group has not been discovered as yet either. The languages of the Southern Australian group are classified into several sub-groups, also more geographic than linguistic.

Austric: W. Schmidt's term for a hypothetical family of languages, into which he classified the Austro-Asiatic family and the Austronesian family as sub-families.

Austro-Asiatic: A family of languages, spoken in South-East Asia (the Chota-Nagpur region of India, parts of Indo-China and of the Malay Peninsula, in Annam, Cambodia and parts of Thailand), hence also called *South-East Asiatic*. It consists of the *Mon-Khmer*, *Annamese-Muong* and *Munda* (or *Kolarian*) branches. Although these branches show sufficient common features to indicate that they constitute a family of languages, several linguists disagree with this classification. Thus, Annamese-Muong and certain Munda dialects have been also classified as Sino-Tibetan languages. W. Schmidt and others have claimed that the entire Austro-Asiatic family is closely related to the Austronesian (Malayo-Polynesian) family and that these two families form a "super-family," which Schmidt named *Austric*.

Austronesian: An alternative designation of the *Malayo-Polynesian* family of languages.

autonomous sound change: See *spontaneous sound change*.

auxiliary: In general, a word which has no complete meaning in itself and is used only in combination with or in reference to another word which has a meaning of its own. (E.g., prepositions, conjunctions, etc.)—(Cf. *auxiliary verb*.)

auxiliary numerals: A set of *classifiers* (q.v.) used in certain languages, e.g., Japanese, in addition to cardinal numerals, to indicate the class to which the noun modified by the numeral belongs.

auxiliary verb: A verb used in combination with another verb, to express the mood, tense, or aspect of the action denoted by that main verb. (E.g., the English *may*, *shall*, etc.).

Avar: A language spoken in the Caucasus; a member of the Avaro-Andi branch of the Eastern Caucasian group of the North Caucasian family of languages.

Avaro-Andi: A branch of the Eastern group of the North Caucasian family of languages; it includes Avar, Andi, Dido, K'varshi and Qaputsi.

Avestan: That form of Old Persian in which the sacred literature of Zoroastrianism (*Avesta*) was written. (Also called *Avestic* and *Zend*.)

Aymará: A family of 11 South American Indian languages, spoken by about 500,000 persons in Ecuador and Bolivia.

Azerbaidjani: A dialect of the Southern Turkic group of the Altaic sub-family of the Ural-Altaic family of languages.

Aztec: An extinct American Indian language, also called *Nahuatl*, member of the Nahuatlan family of languages; the language of the ancient civilization of Mexico prior to Columbus' discovery of America.

B

Ba: A Great Andamanese language.

Babylonian: New Akkadian, i.e., the Akkadian language after 650 B.C.

Babylonian Judaeo-Aramaic: An Eastern Aramaic dialect, the language of the Babylonian Talmud (fourth to sixth centuries A.D.).

back-formation: The derivation of new words, by analogy, from existing words assumed to be derivatives. (E.g., *to sculpt* from *sculptor*, on the analogy of *actor—to act*.)

back vowel: A vowel, the point of articulation of which is in the rear part of the oral cavity, i.e., pronounced with the back part of the tongue arched toward the palate.

Bafflegab: See *Gobbledegook*.

Bahasa Indonesia: See *Malay*.

Bahuvrihi: A term borrowed from the grammarians of ancient India, meaning *"much-riced,"* and used to designate possessive compounds of the type "black-haired."

Balaian: See *Palawi*.

Balinese: A language spoken by about 1,000,000 persons on the island of Bali; a member of the Indonesian sub-family of the Malayo-Polynesian family of languages.

Balochi (Baluchi): A language spoken in Balochistan; it belongs to the Iranian branch of the Indo-Iranian group of the Indo-European family of languages.

Balta: An artificial language, a modified form of Volapük (q.v.), created by Dormoy in 1893.

Balti: The native language of approximately 150,000 persons in the Kashmirian province of Baltistan, a member of the Tibetan (or Bhotian) group of the Tibeto-Himalayan branch of the

Tibeto-Burmese sub-family of the Sino-Tibetan family of languages.

Baltic: A language group, of the Indo-European family, comprising Lithuanian, Lettish (or Latvian) and the extinct Old Prussian. (Customarily classified, with the Slavic group, in the Balto-Slavic sub-family.)

Balto-Slavic: A sub-family of the Indo-European family of languages, consisting of the Baltic and the Slavic language groups.

Baluchi: See *Balochi.*

Bambala: A Kushitic vernacular.

Banda: One of the Ubangi (q.v.) dialects.

Bangui: An African Negro language, member of the Bantu family of languages.

Bantu: A family of African Negro languages, considered by some authors (notably, Delafosse) to be cognate with the Sudano-Guinean family. The Bantu languages (spoken by an estimated 50,000,000 persons in South Africa, south of the Sudanese-Guinean speech area) have the common characteristic that they group their nouns in classes, and each class has a characteristic prefix which is prefixed also to every word referring to or connected grammatically or syntactically with the noun. The number of the Bantu languages is still undecided, ranging, according to different authorities, somewhere between 80 and 100. The most important Bantu languages are: Swahili, Zulu, Congo, Luba-Lulua, Luganda (or Ganda), Nyanja.

Bara: See *Bodo.*

Baraba: A language spoken in western Asia; it belongs to the Eastern Turkic group of the Altaic sub-family of the Ural-Altaic family of languages.

barbarism: Any deviation from or violation of the recognized, current rules of grammar or style, speech or linguistic usage.

Bari: An African Negro language, spoken in the Anglo-Egyptian Sudan, a member of the Sudanese-Guinean family of languages.

Barma: An African language, member of the Sudanese-Guinean family of languages.

Bartholomae's law: The phonetic law which states that in the Indo-Iranian languages, under certain conditions, an aspirated voiced consonant followed by a voiceless consonant becomes unaspirated, and the voiceless consonant becomes voiced and aspirated.

base (of inflection): The simple or basic form of a word to which the inflectional endings are appended. It may be the primary root of the word (*root base*) or the root with a *thematic suffix* (*stem base*).

base of comparison: In phonemics, the relevant features which two or more phonemes have in common. In bilateral *oppositions* (q.v.) this is the *archiphoneme* (q.v.). In all oppositions, this is what permits the setting up of *orders* and *series* (qq.v.).

Bashkir: An Asiatic language; it belongs to the Western Turkic group of the Altaic sub-family of the Ural-Altaic family of languages.

Basic: Short for *Basic English* (q.v.).

Basic English: A system, devised by C. K. Ogden, consisting of 850 selected English words and simple rules for using this vocabulary to express ideas. The purpose of this system is twofold: To serve as a simple and easy international auxiliary language, and as an instrument of semantic training. The vocabulary of 850 words consists of 400 general nouns, 200 names of picturable objects, 150 adjectives, and 100 "operators" (verbal forms, prepositions, particles, etc.); a supplementary general science vocabulary of 100 words and special word-lists for specialized scientific fields are also included in the system, to provide a basic scientific vocabulary in addition to the general vocabulary of 850 words.

basis of articulation: The neutral position of the organs of speech and their various parts which is peculiar to or characteristic of a given speech-community or of the native speakers of a given language.

Basque: A language, without any known or demonstrable relationship or affiliation with any other known language, spoken by about 1,000,000 persons in the Pyrenees region (the northeastern corner of Spain and the southwestern corner of France). Basque (called *Eskuara* or *Euzkara* by the native speakers) is characterized phonetically by an abundance in stops, spirants and palatals, morphologically by an essentially agglutinative structure, and grammatically by the absence of an active voice of the verb. Some linguists assume that Basque is a descendant of the extinct and almost completely unknown *Aquitanian* dialect of *Iberian*, the pre-Roman language once spoken in the Iberian Peninsula. (Cf. *Aquitanian.*) Certain authorities maintain that Basque has certain affinities with the North Caucasian languages.

Batak: A language spoken in Samoa; a member of the Indonesian sub-family of the Malayo-Polynesian family of languages. Some authorities estimate the number of Batak speakers to exceed 1,000,000.

Bats: See *T'ush.*

Bazaar Malay: See *Pasar Malay.*

Beach-la-mar: A contact vernacular (q.v.) used extensively all over the Western Pacific. Its vocabulary is derived, almost entirely, from English. Also called *Beche-le-mar*, *Beche de mer English* and *Sandalwood English.*

Beche de mer English: See *Beach-la-mar.*

Beche-le-mar: See *Beach-la-mar.*

Bemba: An African Negro language, spoken in Northern Rhodesia; member of the Bantu family of languages.

benefactive aspect: A verbal aspect (variously termed also *accommodative*, *applicative* and *indirective*), expressing that the action or state denoted by the verb is performed or exists for or in the interest of another person.

Bengali: An Indic language, spoken in Bengal and the Calcutta region of India; the number of its native speakers is about 75,000,000.

Berber: A group of languages (Tuareg, Shluh, Kabyl, Zenaga, Zenete and the extinct Guanche) which with the extinct Libyan constitute the Libyco-Berber branch of the Hamitic sub-family of the Semito-Hamitic family of languages.

Bhili: A Dravidian language, spoken in Central India, classified in the Gondi group.

Bhojpuri: A dialect of the Indic language *Bihari;* spoken by over 20,000,000 persons in and around the eastern parts of the United Provinces.

Bhotian: See *Tibetan.*

Biblical Aramaic: A Western Aramaic dialect, the language in which the non-Hebrew portions of the Bible were written.

bibliography: (1) The study of books.—(2) A list of books, usually sources of reference.

Bichlamar: See *Beach-la-mar.*

Bicol: A language spoken in the Philippine Islands by about 700,-000 persons; a member of the Indonesian sub-family of the Malayo-Polynesian family of languages.

Bihari: An Indic language, spoken in northeastern India by approximately 37,000,000 native speakers. Its three main dialects are: Maithili, Magahi and Bhojpuri.

bilabial (bi-labial): In phonetical terminology, a consonant produced by a combined movement of both lips, i.e., in the articulation of which the two lips closely approach or touch each other (E.g., [b], [m], [w]).

bilabiodental: A sound formed with the upper lip and upper teeth touching the lower lip.

bilateral opposition: Two phonemes with the same archiphoneme, opposed to each other on the basis of a single relevant feature (the *mark of opposition*).

Bilin: A Kushitic vernacular.

bilingual: (1) With reference to a text, written in two languages. —(2) With reference to persons, speaking two languages customarily and with equal ease.

bilingualism, bilinguality: The quality or property of being bilingual (q.v.).

binary: Consisting of two elements; showing two aspects or characteristics.

binary principle: The theory that every phonemic opposition (q.v.) presents a common denominator both on the acoustic and on the articulatory level in a dichotomy imposed by the nature of language; e.g., the relation strong/weak is perfectly measurable physically and physiologically. (*Roman Jakobson*)

Bindevokal: German for *linking vowel;* the German term for a *bridge-vowel* (q.v.).

biolinguistics: The study of language and communication behavior as biologically determined activities of the organism, with stress on the neurophysiological and genetic factors and aspects.

Bisa: An African Negro language, also called *Wisa,* member of the Bantu family of languages.

Bisaya: A language spoken in the Philippine Islands by about 3,250,000 native speakers; a member of the Indonesian sub-family of the Malayo-Polynesian family of languages. (Also called *Visaya.*)

Bithynian: An extinct language, preserved in some inscriptions and glosses recorded by classical authors. Although some linguists have regarded it as a member of the Thraco-Phrygian group of the Indo-European family of languages, it is generally considered a language of undetermined linguistic affinities, classified as *Asianic.*

Blackfoot: A North American Indian language, classified in the Algonquian family; surviving in Alberta, Canada.

blade: The part of the tongue just past the tip (*apex*) and up to the front (associated with the hard palate).

blend: A word formed as a result of linguistic contamination (q.v.). (Cf. *portmanteau word, telescoped word.*)

blocked syllable: See *closed syllable.*

Blue Language: See *Langue Bleue.*

Bo: See *Ibo.*

Bobangi: An African Negro language, spoken in South Africa; a member of the Bantu family of languages.

Bodo: A Tibeto-Burmese language, also called *Bara,* having many related dialects; a member of the Bodo-Naga-Kachin group.

Bodo-Naga-Kachin: A group of Tibeto-Burmese languages, consisting of Bodo or Bara, Naga, Naga-Bodo, Kachin or Singhpho, and Naga-Kuki, each with several related dialects. This group is often, misleadingly, referred to as the *Middle and South Assamese* languages.

Bohemian: See *Czech.*

Bontok: A language spoken in the Philippine Islands; a member of the Indonesian sub-family of the Malayo-Polynesian family of languages.

Bopal: An artificial language, representing a modified form of Volapük (q.v.), created by St. de Max in 1887.

borrowed word: A word taken over from another language; also, a word of foreign origin, even though modified in form.

borrowing: A *borrowed word* (q.v.).

bound accent: See *fixed stress.*

bound form: Short for *bound linguistic form*: a morpheme which has a distinct meaning when attached (prefixed or suffixed) to a word. (E.g., a declensional ending.)

Bourguignon: A French dialect, spoken in the former province of Burgundy.

boustrophedon: The method of writing in which the individual lines run alternately from right to left and from left to right, or alternately from top to bottom and from bottom to top.

bow-wow theory: See *onomatopœic theory.*

brachylogy: In general, a concise and abbreviated expression or style. Specifically, a grammatically incomplete phrase or expression.

Brahui: A Dravidian language, spoken by about 175,000 persons who form a linguistic island in the mountains of East Baluchistan.

breaking: A literal translation of the German term, *Brechung.* (See *vowel fracture.*)

breathings: The marks appearing in Greek over initial vowels and initial *r* to indicate the presence (', *rough breathing*) or the absence (', *smooth breathing*) of aspiration. The rough breathing is normally transcribed in the Roman alphabet by the letter *h*, while the smooth breathing is left untranscribed.

Brechung: The German term for *vowel fracture* (q.v.).

Breton: A language of the Brythonic branch of the Celtic group of the Indo-European family, spoken by about 1,000,000 people in Brittany (France).

breve: The mark [˘] placed over a vowel to indicate the correct sound in pronunciation; it often merely indicates that the vowel is to be pronounced short.

bridge-letter: The written representation of a *bridge-sound* (q.v.).

bridge-phoneme: See *bridge-sound, bridge-syllable.*

bridge-sound: A sound, usually a vowel, inserted between prefix and root or between root and suffix (especially flexional ending) for easier, clearer or more euphonic pronunciation.

bridge-syllable: A syllable fulfilling the function of a *bridge-sound* (q.v.).

bridge-vowel: See *connecting vowel.*

bright vowel: A synonym of *front vowel* (q.v.).

Briticism: A word, expression or grammatical or syntactical construction characteristic of or confined to the English language as spoken in Great Britain.

broad consonant: In Irish phonetics, a consonant immediately following or preceding a *broad vowel* (q.v.) in the same word.

Broad Romic: The simplified form of Sweet's system of phonetic symbols, *Romic.*

broad transcription: A representation of the gross phonetic features of an utterance, usually very close to a phonemic transcription (q.v.). (Cf. *narrow transcription.*)

broad vowel: A *back vowel* (q.v.).

broken: Prefixed to the name of a language, this adjective means *ungrammatical, insufficiently learned, corrupt,* often also *mispronounced.*

Broken-English: A creolized English, with admixtures of African linguistic features and elements, used as a "contact vernacular" (q.v.) in Liberia and Sierra Leone.

Brythonic: A branch of the Celtic group of the Indo-European family of languages, consisting of Breton, Welsh and Cornish.

Bube: An African Negro language, a member of the Bantu family of languages.

Buduk: A language spoken in the Caucasus; a member of the Samurian branch of the Eastern group of the North Caucasian family of languages.

Bugi: See *Buginese*.

Buginese: A language (also called *Bugi* or *Bugis*) spoken in Celebes; a member of the Indonesian sub-family of the Malayo-Polynesian family of languages.

Bugis: See *Buginese*.

Bukvitsa: A slightly modified version of the Cyrillic alphabet, showing influences of the Glagolitic alphabet, formerly used by Catholic Slavs in Bosnia and Dalmatia.

Bulgarian: A South Slavic language, spoken by over 7,000,000 people in Bulgaria and neighboring regions.

Burgundian: (1) An extinct East Germanic language.—(2) The *Bourguignon* (q.v.) dialect of French.

Burmese: A language (also called *Maghi*), spoken by almost 10,000,000 persons in Burma; a member of the Arakan-Burmese group of the Tibeto-Burmese sub-family of the Sino-Tibetan family of languages.

Burushaski: A language spoken in northwestern India. Although several linguists have considered it to be related to the Dravidian or Munda languages, the current opinion is that it is not related to any other known language.

Buryat: An Asiatic language which constitutes the Northern sub-branch of the Mongol branch of the Altaic sub-family of the Ural-Altaic family of languages.

Bushman: See *San*.

Bush-Negro English: A creolized English spoken by the Bush Negroes of Dutch-Guiana. (Also called *Jew-Tongo*.)

Byelorussian: See *White Russian*.

C

cacography: Misuse or inappropriate choice of words in writing; in general, improper or incorrect use of a language in writing.

cacology: Grammatically or idiomatically incorrect expression; unpleasant or faulty pronunciation or diction.

cacophony: A discordant sound or an unpleasant combination of sounds.

cacuminal: In phonetical terminology, a consonant pronounced with the tip of the tongue turned back toward the hard palate.

cadence: The modulation of the voice in speaking, which produces the "flow of the language"; especially, the rise and fall produced by the alternation of louder and softer syllables in accentual tongues. The term is applied in particular to the fall of the voice at the end of a sentence or at a pause in general.

Calabrian-Sicilian: A generic term for the dialects of Calabria and Sicily, generally characterized by conservatism in the treatment of Latin consonants.

Cambodian: See *Khmer*.

Campidanese: See *Sardinian*.

Canaanite: (1) A subdivision of the Northern subdivision of the West Semitic branch of the Semitic group of languages, comprising Old Canaanite, Hebrew, Phoenician and Moabite.—(2) Old Canaanite (q.v.).

cant: The special vocabulary of a particular group, especially of criminals.

Cantonese: A Chinese vernacular spoken in Kwang-tung (Southern China) by about 30,000,000 persons. The indigenous name of this vernacular is *Yüeh*.

Cape Dutch: An occasionally used name for Afrikaans (q.v.).

Cappadocian: An extinct language, spoken in remote antiquity in the Near East, preserved in inscriptions, dating back to the end of the third millennium B.C., and in glosses recorded by classical authors. This language, of undetermined linguistic affinities, is classified as *Asianic*.

cardinal numeral: A numeral which answers the question "How many?"

cardinal vowel: One of a series of vowel sounds, not taken from any specific languages, having a characteristic tongue-position and well-defined acoustic qualities; to be used for comparison with vowels in different languages. (*Daniel Jones*)

Carian: An extinct language, spoken in antiquity on the west coast of Asia Minor, of undetermined linguistic affinities, preserved in about 80 short inscriptions and glosses recorded by classical authors. Classified as *Asianic*.

caritive: A declensional case in certain languages (e.g., in Caucasian languages), having the same denotation as the English preposition *without*.

Carioca: The dialectal variant of Portuguese spoken in and around Rio de Janeiro, Brazil; one of its outstanding characteristics is the palatalization of final *-te*, *-de* groups.

Carpatho-Russian: See *Ruthenian*.

case: In the flexional languages, a morphological variant of a noun, adjective, pronoun, numeral, or participle, distinguished from other such variants of the same word by a specific declensional ending, by a zero-ending, by an internal vowel change, etc., indicating the grammatical function or syntactical relationship of the word. As applied to non-flexional languages, *case* means in general the grammatical function or syntactical relationship of a word, indicated by a preposition, postposition, suffix or a particle, or even by word order alone.

case-form: In flexional languages, a morphological variant of a noun, adjective or pronoun (in certain languages, also numerals and other parts of speech) indicating by its form, usually its ending, the grammatical or syntactical function.

caste: See *high-caste nouns, casteless nouns.*

casteless nouns: In Dravidian languages, that group of nouns which includes nouns denoting irrational beings (including beings regarded irrational) and inanimate objects. (Cf. *high-caste nouns.*)

Castilian: A Spanish dialect, accepted and used as the standard literary language of Spain and other Spanish-speaking countries.

Catalan: A Romance language (also called Catalonian), spoken in Catalonia and the province of Valencia, in northeastern Spain, Andorra, the Balearic Islands, and a small region of southern France (Corbières), by approximately 6,000,000 people.

catch: See *glottal stop.*

category: See *grammatical categories.*

Caucasian: A collective designation, geographical rather than linguistic, of the *North Caucasian* and *South Caucasian* (qq.v.) language families.

causal clause: A clause introduced by a *causal conjunction* and stating the cause of a fact, event or situation mentioned elsewhere in the sentence.

causal conjunction: A conjunction (q.v.) which introduces a clause expressing a *purpose* (e.g., *in order that*) or an *effect* (e.g., *therefore*).

causative: Expressing a cause or agency.

causative aspect: See *causative form.*

causative case: A declensional case in certain languages (e.g., in Caucasian languages), having the denotation *because of.*

causative form: A verbal form or structure expressing that the subject causes or has another agent perform the action.

causative mood: See *causative form.*

causative suffix, infix, prefix: A particle added to a verb to express that the subject causes another agent to perform the action.

causative verb: A verb expressing or indicating that the subject causes an agent to perform the action.

cedilla: The diacritic mark [¸] used under certain letters to indicate the proper sound to be used in pronunciation. In certain languages, the same mark indicates nasalization of a vowel.

Celtic: A language group, of the Indo-European family, divided into the Goidelic branch (Irish or Irish Gaelic, Scots Gaelic and Manx) and the Brythonic branch (Breton, Welsh, Cornish). The oldest, long extinct member of the group, *Gaulish,* is little known.

Central Algonquian: A sub-division of the Algonquian family of North American Indian languages; its surviving members, spoken in the Great Lakes region, are: Fox, Illinois, Kickapoo, Menomini, Miami, Montagnais, Ojibway (Ojibwa or Chippewa), Potawatomi, Sauk, Shawnee.

Central Italian: The term applied to the group of dialects spoken in central Italy, in the regions of Tuscany, Umbria, Marche and northern Latium. Corsican and the north Sardinian dialects, Gallurese and Sassarese, also belong to the "Central Italian" classification.

Central Turkic: A language-group, a subdivision of the Turkic branch of the Altaic (or Turco-Tartaric) sub-family of the Ural-Altaic family of languages; it comprises Chagatai, Kashgar, Sart, Taranchi, Uzbeg and Yarkand.

centum languages: Those Indo-European languages in which the Proto-Indo-European guttural [k] sound is represented by [k]. (Greek, Italic, Celtic, Germanic, Hittite and Tokharian.)

cerebral: In phonetical terminology, a synonym of *cacuminal* (q.v.).

cessative aspect: A verbal aspect expressing that the action or state denoted by the verb ceases or has ceased to be performed or to exist.

Chagatai: An Asiatic language; it belongs to the Central Turkic group of the Altaic sub-family of the Ural-Altaic family of languages.

Chagga: An African Negro language, spoken in the Kilimanjaro region; a member of the Bantu family of languages.

Ch'ak'ur: A language spoken in the Caucasus; a member of the Samurian branch of the Eastern Caucasian branch of the North Caucasian family of languages.

Chaldean: A designation often, but erroneously, used for Biblical Aramaic (q.v.).

Cham: A language spoken in French Indo-China, a member of the Mon-Khmer branch of the Austro-Asiatic family of languages.

Chambiali: A western Pahari (q.v.) dialect, spoken by about 65,000 persons in Chamba State.

Chameali, Chamiali: See *Chambiali*.

Chapogir: A Tungus dialect.

Chari: A Great Andamanese language.

Chechen: A branch of the Eastern Caucasian languages, comprising the Ingush and T'ush or Bats dialects.

Checheno-Lesghian: See *Eastern Caucasian*.

checked syllable: See *closed syllable*.

Cheremiss: A Finno-Ugric language, spoken by about 375,000 persons in Asiatic Russia. Some linguists consider Cheremiss a member of a Lapponic group composed of Lapp, Cheremiss and Mordvin, while others regard these three languages as distinct branches of the Finno-Ugric (or Uralic) sub-family of the Ural-Altaic family of languages.

Cherkess: See *Circassian*.

Cherokee: A North American Indian language, member of the Iroquoian family; spoken in the southern United States.

Cheyenne: A North American Indian language, member of the Algonquian family; surviving in Montana.

Chi: An African Negro language, member of the Sudanese-Guinean family of languages.

Chinese: A sub-family of the Sino-Tibetan family of languages, comprising *Wen-li* (the traditional standard written language of China), *Kuo-yü* (the new "National Tongue"), and the many Chinese dialects and vernaculars, spoken altogether by almost 600,000,000 persons. The most important Chinese vernaculars are: *North Mandarin*, the language of the Peiping region and the basis of the new "National Tongue," *Kuo-yü*, now used by about 300,000,000 persons; *Wu*, spoken around the Yang-tse Delta by about 40,000,000; Cantonese or *Yüeh*, spoken by about 30,000,000; *Min*, spoken in the province of Fu-kien by about 30,000,000 persons.

Chinook Jargon: A contact vernacular originated in Oregon, as a mixture of French, English and indigenous Indian dialects.

Chippewa: See *Ojibway*.

Christian Palestinian Aramaic: A Western Aramaic dialect, used in the fifth and sixth centuries A.D. in portions of the Bible and in Bible translations made from the Greek.

chromatic accent: The musical accent in speech, resulting from the flow of *pitch* (q.v.). This term is used by many authors as a synonym for *pitch*.

Chuana: An African Negro language, spoken in Bechuanaland; member of the Bantu family of languages.

Chukchi: A language, spoken by about 10,000 persons in northeastern Asia; a member of the Chukchi-Kamchadal family of languages, classified in the *Hyperborean* or *Palaeo-Asiatic* group.

Chukchi-Kamchadal: The family of languages, spoken in extreme northeastern Asia, consisting of Chukchi, Kamchadal and Koryak; classified, with the linguistically unrelated Ainu and Gilyak, in the *Hyperborean* or *Palaeo-Asiatic* group of languages.

Church Slavonic: The South Slavic language into which Kyrillos and Methodos translated the Gospels in the ninth century A.D.; it is extinct as a vernacular, but has remained the official language of the Slavic Greek Orthodox Church. (Also called *Old Church Slavic* and *Old Bulgarian*.)

Chuvash: An Asiatic language, belonging to the Western Turkic group of the Altaic sub-family of the Ural-Altaic family of languages; it shows marked differences from the other Turkic languages.

Chwee: See *Twi*.

Cilician: An extinct Near-Eastern language, of undetermined linguistic affinities, preserved in a few inscriptions and glosses recorded by classical authors. Classified as *Asianic*.

Circassian: A language (also called *Cherkess*) spoken originally in the Caucasus, although most of the native speakers have emigrated to Asia Minor and Syria; a member of the Adyghe group of the Western Caucasian branch of the North Caucasian family of languages.

circumflex accent: The diacritic mark [^] used over certain letters to indicate the proper sound in pronunciation.

class: The totality of linguistically, phonetically, morphologically, etc. comparable or equivalent elements.

class-meaning: That common feature of meaning which is present in every lexical form (q.v.) within a given form-class.

class words: The words of a given language arranged into classes on the basis of the way they function in specific frames; e.g., all words which can be inserted in the frame: "The —— is good," may be considered members of the same class. (*Charles C. Fries*)

classical: The stage or version of a language, especially of an ancient or extinct language, appearing in literary texts of high standing or renown, usually employed as the basis or means of teaching that language.

classificatory language: A term usually applied to the languages of the Bantu family, in which certain prefixes are used to indicate the class to which any given word belongs; the modifiers of the principal words carry the same prefix as the latter.

classifier: (1) A word or prefix used in various languages to indicate the grammatical or semantic classification of words. (Cf. *classificatory language, numerative classifier*.)—(2) In the ideographic writings, especially Chinese, an additional symbol added to the *phonetic* (q.v.) to form a compound ideographic character.

clause: In general a subdivision of a sentence containing a subject and a predicate (or a word which implies or replaces a predicate).

click: A speech-sound, produced by an inspiration of air, characteristic of the Bushman and Hottentot languages, and also of the Kafir-Sotho group of the Bantu languages.

clipped word: A word that has lost its initial or final part or both (e.g., *cab* for *cabriolet*, *flu* for *influenza*, etc.).

close vowel: See *closed vowel*.

closed stress: Sweet's term for the stress when the consonant is heard while the vowel still has its maximum intensity.

closed syllable: A syllable ending in a consonant. Also called *blocked* or *checked syllable*.

closed vowel: A vowel pronounced with the mouth opened less than in the production of another vowel sound.

closure: The phonetic process by which some part or parts of the speech mechanism momentarily cut off the stream of air, producing an occlusive or stop sound.

cluster: In phonetics, a group of phonemes, not necessarily constituting a syllable.

Cocoliche: An "immigrant language" in Argentina, consisting of a mixture of Italian and Spanish.

cognate words: Two or more words in different languages which have the same root.

cohortative mood: In some languages, a distinct mood, used in utterances expressing an exhortation, encouragement, suggestion, etc. The designation is applied by grammarians in general to the imperative or subjunctive moods when used in such sentences. (Also called *hortatory mood.*)

coinage: The creation of a new, artificial word; also, the process of creating such word.

coined word: An artificial word, deliberately created for a certain purpose.

collateral clause: A subordinate clause (q.v.).

collective noun: A noun designating a group of individual persons or objects.

collocation: The arrangement of words in a sentence in order properly to convey the intended meaning.

colloquial style: The language or the style of writing used by educated persons in familiar or informal discourse.

colloquialism: An informal expression or linguistic form of the conversational type; generally considered out of place in formal discourse or literature, although widely used in daily speech.

colon: The punctuation mark [:].

colonizing language: See *language of colonization.*

combinatory variants: Variants (q.v.) due to position in the environment; also called *conditional* or *positional* variants.

comitative: In certain language groups (e.g., Finno-Ugric), a case having the denotation *with* or *accompanied by.*

comitative aspect: A verbal aspect expressing that the action or state denoted by the verb is performed or experienced together or jointly with somebody or something else.

comma: The punctuation mark [,].

Commercialese: See *Gobbledegook.*

common case: The uninflected form of a word which in uninflected languages is used, with or without prepositions, in all instances where inflectional languages would use different case forms.

common gender: In the grammars of languages which classify words according to grammatical genders, this term is applicable to adjectives, pronouns and occasionally also nouns which have only one form for all genders; in the grammars of languages which are innocent of gender, or in which grammatical gender is merely a designation of sex or is unimportant, the term is applicable to pronouns and nouns which may denote men, or women, or men and women alike.

common language: That version of a language which is accepted and employed by various groups or strata of the speakers of the language, as a result of the suppression or levelling of local dialects, among the better educated classes at least.

common noun: A noun which may designate any member of a group of persons, objects, etc., and is not the name of any specific member of the group. (Antithesis: *proper noun.*)

common syllable: A syllable that may be accented or unaccented, long or short, according to its position.

comparative case: A declensional case in certain languages (e.g., in Chechen), having the denotation *more* (or *less*) *than.*

comparative degree: That form of an adjective or adverb which expresses that one thing possesses a certain quality to a greater extent than another thing.

comparative grammar: That branch of *explanatory grammar* (q.v.) which examines and compares the grammatical features and phenomena of two or more related languages, in order to ascertain the nature and degree of their relationship.

comparative linguistics: That branch of linguistics which discloses and studies similarities between related languages; the study of related languages, with particular emphasis on similarities and differences.

comparison: The change in the form, or other modification, of an adjective or adverb in order to denote degrees of quality, characteristics, etc. (Cf. *linguistic comparison, base of comparison.*)

compellative: A term occasionally used instead of *vocative* (q.v.).

complement: In general, a word, term or phrase used in order to complete the meaning of another term.

complementary distribution: The arrangement in which two phonemes which cannot appear in the same environment (i.e., *positional variants*) are said to be (e.g., the *l's* in *Lil*).

complete predicate: A simple predicate (i.e., a verb or verb-phrase) used in combination with modifiers or other complements.

complete verb: (1) A *verb of complete predication* (q.v.).—(2) A verb, the conjugation of which contains all conjugational forms of verbs of the same class.

complex sentence: A sentence containing a modifying clause.

complex word: A *compound* or a *derivative* word (qq.v.).

composite word: A compound word (q.v.).

composition: Compounding (q.v.).

compound: Consisting of two or more parts, elements or components. (The term *compound* is frequently used as a noun, instead of the term *compound word*—q.v.)

compound phoneme: A combination of two or more simple primary phonemes (e.g., a diphthong).

compound predicate: Two or more simple predicates (i.e., verbs or verb-phrases), with or without conjunctions, used in the same sentence.

compound tense: A tense formed with the aid of an auxiliary verb or other word.

compound word: A word which is composed of two or more words, the combination of which constitutes a single word with a meaning often distinct from the meanings of the individual components.

compounded flexion: In Irish grammar, the conjugation of verbs compounded with a prefix.

compounding: The process of forming new words (*compound words*) by combining existing words (called the *components*).

complementary distribution: Two allophones (q.v.) which cannot appear in the same environment (i.e., *positional variants*) are said to be in complementary distribution; e.g., the clear *l* and the dark *l* in *Lil.*

concessive conjunction: A conjunction (q.v.), usually one of a pair of correlative conjunctions (q.v.) expressing a state, condition or situation. (E.g., *although.*)

concord: The agreement of a word with another word or other words in a sentence as to number, case, gender, person, etc. According to Jespersen, *concord* is "the agreement between secondary words and the principals they belong to." (Cf. *grammatical agreement.*)

concordance: See *concord.*

concrete term: A term denoting a person, animate or inanimate being, or in general anything physically real and perceptible by the senses or organs of perception. (Opposed to *abstract term.*)

conditional mood: The verbal form expressing a condition or hypothetical state. The mood used in the consequence clause of a conditional sentence.

conditional sentence: A sentence which states what may or could or will happen (*consequence clause*) IF something else will have happened or be the case (*hypothetical clause*).

conditioned sound change: A phonetical change in a word under the influence of neighboring or near-by phonetical features or elements. (Also called *dependent* or *heteronomous sound change*.)

conditioned stress: Stress placed on a syllable determined by certain phonetical, morphological or functional conditions.

conditioned variants: Variants (q.v.) due to position in the environment. (Also called *combinatory* or *positional variants*.)

conformative: See *similative*.

Congo: A language spoken in the Belgian Congo; a member of the Bantu family of languages.

congruence: Morphological or other formal agreement or concord.

conjugate: To indicate differences as to number, person, tense, mood, etc., by inflection, prefixes, auxiliaries, etc.

conjugation: The scheme of the modifications of the verb, by means of inflection, prefixes, auxiliaries, etc., to express various tenses, moods, voices, persons and numbers.

conjunct flexion: See *compounded flexion*.

conjunction: A word used to connect words or sentences, indicating the relationship of these connected elements. Conjunctions can be classified as *coordinating* and *subordinating*, as *connective* and *disjunctive*, also as *affirmative, adversative, copulative* and *continuative, causal, concessive, hypothetical, correlative, negative* and *temporal* (qq.v.).

conjunctive: Serving as a connecting link between two terms.

conjunctive adverb: An adverb which can be used as a coordinating connecting word between two clauses.

conjunctive pronoun: In the Romance languages, a personal pronoun in an oblique case (q.v.), used in conjunction with a verbal form.

connecting vowel: A vowel inserted at times between the stem or root of a word and an inflectional ending, or in general between two elements of word-formation, for the sake of ease or euphony in pronunciation.

connective conjunction: A conjunction (q.v.) connecting two words, word-groups or clauses having a cumulative effect. (E.g., *and*.)

connotation: The ideas and associations linked with a word; the meanings or ideas which a word suggests or implies (also called the *intensional meaning*).

consequence clause: In a conditional sentence, the clause which states the expected or logical result of the condition expressed by the *hypothetical clause* (q.v.). Also called *apodosis*.

consonance: In prosody, the agreement of final consonantal sounds of two or more words, the final vowel sounds of which are different.

consonant: (1) A sound produced by an obstruction or blocking or some other restriction of the free passage of the air, exhaled from the lungs, through the oral cavity.—(2) A letter representing such a sound.

consonantal digraph: A combination of two consonant letters representing one single consonant sound.

consonantal trigraph: A term occasionally applied to any combination of three consonant letters which represents one consonant sount. (E.g., the German *sch*.)

consonantal writing: A system of alphabetic writing in which only consonants are written. (Some authorities regard the characters of these systems actually as syllable signs.) (Cf., e.g., *defective writing*.)

consonantism: The scientific study, historical or descriptive, of the consonant system of a language or dialect.

consonantization: The change of a vowel or semi-vowel into a consonant.

constituents: The component morphemes of a complex form; the constituents of "John ran" are the simple forms "John" and "ran." In the statement "Poor John ran away," the *immediate constituents* are the complex forms, "Poor John" and "ran away," which may be subdivided into the *ultimate constituents*, "poor," "John," "ran," "a-," "-way." (*Bloomfield*)

constricted: In phonetical terminology, said of a phoneme the articulation of which involves a contraction of the larynx.

constructio ad sensum: Latin for *construction according to sense;* a term synonymous with the Greek term *synesis* (q.v.).

construction: The manner of grouping and combining elements of speech; specifically, *syntactical construction* (q.v.).

contact anticipation: Assimilation (q.v.) in which a phoneme or group of phonemes becomes identical with or similar to the phoneme or group of phonemes immediately following it.

contact vernacular: A term used by Bodmer and Hogben (*The Loom of Language*) to designate any vernacular developed in and for dealings between European colonizers and natives of various colonial parts of the world. (E.g., Pidgin English.)

contagion: See *semantic contagion.*

contamination: The effect exercised by one element of speech upon another with which it is customarily or accidentally associated, resulting in a *portmanteau* or *telescope word* (q.v.).

content: The intrinsic meaning of a linguistic symbol.

context: The sounds, words or phrases immediately preceding or following the sound, word or phrase under consideration; also, the relation to or connection with such preceding or subsequent sounds, words or phrases.

contextual variant: See *positional variant.*

Continental West Germanic: A collective term for the West Germanic languages spoken on the European continent (i.e., German, Dutch and Flemish, and their various dialects).

continuant: In phonetical terminology, a consonant which can be prolonged in pronunciation, i.e., held continuously without a change in its quality, in contradistinction to a *stop* (q.v.). Also called *spirant* and *fricative.*

continuative: A verbal mood or aspect (e.g., in Bantu dialects) expressing that the action is viewed as a continuous development.

continuative conjunction: A conjunction (q.v.) which connects a dependent clause to an independent or main clause.

continuous script, continuous writing: In paleography, a system of writing in which the individual words are not separated by blank spaces.

contraction: (1) The shortening of a word or expression; also, the shortened form resulting from this process.—(2) The combination of two or more sounds or sound-elements in one single sound.

contrast: Often used as a synonym for *opposition* (q.v.). A. Martinet has urged the useful distinction that *opposition* be reserved for phonemic distinctions (*p*in vs. *b*in) and *contrast* for non-distinctive, phonetic features (*p*in vs. s*p*in.)

coordinate: Of the same order or importance.

coordinated adjectives: Two or more adjectives, both or all of which modify the same substantive with equal effect.

coordinating conjunction: A conjunction (q.v.) connecting two words, word-groups or clauses and indicating that both connected elements are independent and of equal function or importance.

coordination: The arrangement on the same level of importance or function of two or more terms or elements—in contradistinction to *subordination*.

Coptic: A Hamitic language, descendant of ancient Egyptian; the vernacular of Egypt in the third to tenth centuries A.D.

copula: A word expressing the relationship between the subject and predicate of a sentence. (The various forms of the verb *to be* or its equivalents are typical examples of copulas.)

copulative: Connecting; constituting a copula (q.v.).

copulative compound: A compound word or expression, the meaning of which would not be changed, and in fact would be clarified, by the insertion of the conjunction *and* or an equivalent between the component words. (Also called *dvandva compound*.)

copulative conjunction: A conjunction (q.v.) which coordinates terms (words, word-groups or clauses) of equal importance or function. (E.g., *and*.)

Cornish: The now extinct language of Cornwall; a member of the Brythonic branch of the Celtic group of the Indo-European family.

coronal articulation: In phonetical terminology, the formation of a sound with the blade of the tongue making contact with some part of the oral cavity.

correlation: The relationship between a voiced series and a voiceless series (cf. *series*) is expressed as a correlation of voice; the relationship between an aspirate series and an inaspirate series, as a correlation of aspiration.

correlative: (1) Said of two or more mutually interdependent terms or of two or more words or groups of words which are customarily used together.—(2) See *correlative conjunctions*.

correlative conjunctions: Pairs of conjunctions (q.v.) which complement the meaning of each other. (E.g., *either—or*.)

correspondence: Similarity, analogy; concordance.

corrupt: (1) Grammatically, morphologically, phonetically, idiomatically, etc. incorrect.—(2) Creolized (q.v.).

Corsican: A Central Italian dialect spoken on the island of Corsica; its closest links are with the Gallurese and Sassarese of northern Sardinia, and the Tuscan of the Italian mainland.

Cossaean: An extinct language (also called *Kassite*) classified as *Asianic*, spoken in the Zagros Mountains area, east of Mesopotamia, with written records dating as far back as the 17th century B.C. No affinity to any other known language can be demonstrated.

Cottian: An extinct language, also called *Kottish*, related to Yenisei-Ostyak; formerly spoken on the Agul in eastern Siberia.

crasis: Syneresis (q.v.) resulting from the fusion of the final vowel of a word with the initial vowel of the immediately following word.

Cree: A North American Indian language, belonging to the Algonquian family, surviving in lower Saskatchewan, on the east shore of Hudson Bay, James Bay, near Lake Winnipeg.

Creek: See *Mushkogee*.

Creole: The creolized (q.v.) French spoken in Haiti and Mauritius, more specifically called *French Creole,* to distinguish it from the *Dutch Creole* spoken in the West Indies, and from the *Portuguese Creole* of the Cape Verde Islands.

creolization: The "degeneration" of a language into a *creolized language* (q.v.).

creolized language: A trade language or "contact vernacular" (qq.v.) which has become the only language used for daily speech and communication by an economically, socially or politically subject group, class or race; characterized by extreme morphological simplification of the language of colonization (q.v.) from which it is derived.

crest of sonority: A synonym for *syllabic* (q.v.).

Cretan: An extinct and still unknown language, spoken in ancient Crete, preserved in three still undeciphered inscriptions, and in four brief texts written with Greek characters. Classified as *Asianic.*

critical transcription (*or* **edition**): A transcription of an ancient or medieval document in which the transcriber makes adaptations and changes designed to reconstruct a hypothetical original form, or to present the document in the most comprehensible and logical fashion. (Cf. *diplomatic transcription.*)

criticism: Evaluation and judgment according to recognized standards, based on study and analysis.

Croatian: See *Serbo-Croatian.*

Csángó: A variety of Hungarian spoken by a rapidly dwindling linguistic island in Bukovina, near the Carpathians; it is heavily interlarded with Romanian and Slavic words and constructions.

culminative function: The use of accent to determine the number of full words in an utterance.

cultural language: A language learned by the speaker in school or acquired through social, business, or other dealings with its native speakers. E.g., German is a cultural tongue in this sense all over Central Europe, Scandinavia and the Netherlands.

cultural word: Any word which expresses ideas characteristic of the social or communal or cultural life of a community.

cuneiform: The syllabic writing, with vestiges of ideographic symbols, consisting of wedge-shaped signs, invented by the Sumerians, and used by the Assyrians and other nations of ancient Mesopotamia (from about 4000 B.C. to the first millennium B.C.). The symbols were impressed into wet clay.

cursive aspect: A verbal aspect (q.v.) considering the action in its development, but without consideration for its duration.

cursive writing: Any simplified script used for quick, daily use.

curtailed word: A word created by shortening another word.

Cushite: See *Kushitic*.

Cymric, Cymraeg: Alternative names of *Welsh* (q.v.).

Cyprian: See *Cypriote*.

Cypriote: An extinct and still unknown language, spoken in ancient Cyprus, preserved in twelve inscriptions, assumed to date from the fourth century B.C. Classified as *Asianic*.

Cyrillic writing: The script used in Russia, Bulgaria, Serbia, and the Ukraine, devised by Cyril and Methodius, in the 9th century A.D., mainly on the basis of the Greek alphabet.

Czech: A West Slavic language, spoken by about 12,000,000 native speakers. (Formerly also called *Bohemian*.)

D

Daco-Romanian: The Romanian language as spoken in Romania proper.

Dahl's law: The phonetic law applicable to the Bantu languages, stating that in certain languages of that group when a vowel or diphthong is immediately between two unvoiced consonants, the first of these consonants becomes voiced.

Dahomian: See *Fon*.

Dalmatian: An extinct Romance language, spoken formerly on the eastern coast of the Adriatic. Its two recorded dialects were: *Veglian*, which became extinct with the death of Antonio Udina in 1898, and *Ragusan*, known only from a few medieval documents.

Danish: A Scandinavian (North Germanic) language, spoken by about 4,000,000 native speakers.

Dano-Norwegian: See *Riksmål*.

Dargva: A branch of the Eastern Caucasian group of the North Caucasian family of languages.

dark vowel: A synonym of *back vowel* (q.v.).

Darmesteter's law: The law which states that in the transition from Latin to French the syllable immediately before the stressed syllable becomes silent or disappears, except if it contains the vowel *a*.

dash: The punctuation mark [—].

dative: In Indo-European languages, that case form in which a noun, pronoun, adjective or numeral is used when it is the indirect object (q.v.) of the sentence.

Dayak: A language spoken in Borneo; a member of the Indonesian sub-family of the Malayo-Polynesian family of languages.

dead language: A language no longer used as a general medium of spoken communication.

dead metaphor: A metaphor (q.v.) which has lost its metaphorical character.

declension: In inflectional languages, the system of the inflection of a noun, pronoun, adjective or numeral, intended to show differences of case, gender and number.

decline: To indicate the relationship of a noun, pronoun, adjective or numeral to another word or other words in the sentence by means of inflectional endings.

deep vowel: A synonym for *back vowel* (q.v.).

defective: Lacking a certain form or certain forms of declension, conjugation or comparison, which the great majority of the words of the same class have.

defective writing: In the Hebrew system of consonantal writing, the method of writing consonants only. (Cf. *plene writing.*)

definite: In general, referring or relating to a specific or determined person, thing or idea.

definite article: A particle inserted before or prefixed (in certain languages added as a suffix) to nouns to indicate that the noun is used to denote a specific member of the class which it designates.

definite conjugation: See *objective conjugation.*

definite declension: In German grammar, a synonym for the *weak declension* (q.v.) of the adjective.

deflexion: Loss of inflexion.

delabialization: (1) The process of depriving a sound of its labial (q.v.) character.—(2) Unrounding (q.v.).

delative: A declensional case in certain non-Indo-European languages, having the denotation of a descending motion.

demarcative function: The use of phonemic and non-phonemic features, including accent, to mark off the boundaries of words and morphemes.

demonstrative adjective: A demonstrative pronoun or a word of the same or similar class, used adjectivally, i.e., with a substantive which it is to modify.

demonstrative pronoun: A pronoun which refers to one or more specific persons, objects, etc.

Demotic Greek: The modern Greek vernacular or colloquial form of the Greek language, characterized by a simplification of grammatical form and by the use of Turkish and other loan-words. (The indigenous term for this vernacular is *Dhēmotikē*).

Dene: A group of North American Indian languages (Athapascan family), spoken in northwestern Canada.

denotation: The expressed or *extensional meaning* of a word or term.

dental: In phonetical terminology, a consonant pronounced with the tongue touching the tips of the upper teeth.

dependent clause: A subordinate clause (q.v.).

dependent sound change: See *conditioned sound change*.

deponent verb: In Latin grammar, a verb having a passive form i.e., conjugated according to the paradigms of the passive voice, but having an active meaning. (Cf. *middle voice*.)

derivation: (1) The formation of a new word from an existing word, root or stem, by the addition of a prefix or suffix, or by other means.—(2) The indication of the sources and development of the elements composing a word.

derivational: Representing, relating to or obtained by derivation.

derivational compound: A compound in which one of the components appears in a derivational form. (E.g., thick-headed.)

derivative: In general, a word formed from another word by internal vowel change ("primary derivative") or by the addition of a prefix or suffix ("secondary derivative").

descriptive adjective: An adjective denoting a quality or characteristic (answering the question "of what kind?").

descriptive grammar: The presentation of grammar in terms of actual usage on different levels, comparing the formal and informal, standard and non-standard, written and spoken, etc., in the light of linguistic science.

descriptive linguistics: Synchronic linguistics (q.v.).

descriptive phonetics: Synchronic phonetics (q.v.).

desiderative: The verbal mood or aspect expressing a desire.

destinative: A declensional case in certain languages (e.g., in Basque), having the denotation of the English preposition *for*.

deteriorative suffix: See *pejorative suffix*.

determinative: (1) A sound or syllable added to the base or stem of a verb, i.e., interpolated between base and inflectional ending, to modify the *aspect* (q.v.) of the verb.—(2) In systems of ideographic writing (e.g., in Chinese writing), a semantic but non-phonetic sign which is added to the basic ideogram to indicate its proper meaning in the context by identifying the category to which the depicted concept, thing, etc., belongs.

determinative clause: An adjectival clause which serves as a compound demonstrative adjective.

determinative compound: A compound word in which a noun or adjective is combined with another noun, adjective or adverb which determines, modifies or qualifies it. (Defined by Graff as a compound "in which one component plays the part of a genitive or some objective [oblique] case with respect to the other.")

determiners: Words which serve to mark the so-called Class I forms in the Fries classification system; e.g., words which can be substituted for "the" in the frame, "(The) concert is good!"

Devanagari: The form of script used for writing ancient Sanskrit and several of the modern languages of India, notably Hindi.

devoiced plosive: In phonetical terminology, a consonant produced by a weak exhalation of an unaspirated voiced plosive.

devoicing: In phonetical terminology, the deprivation of a voiced consonant of its voiced quality. (Also called *unvoicing*.)

Dhēmotikē: See *Demotic Greek*.

diachronic: For the use of this adjective, cf. *diachronic grammar*, *diachronic linguistics* and *diachronic phonetics*.

diachronic grammar: Historical grammar (q.v.).

diachronic linguistics: The study of words, speech, languages and linguistic changes from the point of view of evolution in the course of time.

diachronic phonetics: That branch of phonetics which endeavors to study and classify the phonetic laws which explain and account for phonetic changes in the course of time.

diacritic mark; diacritic sign: A sign placed over, below or across a letter, at times merely as an orthographic sign, but in most instances to indicate the correct sound represented by that letter in the given word. (Often referred to as *written accent* or *graphic accent.*)

diaeresis: (1) The diacritic mark [¨] placed over one of two adjacent vowels, to indicate that it does not form a diphthong with the other vowel, but is to be given its full, independent phonetic value in pronunciation.—(2) (Cf. *umlaut.*)

dialect: A specific form of a given language, spoken in a certain locality or geographic area, showing sufficient differences from the standard or literary form of that language, as to pronunciation, grammatical construction and idiomatic usage of words, to be considered a distinct entity, yet not sufficiently distinct from other dialects of the language to be regarded as a different language.

dialect geography: The study of local linguistic differences within given speech-areas.

dialect atlas: A set of maps marking off the boundaries of selected features of a given dialect, such as sounds, vocabulary, grammatical forms, etc.

dialectal: Having the characteristics or forming part of a dialect.

dialectology: The study of dialects.

diathesis: The relationship of the subject to the verb, according as the subject is the agent or the target of the action. (In old grammars, *diathesis* was used in the meaning of *voice.*)

diction: The selection and use of words in speech.

dictionary: A book containing the words of a given language (usually in alphabetical order) with definitions of their meanings; also, a book listing the words of a language with their equivalents in a foreign language or foreign languages; also, a book listing, in alphabetical order or grouped by some convenient method, the terms of a given field of knowledge or study, discipline, profession, etc., with their definitions or explanations or foreign-language equivalents.

Dido: A language spoken in the Caucasus; a member of the Avaro-Andi branch of the Eastern Caucasian group of the North Caucasian family of languages.

dieresis: See *diaeresis.*

differentiation: (1) In general, the abolition of similarity or identicalness.—(2) In phonetics, specifically, the tendency or process of changing one of two adjacent identical phonemes into a different phoneme. (Cf. *dissimilation.*)

digamma: The ancient, obsolete Greek letter ϝ, which in many Greek dialects had the phonetic value of [w].

digraph: A combination of two letters (either vowel or consonant signs) representing one spoken sound. (E.g., the English *th.*)

Dil: An artificial language, a modified form of Volapük (q.v.), created by Fieweger in 1893.

diminutive: A word derived from another word by the addition of a *diminutive suffix* (q.v.).

diminutive aspect: A verbal aspect, expressing that the action or state denoted by the verb is of a minor degree, intensity or importance.

diminutive suffix: A suffix conveying the notion of smallness or daintiness, occasionally also a pejorative (q.v.) meaning.

ding-dong theory: See *nativistic theory.*

Dinka: An African Negro language, spoken in the Anglo-Egyptian Sudan; a member of the Sudanese-Guinean family of languages.

diphthong: A union of two vowels pronounced in one syllable. (Cf. *falling diphthong, rising diphthong.*)

diphthongization: The change of a vowel to a diphthong.

diplomatic transcription (*or* **edition**): A transcription of an ancient or medieval document in which no changes or adaptations are made, but the text is transcribed precisely as it appears in the available manuscript. (Cf. *critical transcription.*)

diptote: In certain languages, this term is applied to designate substantives which have defective declensions, consisting of only two cases.

direct case: The nominative case, in contradistinction to the *oblique cases* (q.v.). Some grammarians use the term, *direct case,* as including both the nominative and the vocative cases.

direct discourse: A sentence, group of sentences, or in general any form of discourse in which the words, statements, etc. of another person are quoted verbatim.

direct object: The person or thing directly affected by the action expressed in the sentence.

direct question: A question in the form as asked in the course of direct communication or quoted in direct discourse.

direct quotation: The word-for-word repetition of a statement or words of another person.

directive: (1) In general, a term applied by *Bodmer* especially to any preposition, postposition or suffix which expresses location, direction, time, agency, etc.—(2) In certain African languages, a verbal ending or suffix, indicating that the action is performed or takes place for the sake of somebody or toward a definite goal.

directive case: A declensional case in certain African languages, having the same denotation as the English *for the sake of* or *for the purpose of.*

discourse: In general, any form of oral or written communication or composition. (Cf. *direct discourse, indirect discourse.*)

discriminative: A declensional case in certain languages, in which a noun is used when it is the agent of an action.

disjunction: (1) In general, separation, abolition of unity or contiguity.—(2) Specifically, the separation of two or more terms of a unit or group by the interpolation of another word or word-group.

disjunctive conjunction: A conjunction (q.v.) placed between two words, word-groups or clauses and having a dissociative, contrasting or separating effect. (E.g., *or, but.*)—Cf. *adversative conjunction.*

disjunctive opposition: Phonemes in different *series* and *orders* (qq.v.) opposed to each other.

disjunctive pronoun: In the Romance languages, a personal pronoun, in an oblique case-form (q.v.), used alone, or after a preposition, or as a stressed subject or object.

displaced speech: The use of linguistic signs (words) to indicate objects which are not present in the specific situation, as in the question, "When will dinner be ready?"

dissimilation: The process in which one of two identical or similar phonemes changes or displaces the other one. When the preceding phoneme changes under the influence of the following one, the dissimilation is called *regressive;* the change of a phoneme under the influence of a preceding phoneme is called *progressive dissimilation.* (Cf. *differentiation.*)

dissonance: An unpleasant combination of sounds.

dissyllabic: Consisting of two syllables.

distant assimilation: Assimilation (q.v.) of not contiguous phonemes.

distinctive function: The use of phonemically relevant features to distinguish linguistic signs.

distribution: The syntagmatic arrangement of elements in the *spoken chain* (q.v.). (Cf. *complementary distribution.*)

distributive: (1) In general: implying a separation or individualization, or indicating that the idea, property, etc. in question applies to each and every member of a group or to objects or persons considered individually.—(2) See *distributive numeral.*

distributive aspect: A verbal aspect expressing that the action or state denoted by the verb is performed or experienced simultaneously by more than one individual or object.

distributive numeral: A numeral referring to units or groups, each consisting of the indicated number of members considered. (E.g., *by twos, by the dozen.*)

Djong: See *Mo-so.*

Dog-Aramaic: A designation of the language in which several extant ancient Aramaic written documents and inscriptions are couched—i.e., Aramaic mixed with a foreign language or strongly influenced by a foreign form of speech.

Dogon: An African Negro language, member of the Sudanese-Guinean family of languages.

Dogra: A dialect of the Indic language *Punjabi;* spoken by about 1,500,000 persons in and around the State of Jammu. (Also called *Dogri.*)

domesticated word: A term occasionally applied to designate a word borrowed from a foreign language and adopted for use in its original form.

Doric: A group of ancient western Greek dialects, including Laconian, Messenian, Argolic and Cretan.

dorsal: A sound made with the *dorsum* (q.v.).

dorsum: The back part of the tongue, associated with the soft palate (*velum*).

double negative: The use of more than one negative word in the same sentence to express one negation.

doublets: In general, alternative forms. Usually, the term *doublets* is employed to mean *etymological doublets*, i.e., two or more words of the same language which were derived from the same basic word but are currently used as having different meanings. (E.g., the English *frail* and *fragile.*) (See also *morphological doublets.*)

downward comparison: The comparison of adjectives or adverbs to denote a lesser quantity or intensity of the characteristic or quality expressed.

Dravidian: A family of languages, spoken by over 100,000,000 persons in central and southern India, on the east coast of India, in northern Ceylon and in the mountains of eastern Beluchistan. Its main branches are: Tamil-Kurukh (Tamil, Malayalam, Kanarese, Tulu, and Kurukh), Kui-Gondi (Kui, Gondi, Bhili, Kolimi and Naiki), Telugu, and Brahui.

drift: A consistent diachronic change in the pattern of a language, i.e., the movement of language "down time in a current of its own making" (*Edward Sapir*), resulting in the breaking up into dialects because of specific phonetic tendencies.

dual: The grammatical number denoting *two*, which many languages use in addition to the singular and plural.

Duala: An African Negro language, spoken in Cameroon; a member of the Bantu family of languages.

duration: With reference to speech sounds or phonemes, the relative length of time during which the vocal organs remain in the position required for the articulation of a given sound. (Synonymous with *quantity*.)

durative aspect: The verbal *aspect* (q.v.) which considers the action in its duration and development. Often used as an alternative term for *imperfective aspect* (q.v.).

Dutch: A West Germanic language, spoken by about 13,000,000 native speakers in the Netherlands and the Dutch colonies and possessions. (See *Flemish* and *Afrikaans*.)

Dutch Creole: A creolized (q.v.) Dutch spoken in the West Indies.

dvandva compound: See *copulative compound*.

dynamic accent: Stress (q.v.).

dynamic action: See *middle voice*.

dynamic linguistics: The linguistic discipline which considers languages from the aspect of their development and history.

dynamics: Jespersen's term for historical grammar endeavoring to explain grammatical phenomena which it considers to be related.

E

East Germanic: The extinct branch of the Germanic group of the Indo-European family of languages, which consisted of Gothic, Burgundian and Vandal.

East Romance: A term used by some Romance scholars to include Romanian, Dalmatian and centro-southern Italian.

East Semitic: A branch of the Semitic group of languages, represented only by the extinct Akkadian language (called also Assyrian or Old Akkadian in its early period, and Babylonian or New Akkadian in its late period).

East Slavic languages: A branch of the Slavic group of the Indo-European family of languages, comprising Russian (also called Great Russian), Ukrainian (also called Little Russian) and White Russian.

East Tokharian: The designation (*Osttocharisch*) applied by W. Krause to *Tokharian A* (see *Tokharian*).

Eastern Algonquian: A subdivision of the Algonquian family of North American Indian languages; its surviving members are: Malisit, Micmac, Penobscot and Passamaquoddy (northeastern United States and central and eastern Canada).

Eastern American English: The dialectal variant of American English spoken generally in New England, New Jersey, Delaware, Maryland, and the eastern portions of New York and Pennsylvania.

Eastern Aramaic: A branch of Aramaic, a Northern West Semitic language, consisting of the extinct dialects called Babylonian Judaeo-Aramaic, Mandaean, and Harranian, furthermore Syriac and various modern dialects spoken in parts of Mesopotamia and of Persia.

Eastern Caucasian: A group, also called *Checheno-Lesghian,* of the North Caucasian family of languages. It is divided into the following branches: Chechen, Avaro-Andi, Samurian, Dargva, Artshi, Udi, Lak (Kazikumyk) and Kinalugh.

Eastern Hindi: An Indic language, spoken in Oudh, the United Provinces, Baghelkhand, and in the eastern part of the Central Provinces, by an estimated total of 25,000,000 persons.

Eastern Laotian: Tai Lao (q.v.).

Eastern Mongol: A language group within the Mongol branch of the Altaic sub-family of the Ural-Altaic family of languages; it consists of Khalkha, Shara and Tangut, and the near-extinct Afghan Mongol. Some linguists classify also Yakut (usually considered a Turkic language) as a member of the Eastern Mongol group.

Eastern Turkic: A language group, a subdivision of the Turkic branch of the Altaic (or Turco-Tartaric) sub-family of the Ural-Altaic family of languages. It is occasionally referred to as Altaic proper. It comprises Altaic, Abakan, Baraba, Karagas, Soyonian and Uighur.

echo-word: An onomatopoetic word (q.v.).

echoism: See *onomatopoeia*.

eclipsis: (1) A synonym for *ecthlipsis* (q.v.).—(2) In the grammars of the Celtic languages, the term for certain phonetical changes, especially a nasalization, of the initial phonemes of words when they directly follow certain words or flexional forms.

economy: The tendency of a language to follow the so-called "law of least effort," commensurate with communicative needs. (*A. Martinet*)

ecphoneme: An obsolete name of the *exclamation point* [!].

ecthlipsis: The suppression or omission of a consonant, whether in speech or in writing.

effective aspect: An alternative term for the *perfective* verbal aspect (q.v.).

Efik: An African Negro language, spoken by about 50,000 persons in the Calabar district of Nigeria (West Africa); a member of the Sudanese-Guinean family of languages.

Egyptian: (1) A branch of the Hamitic sub-family of the Semito-Hamitic family of languages, consisting of Egyptian proper and its descendant, Coptic.—(2) The language of ancient Egypt, and parent language of Coptic, divided into Old Egyptian (3400-2200 B.C.), Middle Egyptian (2200-1580 B.C.) and New Egyptian (1580 B.C. to the third century A.D.).

Ehue: See *Ewe*.

ejective consonant: In phonetical terminology, a *plosive* (q.v.) pronounced with a simultaneous *glottal stop* (q.v.).

Elamite: An extinct language, classified as *Asianic*, spoken in the area of modern Iran from at least 2500 B.C. till the first century A.D. No relationship to any known language can be demonstrated. Elamite is called also *Susian;* Old Elamite is often called *Anzanite*, while New Elamite is often referred to as *Hozi*.

elative: (1) The absolute superlative (q.v.) of an adjective or adverb.—(2) See *elative case*.

elative case: A Finno-Ugric declensional case, having same denotation as the English *out of*.

electrical vocal tract: A machine, demonstrated by H. K. Dunn, designed to synthetize vowel sounds with the aid of electronic circuits.

element: In general, a constituent part, or a part of a unit separable by analysis.

elements of a sentence: The constituent parts of a sentence.

elision: The suppression or omission of a vowel or of an entire syllable, usually for euphony (in poetry, often used in order to conform with a given meter). Occasionally used as a synonym for *ellipsis* (q.v.—*1*).

ellipsis: (1) The omission of a word or words considered essential for grammatical completeness, but not for the conveyance of the intended meaning.—(2) A series of dots (...) or asterisks (* * *) to indicate the omission of a word or words.

elliptical: Having a part omitted.

elliptical construction: Having an essential part or element omitted.

Elu: Classical, literary Sinhalese, free of foreign admixtures. (Cf. *Sinhala.*)

emotive: Relating or appealing to or based on emotions or sentiments rather than reasoning or intelligence.

emotive speech: Speech or utterance intended to express or convey emotion.

emphasis: Special importance placed on an element; also, the indication of such special importance.

emphatic: Conveying or indicating special intensity, stress or emphasis.

emphatic articulation: In the Semitic languages, a form of articulation which imparts a special character to certain consonants.

emphatic mood: The verbal mood, whether synthetic or periphrastic (qq.v.) which expresses special stress or emphasis. (E.g., the emphatic imperative of Latin, or the periphrastic construction *I do see him* in English, etc.)

emphatic pronoun: A personal pronoun used for emphasis.

empty word: In Chinese grammar, a designation approximately equivalent to *particle* or *pointer word* (qq.v.)—i.e., a word which serves to indicate or define the function or syntactical relationship of a *full word* (q.v.) in a sentence.

enclisis: The pronunciation of a word without its independent accent, as a part of the immediately preceding word; in many languages, the enclitic word is often written as forming one word with the preceding one.

enclitic: Said of a word which bears no accent of its own, but is pronounced as forming a phonetic unit with the accented word preceding it.

encyclopedia: A comprehensive summary of knowledge in a given field or branch of science.

ending: (1) In general, the final sound or syllable of a word.— (2) Specifically, a flexional suffix added to a word or word stem to indicate variation in case or number (*case ending*), tense, mood, person (*personal ending*), or other grammatical function or syntactical relationship. (In many languages, possession is also expressed by *personal endings*—e.g., in the Finno-Ugric and Semitic languages.)

endocentric construction: A syntactical construction which as a unit has the same function or belongs to the same linguistic, grammatical, syntactical, etc. class as one or more of its constituent elements.

endophasia: Non-vocal, inaudible language, conscious or subconscious.

energetic mood: A synonym for *emphatic mood* (q.v.).

English: A West Germanic language, the native tongue of approximately 250,000,000 persons, spoken in the British Isles, the United States of America, in Canada, Australia, New Zealand, South Africa, etc.

environment: In linguistic usage, a synonym for *context* (q.v.).

epanalepsis: In general, the repetition of a word, for emphasis or rhetorical effect. Specifically, the use of a personal pronoun instead of repeating a word previously mentioned; this construction is current and permissible in many languages (e.g., in French: *votre père, comment va-t-il?*).

epenthesis: The interpolation in a word or sound-group of a sound or letter which has no etymological justification for appearing there. (E.g., the *b* in *doubt*.) The interpolated element is called an *anaptyctic* or *excrescent* sound or letter. The epenthetic sound is often used to facilitate a difficult transition between two other adjacent sounds (e.g., Latin *venire habeo* > *ven're* > Spanish *vendré*, or Germanic *knîf* > French *canif*).

epexegesis: Explanation, elucidation, interpretation.

epexegetical: Explanatory or defining (E.g., in the expression, "the city of Paris," the possessive form of *Paris* is termed an "epexegetical genitive.")

epicene: A noun which can be used as of male or female gender, i.e., which may designate a male or a female being.

epigraphy: The study, deciphering and interpretation of ancient inscriptions or records carved or engraved into stone, moulded on clay, or otherwise made and preserved in some other hard, solid material. (Cf. *paleography*.)

episememe: The smallest meaningful grammatical unit; the meaning of a *tagmeme*. (*Bloomfield*)

epithesis: A synonym for *paragoge* (q.v.).

epithet: A word or phrase which denotes a real or essential or distinctive quality of a person or thing and forms a closely linked unit with the word designating the latter, as a qualifier, attributive or predicate adjective.

epithetologue: A term applicable to nouns and adjectives (including participles used adjectivally).

eponym: The person from whose name (or that name itself) the name of a group or country or other geographical or sociological unit is derived.

equative case: A declensional case in certain languages (e.g., Georgian), having the same denotation as the English *as*, *like* or *in the capacity of*.

equative degree: A degree of the comparison of adjectives in certain languages, expressing an equality of the quality, property, etc. designated by the adjective.

ergative case: In Basque, a language which has no active voice, a case in which a substantive is used when it is the agent in a sentence the verb of which is by form or sense in the passive voice.

Erse: An obsolete and not recommended popular name of the *Irish* language; it is not used by the Irish themselves.

Eskimo-Aleut: A family of languages, spoken in western and northern Alaska, along the northern coast of North America, along the shores of Hudson Bay, the shores of Labrador and Greenland, also in extreme northeastern Asia (*Eskimo*) and in the Aleutian Islands (*Aleut*). One of the main characteristics of these languages is their extreme degree of incorporation (polysynthetism). Some linguists regard these languages as related to Altaic, others consider them members of the Finno-Ugric sub-family, but neither of these relationships has been proved conclusively.

Eskuara: See *Basque*.

Esperantido: An artificial language, a modified version of Esperanto (q.v.), created by R. de Saussure.

Esperanto: An artificial language created, to serve as a world-wide interlanguage, by Dr. Ludwig L. Zamenhof, first published in 1887. At the present time, the number of the speakers and users of Esperanto is estimated at 8,000,000.

essive: A declensional case in certain languages (e.g., Finno-Ugric languages), denoting a continued or permanent state of being.

Estonian: A language of the Finnish group of the Finno-Ugric (or Uralic) sub-family of the Ural-Altaic family of languages; the native tongue of approximately 1,000,000 persons.

Estrangelo: The old Syriac script developed by Christian missionaries and in exclusive use for the writing of Syriac until the fifth century A.D.

Eteocretan: See *Cretan.*

Eteocyprian: See *Cypriote.*

Ethiopian: See *Ethiopic.*

Ethiopic: (1) A sub-group of the Southern West Semitic languages, consisting of Ge'ez (also called Ethiopic) and its modern descendant Tigriña (also called Tigray), furthermore of Tigre, Amharic, Argobba, Gafat, Gurage and Harari.—(2) The Ge'ez language (q.v.).

ethnolinguistics: The study of the relations between linguistics and ethnology, and their mutual influence.

ethnology: The science and study of the races of mankind, their character, history, cultures, customs and institutions.

Etruscan: An extinct language, of undetermined linguistic affinities, spoken in pre-Roman and Roman Italy (the oldest records date from the eighth century B.C.). Classified as *Asianic.*

etymological: Pertaining or according to etymology.

etymological doublets: See *doublets.*

etymology: That branch of linguistics which deals with the origin and history of words, tracing them back to their earliest determinable base in the given language group.

etymon: The word which is the key to the etymology of a given word. Often used as a synonym for *radical* (q.v.).

euphemism: The substitution of a word of more pleasant connotation for one of unpleasant or disagreeable connotation. (E.g., *to pass away* for *to die*.)

euphonic: Having an agreeable or pleasing sound; contributing to euphony.

euphony: A pleasing sound or combination of sounds.

Europan: An artificial language, created by Weisbart.

Euzkera: See *Basque*.

evolution: A process of change and development, involving continuity.

evolutionary linguistics: The term introduced by F. de Saussure (*linguistique évolutive*) to designate *diachronic linguistics* (q.v.).

Ewe: An African Negro language, spoken in Togoland and part of the Gold Coast (also serving as a *lingua franca* over a large area); a member of the Sudanese-Guinean family of languages.

exclamation: A word or phrase expressing or conveying a strong emotion, often at the expense of grammatical completeness.

exclamation mark: The punctuation mark [!].

exclamatory pitch: The change in *pitch* (q.v.) when the speaker is under a strong emotion or responds to a strong stimulus.

exclusive personal pronoun: One of the plural personal pronouns found in certain languages, meaning "we without you," or "we without them," or "you without us," or "you without them," etc., in contradistinction to the *inclusive pronouns* (q.v.).

exclusive relationship: See *complementary distribution*.

excrescent: Said of letters or sounds inserted into words without etymological justification. (Cf. *epenthesis*.)

exhortative mood: A designation applied to the imperative and subjunctive moods when used in sentences expressing or implying an exhortation, encouragement, suggestion, etc.

existential sentence: Jespersen's term for a sentence which states or denies the existence of something (in English, the sentences beginning with *there is, there is not*, etc.).

exocentric construction: A syntactical construction which as a unit has a different function or belongs to a different class from any of its constituent elements.

exogenous: Produced or determined by an external or extraneous factor or factors.

exolinguistics: A term preferred by some authors to *metalinguistics* (q.v.).

exophasia: Vocal, audible language.

experiential word: In semantics, a word which denotes a thing with which the speaker has had direct, first-hand personal experience or contact.

experimental phonetics: The practical study of speech-sounds, as to their production (*physiological phonetics*) or propagation in the air (*acoustic phonetics*) without consideration of their meanings or semantic contents.

expiratory stress: A synonym for *stress,* indicating that it is produced by the expulsion of air.

explanatory grammar: That branch of grammar which observes and studies grammatical phenomena and explains their reasons, causes and origins. (*Sweet*)

expletive: Said of a syllable, word or word group which is inserted in a word or sentence, to satisfy some grammatical or syntactical rule or custom, but the omission of which would not alter or affect the meaning of the word or sentence. (E.g., the word *there* in the sentence "There are many people here.")

explosion: In phonetical terminology, the sudden opening of a closure of the oral air passage, resulting in a sudden exhalation of air.

explosive: See *plosive.*

expression: (1) In general, the manner of conveying or stating an idea. (2) Specifically, a phrase having a distinct meaning and/or form; also, a word.

expressive: Currently used (e.g., Troubetzkoy, etc.) to designate the first of the three important aspects of language, viz., that characterizing the speaker. (Cf. *appellative* and *representational.*)

extension: See *analogical extension, extensional meaning, morphological extension, semantic extension.*

extension of meaning: See *semantic extension.*

extensional meaning: The individual thing or things to which a name or term applies or which it denotes. Synonymous with *denotation*. (Also called, simply, *extension*.)

external hiatus: See: *hiatus*.

external punctuation marks: Signs indicating division of a text into sentences.

externalization: The mental act or process by which sensory data originally considered to be internal are projected into the external world.

F

fact mood: A rarely used alternative designation of the *indicative mood*.

factitive: A synonym for *causative* (q.v.).

factive: A declensional case in certain languages (e.g., Japanese, Finno-Ugric languages, etc.), denoting the idea of becoming or turning or being transformed into something. (Called also *mutative* or *translative*.)

Faliscan: An extinct language, member of the Latino-Faliscan branch of the Italic group of the Indo-European family of languages.

falling diphthong: A diphthong in which the syllabic or stressed element precedes the non-syllabic one.

familiar form: Those forms of verbs, pronouns (in certain languages, such as Japanese, also of other parts of speech) which indicate or imply familiarity, affection, kinship, etc., occasionally also contempt or lack of respect, on the part of the speaker toward the person or persons addressed.

familiar style: (1) Colloquial style (q.v.); (2) cf. *familiar form*.

family of languages: See *language family*.

Fanti: An African Negro language, member of the Sudanese-Guinean family of languages.

Faroese: A Scandinavian dialect spoken in the Faroe Islands.

faucal: Produced in the area between pharynx and glottis.

Federal English: Noah Webster's term for the American form of the English language.

Federalese: See *Gobbledegook*.

feminine: One of the grammatical *genders* (q.v.).

feminization: The formation of a feminine noun from a masculine one by changing its ending or by adding an ending characteristic of the feminine gender.

Fi: An alternative name of *Efik* (q.v.).

figurative idiom: A phrase in which the individual words have a metaphoric meaning. (Cf. *metaphor.*)

figurative meaning: Non-literal or metaphoric meaning (cf. *metaphor.*)

figure: In general, a deviation from the ordinary usage.

figure of etymology: Any deviation from the current or standard form of a word.

figure of rhetoric. An expression or construction intended to produce special effects by deliberate deviation from the ordinary or standard use.

figure of speech: In modern terminology, a *metaphor* or a *simile* (qq.v.). Often used instead of the term *figure of rhetoric* (q.v.).

figure of syntax: Any deviation from the standard or ordinary syntactical construction.

Fiji, Fijian: The language of Fiji; a member of the Melanesian group of the Malayo-Polynesian family of languages.

final accent: Accent or stress falling on the last syllable of a word.

final glide: See *off-glide.*

finite form: Any verbal form which expresses the relationship of the action to a given, definite subject (i.e., the verbal forms which show or imply distinction as to grammatical person, by means of suffixes and/or personal pronouns), in contradistinction to the *infinite forms.* (While this distinction is important in the Indo-European languages, and to a certain extent in the Semitic and Finno-Ugric languages as well, it is meaningless in many other languages or language groups.)

finite mood: A collective designation occasionally applied to designate the *finite forms* (q.v.) of verbs.

Finnish: A language of the Finnish group of the Finnish-Lapponic branch of the Finno-Ugric (or Uralic) sub-family of the Ural-Altaic family of languages; the native tongue of approximately 3,000,000 persons.

Finnish group: A group of languages within the Finnish-Lapponic branch of the Finno-Ugric (or Uralic) sub-family of the Ural-Altaic family of languages; the languages classified into this group are: Finnish, Estonian, Karelian, Ingrian, Livonian, Ludian (or Lüdish), Olonetzian, Vepsian and Votian.

Finnish-Lapponic: A branch of the Finno-Ugric (or Altaic) sub-family of the Ural-Altaic family of languages; it includes the Finnish group (Finnish, Estonian, Karelian, Ingrian, Livonian, Ludian or Lüdish, Olonetzian, Vepsian and Votian) and Lapp. (Cheremiss and Mordvin are frequently classified with Lapp in a Lapponic group, while other linguists consider them two distinct branches of Finno-Ugric.)

Finno-Ugric: A sub-family (also called Uralic) of the Ural-Altaic family of languages. It is divided into the following branches: Finnish-Lapponic, Ugric (Hungarian and the Ob-Ugrian group), Permian and Samoyedic. (Certain linguists consider Cheremiss and Mordvin as two distinct branches, while others classify them with Lapp in a Lapponic group of the Finnish-Lapponic branch.) The linguistic characteristics of this sub-family are: Extreme agglutinative structure and vowel harmony (q.v.).

first-future tense: A designation at times applied to the simple future tense, in contradistinction to the *future-perfect* (or *second-future*) tense.

first participle: An obsolete term for the *present participle*.

first person: The speaker of a sentence.

fixed accent: See *fixed stress*.

fixed stress: With reference to a word, stress which always rests on the same syllable, regardless of flectional or other changes and of syntactical function.

fixed word order: Word order which cannot be altered without changing or altogether destroying the meaning of the utterance.

flapped: In phonetical terminology, said of a variety of the *rolled* (q.v.) consonant, produced by a single tap of the tongue.

flection (*or* **flexion**): Synonyms for *inflection* (q.v.).

Flemish: A variant of Dutch, spoken in Belgium by approximately 4,500,000 persons.

flexible: Capable of being inflected.

flexional: Relating to, derived through or characterized by inflections.

flexional language: Any language which expresses grammatical relations of words and shades or modifications of their meanings by affixing prefixes or suffixes to the roots of the words. This term thus applies both to *agglutinative* and *amalgamating* languages (qq.v.).

floating element: In grammatical terminology, an unnecessary or superfluous word in a sentence.

folk etymology: Any change in the written form or pronunciation of words, in order to make them look or sound more similar to more familiar words, with little or no regard to similarity in meaning or derivation.

Fon: An African Negro language, also called *Dahomian*, member of the Sudanese-Guinean family of languages.

foot: In prosody, a metrical unit containing a specific number of accented and unaccented syllables in a specific combination.

foreignism: A word or idiom or linguistic usage borrowed from the speech of another country.

form-class: A group into which forms showing recognizable phonetical or grammatical similarities are classified.

form-word: Sweet's term for words which do not denote any idea in themselves. (E.g., articles, prepositions, etc.)

formal grammar: That branch of study which treats principally of the form of words and the changes of their external forms (endings, etc.).

formal language: (1) A synonym for *formal speech* (q.v.)— (2) A synonym, occasionally used, for *flexional language* (q.v.).

formal speech: That form of a language which is used in literature, official documents, and in general in all formal writing or speech—as distinguished from *colloquial speech* or *vernacular* (q.v.).

formative: A sound or syllable or group of syllables, usually without any recognizable meaning when used independently, added to words to change their meanings or functions, or as a means of word-formation or derivation.

formless language: A general term applicable to the nonflexional languages in general, and to the isolating languages (q.v.) in particular.

Formosan: The language of Formosa Island; a member of the Indonesian sub-family of the Polynesian family of languages.

formula: Jespersen's term for a word-group used as an indivisible and invariable unit of conversation.

fortis: A strongly, tensely articulated consonant.

fossil form: See *survival*.

fossilized: Antiquated, obsolete; having lost flexibility.

Fox: A North American Indian language (Central Algonquian), surviving in the Great Lakes region.

fracture: See *vowel fracture*.

Francien: The medieval dialect of the Ile-de-France section of northern France, which ultimately became the basis for the official French language. (Also spelled *Francian*.)

Franco-Provençal: A term created by Ascoli to describe a group of dialects in eastern France, western Switzerland and northwestern Italy, which partake of the general characteristics of both northern French and Provençal.

Franconian: A group of medieval West Germanic dialects, combining the characteristics of Low and High German, and subdivided into *Lower Franconian* (which combined with Frisian and Saxon to produce Dutch), and *Middle* and *Upper Franconian* (which combined with Hessian and Thuringian to produce Middle German).

Franco-Venetian: An artificial literary language, consisting of a mixture of Old French and medieval Venetian, evolved by French *jongleurs* for the purpose of reciting the Old French *chansons de geste* to north Italian audiences.

free accent: See *free stress*.

free combination: Jespersen's term for an expression formulated by a speaker or author to fit a certain situation.

free form: Short for *free linguistic form*: any morpheme which can be used as an independent word, i.e., which has a distinct meaning of its own when used alone.

free stress: Stress which may fall on any syllable of a word or expression, according to the flexional form or syntactical function in which it is used.

free syllable: See *open syllable*.

free translation: The rendering of the meaning of a statement, expression, text, etc., in another language, without following the original accurately.

free variants: Variants (q.v.) which are not conditioned by the environment, but are optional with the individual speakers; e.g., the *t* in *net* may be articulated by the same speaker sometimes with aspirated release (q.v.) and sometimes without this non-distinctive or irrelevant feature.

free variation: The relationship in which free variants (q.v.) are said to be with respect to each other. (Cf. *complementary distribution*.)

free word accent: See *free stress*.

free word order: Word order which can be modified at the discretion of the speaker.

French: A Romance language, the native tongue of approximately 65,000,000 persons in France, Belgium, Switzerland, Canada and Haiti.

French Creole: See *Creole*.

frequency: Cf. *functional yield*.

frequentative aspect: A verbal aspect expressing the repetition of the action.

frequentative verb: A verb which denotes or implies a repetition or habitual performance of an act.

fricative: In phonetical terminology, a consonant (also termed *spirant* and *continuant*) pronounced by a narrowing of the air-passages, thus producing an audible friction as the air is expelled from the lungs.

Frisian: The language of about 3,500,000 persons in Friesland (in the Netherlands). A member of the Anglo-Frisian subdivision of the West Germanic branch of the Germanic group of the Indo-European family of languages. The East Frisian dialect is more closely related to Northumbrian (q.v.), West Frisian to Kentish (q.v.).

Friulian: A variety of Rumansch, spoken in the northern and northeastern sections of the Italian region of Venetia. It is linked with the Swiss Rumansch of the Engadine and the Grisons, but is also heavily influenced by Venetian.

front: The part of the tongue starting at the end of the *blade* and reaching to the *dorsum* (qq.v.) (associated with the hard palate).

front vowel: A vowel, the point of articulation of which is in the front part of the oral cavity, i.e., pronounced with the front part of the tongue arched toward the palate.

frontal: A sound made with the front part of the tongue, in the area of the hard palate.

fronted: A sound produced with the tongue advanced from a given position.

Fula: An African Negro language, also called *Peul,* member of the Sudanese-Guinean family of languages.

full stop: The British term for the punctuation mark [.], in the United States more commonly called a *period.*

full word: In Chinese grammar, any word which expresses a concept or idea or designates a person, object, quality, etc.—i.e., verbs, substantives and adjectives.

function: In grammatical terminology, the part played by a word or ending in a sentence.

functional: (1) Having a certain function (q.v.); (2) relating to or dealing with a specific function or linguistic functions in general.

functional and structural theory: the view that every language is a coherent structure in which the component elements have a specific function to perform, namely, to keep the linguistic signs distinct from each other, thus making human speech possible. The variability of human speech is thus due to the changing needs of society, reflecting themselves in changes in the functions of the elements, resulting in modifications of the linguistic structure.

functional change: (1) See *transmutation*.—(2) In phonology, the changes in a phonemic system caused by the necessity for phonemes to function differently as new conditions arise.

functional linguistics: Linguistic study in which phonemes and other linguistic elements are viewed and classified according to their function in the given language.

functional words: The term used by M. Schlauch (*The Gift of Tongues*) for words which serve to indicate the relationship or functions of other words (e.g., prepositions, conjunctions, etc.).

functional yield: The degree of use to which *oppositions* (q.v.) are put. English has many examples of *p* vs. *b* (*pat, bat; cap, cab; clapper, clabber; etc.*), i.e., a large functional yield. Conversely, we can find a bare dozen examples of the opposition mou*th*, mou*th* (v.); e*th*er, ei*th*er, etc. (*A. Martinet*).

fusion: The union of two adjacent sounds or other linguistic elements to form a new sound or element, in which the two component parts are not directly discernible.

futhark: The runic alphabet, so named after the first six letters of its conventional order (f, u, θ, a, r, k).

future: Any verbal tense or tenses which expresses that the action will take place at a later time.

future anterior: See *future perfect tense*.

future perfect tense: In the Indo-European languages, the tense which indicates that the action expressed by the verb will be completed by a specified time in the future or before another action will commence.

future tense: The tense which expresses that the action will take place in the future.

G

Ga: An African Negro language, spoken in the Gold Coast area, a member of the Sudanese-Guinean family of languages.

Gaelic: (1) See *Irish* and *Scots Gaelic*.—(2) Occasionally, a synonym for *Goidelic* (q.v.).

Gaelicism: In English linguistics, a word, expression or construction peculiar to Scotland.

Gafat: An Ethiopic dialect.

Galician: The dialect spoken in Galicia; considered to be a part of the Portuguese, rather than the Spanish dialectal system. (The Spanish name of this dialect is *Gallego*.)

Galla: A Kushitic language, of the Hamitic sub-family of the Semito-Hamitic family of languages, spoken by about 8,000,000 persons in and around Ethiopia.

Gallego: See *Galician*.

Gallicism: In general, a word, expression or construction peculiar to, or reminiscent of, the French language.

Gallo-Italian: The designation of a group of Romance dialects spoken in Italy (Emilian, Ligurian, Lombard and Piedmontese) which show marked differences from standard literary Italian and interesting similarities to Provençal or French.

Galoa: See *Mpongwe*.

Ganda: See *Luganda*.

Gascon: A southern French (Provençal) dialect, spoken in Gascony; closely linked to the Béarnais of the province of Béarn, and more remotely to the dialects of Languedoc and Provence.

Gaulish: An extinct, little-known member of the Celtic group of languages. It was spoken in Gaul, even after the fall of the Roman Empire.

Ge'ez: The language of ancient Ethiopia, also known as *Ethiopic*, which ceased to be a living language in the 14th century A.D., but has been retained as the official and liturgical language of the Abyssinian Church. Its modern descendant is the vernacular called *Tigriña* or *Tigray*.

gemination: Doubling—especially with reference to consonant sounds. In alphabetic writing, gemination is usually indicated by a double consonant or vowel letter. (E.g., the double *t* in the Italian *atto,* or the double *u* in the Finnish *kuusi.*) In speech, gemination involves a lengthening of the sound or of the period of complete closure preceding the release of a plosive.

gender: A grammatical distinction or classification of words, found chiefly in the Indo-European and Semitic languages. While most of these languages distinguish between a *masculine* and a *feminine gender,* and most Indo-European languages have also a *neuter* gender, certain languages distinguish an *animate* and an *inanimate* gender.

gender noun: In languages in which grammatical gender is non-existent or unimportant, this term is applied to nouns which indicate the sex of the being designated (e.g., *boy, girl*).

genderless: Not indicating gender.

genderless language: Any language which does not distinguish words as to grammatical gender (q.v.).

genderless noun: In languages in which grammatical gender (q.v.) is non-existent or unimportant, this term is applicable to nouns which designate inanimate objects, abstract ideas, etc., or which do not indicate the natural sex of the living being which they designate.

genemmic phonetics: The study of speech sounds after they have been produced, as in *acoustic phonetics.*

General American: The dialectal variant of American English spoken throughout the central and western United States and in most of Canada. (Also called *Midwestern American.*)

general grammar: See *universal grammar.*

General Semantics: A philosophy of language-meaning, first propounded by Alfred Korzybski, whose work is being continued at present by S. I. Hayakawa.

generic: Generalizing or implying generalization.

generic term: A non-specific, non-distinctive term, applicable to a great number of individual members of a class or group.

generous plural: A term applied to a pluralized form of a word that already bears a plural connotation. (E.g., the Southern American *you-all*.)

genetic phonetics: The study of the production of speech sounds, as in *articulatory phonetics*.

genetic relationship: The family relationship of languages which descend from a common ancestor.

genitive: In Indo-European languages, that case in which a noun is used primarily when the speaker wants to express that the person or thing denoted by the noun is the possessor of something.

geographical linguistics: See *linguistic geography*.

Georgian: A language spoken in the Caucasus by over 1,000,000 persons; a member of the South Caucasian (also called *K'art'-velian* or *K'art'uli'ena*) group of the South Caucasian family of languages.

Gergito-Solymian: An extinct and little known ancient language, of unknown linguistic affinities, preserved in inscriptions and in glosses recorded by some classical authors. Classified as *Asianic*.

German: A West Germanic language, the native tongue of approximately 100,000,000 persons.

Germanic: A group of languages, of the Indo-European family, customarily divided into the *East Germanic*, *North Germanic* and *West Germanic* (qq.v.) branches. (Also called *Teutonic*.)

Germanic sound shifts: The first sound shift, which occurred before the Christian era, separating Proto-Germanic from the rest of the Indo-European family, and the *Second* or *High German sound shift*, between the first century B.C. and the eighth century A.D., separating the Germanic languages into a High German and a Low German dialect group.

Germanism: A word, expression or syntactical construction characteristic or reminiscent of the German language.

gerund: In the Indo-European languages, a verbal noun which may govern cases like a verb.

gerundive: In Indo-European languages, an adjective having certain characteristics of verbs.

Gheg: One of the two predominant dialects of Albanian, spoken in northern Albania and parts of Dalmatia.

ghost-form: See *ghost-word.*

ghost-word: A word created by false etymology or other error (in writing, printing or pronunciation, etc.) of a lexicographer, author, scribe, etc.

Gilyak: A northeastern Asiatic language, spoken by a few thousand persons. While considered linguistically unrelated to any other known language, it is classified as a member of the *Hyperborean* or *Palaeo-Asiatic* group of languages (a geographical rather than a linguistic classification).

gingival: In phonetical terminology, a synonym of *alveolar* (q.v.).

Gitano: The Romani dialect spoken by Spanish Gypsies.

Glagolitic alphabet: An old form of script used by Slavic-speaking peoples.

glide: A transitional sound produced when the vocal organs shift from the articulation of one sound to the articulation of another sound. (Cf. *on-glide, off-glide.*)

glide-vowel: See *glide.*

gloss: An interlinear or marginal notation in an ancient or medieval manuscript, giving a translation or explanation of a word or brief passage.

glossary: A word-list; a brief dictionary listing terms used in a certain field of study or in a certain literary work, with the explanation or definition of their meanings.

glossematics: Hjelmslev's term for the study of *glossemes* (q.v.).

glosseme: "The smallest meaningful linguistic unit." (*Bloomfield*)

glossolalia: The language coined and used by the insane.

glossology: A synonym for *linguistics.*

glottal: A sound phonated in the larynx (hence also called *laryngal* or *laryngeal*) by a narrowing or closing of the vocal cords. (E.g., [h] and the *glottal stop* [ʔ]—q.v.)

glottal catch: See *glottal stop*.

glottal stop: A sound formed by closing the glottis and suddenly releasing the air with an explosive effect. This sound (the international phonetic symbol of which is [?]), is a full-fledged phoneme in many Oriental and African languages.

glottalized: Made with pressure applied in the glottis.

glottis: The opening at the upper part of the larynx, between the vocal cords.

glottochronology: A term proposed by M. Swadesh (1950) for a method of deducing, on the basis of statistical comparisons, family relationships of languages, as well as the probable date when branches of a given language group or family separated from the common parent language.

glottology: A synonym for *linguistics*.

gnomic present tense: The present tense when denoting a permanent situation or periodically recurrent action, without particular emphasis or definite indication of the temporal aspect.

Gobbledegook (Gobbledygook): A term coined by Maury Maverick for the complicated, overinvolved, and often incomprehensible jargon of government bureaucracy; later extended to cover also such professional jargons as the *Medicalese* of the physicians and the *Pedageese* of the educators. Known also as *Bafflegab, Officialese, Federalese*.

Goidelic: A branch of the Celtic group of the Indo-European family of languages, consisting of Irish (Irish Gaelic), Scots Gaelic and Manx.

Gondi: (1) A Dravidian language; spoken in Central India.— (2) A language group (Gondi, Bhili, Kolami and Naiki) which with Kui constitutes the Kui-Gondi branch of the Dravidian family of languages.

Gothic: A now extinct East-Germanic language.

Gothonic: Jespersen's term for *Germanic* (q.v.).

Gotlandic: A Scandinavian dialect. Also called *Gutnian*.

govern: With reference to a word or grammatical form, the meaning of this verb is: to require another word to which it refers, or which is dependent on it, to be used in a certain case, mood or form, or a dependent clause to begin with a certain conjunction, etc.

governed word: A word which is governed (q.v.) by another word.

governing word: A word which governs (q.v.) another word or a dependent clause.

government: The syntactical influence of a given word on another word to which it refers or which is dependent on it, requiring the latter to be used in a specific case, mood or grammatical or syntactical form, to be preceded by a specific preposition, or a dependent clause to begin with a certain conjunction, etc. (Also called *rection* or *syntactic regimen*.)

Grabar: Early Armenian (q.v.), still used as the learned and liturgical language. (Cf. *Ashksarhik*.)

gradation: See *vowel-gradation*.

grammar: The science of the structure of a language and the rules and principles of its generally accepted use.

grammarian: A student of or an expert on grammar.

grammatical: Pertaining to or conformable with the grammar of a language and its rules.

grammatical agreement: The correspondence of a word with another word or other words as to number, person, case or gender.

grammatical analysis: The determination of the grammatical categories to which the words in a sentence belong, as well as their functions in the structure of the sentence.

grammatical categories: The classes into which the words of a language are divided according to their formation, nature or functions. (Nouns, verbs, adjectives, etc.)

grammatical equivalents: Words, or groups of words, the meaning of which is so similar that their substitution for each other does not change or affect the meaning of the sentence.

grammatical form: A tactic form (q.v.) with its meaning.

grammatical gender: The classification of a word or words as to gender (q.v.) regardless of logical considerations, such as the natural sex of the person or being designated.

grammatical meaning: The meaning of a *grammatical form* (q.v.).

grammatical order: A synonym for *syntactic order* (q.v.).

grammatical stress: The natural emphasis given in spoken language to the principal words in the sentences.

grammatical structure: With reference to a given language, the totality of the grammatical, syntactical and other linguistic features.

grammatology: The study and science of writing.

graphemics: The study of systems of writing and their relationships to linguistic systems. (Also called *graphonomy*.)

graphic accent: Diacritic mark (q.v.).

graphonomy: An alternative term for *graphemics* (q.v.).

Grassman's law: The phonetic law formulated by H. Grassman, applying to the Greek language, stating that when two adjacent syllables started originally with aspirates, one of these aspirates (usually the first one) loses the aspiration.

grave accent: The diacritic mark [`], placed over vowels to indicate the proper sound in pronunciation. (In certain languages, e.g., Italian, the mark merely indicates the stressed syllable, without changing the pronunciation of the vowel.)

Gre: An African Negro language (also called *Grebo*), spoken in the Gold Coast area; a member of the Sudanese-Guinean family of languages.

Great Andamanese: A branch of the Andamanese family of languages, consisting of a northern group (subdivided into a subgroup comprising Ba, Chari, Kora and Yeru, and another subgroup composed of Juwoi, Kede, Kol and Puchikvar), and a southern group (Bale and Bea).

Great Russian: See *Russian*.

Grecism: A synonym for *Hellenism* (q.v.).

Greek: A member of the Indo-European family of languages. Modern Greek is the native language of 7-8,000,000 persons.

Grimm's law: The law, formulated by Jacob Grimm in 1822, stating the regularity of consonantal sound shifts in the languages of the Teutonic family. This shift, observable and demonstrable with fairly universal regularity, can be summed up as follows: The Indo-European aspirates *bh*, *dh* and *gh* become in Germanic, respectively, the voiced plosives *b*, *d*, and *g;* the voiced plosives *b*, *d*, *g* become, respectively, the voiceless plosives *p*, *t* *k;* the unvoiced plosives *p*, *t*, *k* become, respectively, the fricatives *f*, *th* [θ] and *h*.

groove-spirant: A sound produced by means of a front-to-back channel in the tongue.

gross acoustic feature: See *acoustic feature.*

Grusinian: See *Georgian.*

Guanche: An extinct language, of the Berber group of the Hamitic sub-family of the Semito-Hamitic family of languages, spoken in the Canary Islands until the late seventeenth century A.D.

Guaraní: A South American Indian language, member of the Tupi-Guaraní family; the vernacular of the Indians of Paraguay, also spoken in parts of Brazil.

Gudella: A Kushitic vernacular.

Guinean: See *Sudanese-Guinean.*

Gujarati: An Indic language, spoken by about 16,000,000 persons in the western Indian province of Gujarat, in the state of Baroda and neighboring states.

Gulla Negro: A creolized English spoken on some South Carolinian islands and seacoast areas.

Gurage: An Ethiopic dialect.

Gurkhali: See *Nepali.*

Gurma. An African Negro language, member of the Sudanese-Guinean family of languages.

Gurung: A Himalayan dialect, a member of the Tibeto-Himalayan branch of the Tibeto-Burmese sub-family of the Sino-Tibetan family of languages.

Gutnian: See *Gotlandic.*

guttural: See *velar.*

Gypsy: Cee *Gitano* and *Romani.*

H

Haida: See *Na-Dene*.

Hakka: An obscure group of dialects spoken in southern China, said to be affiliated with the Miao group.

Hamitic: The sub-family of languages which with the Semitic sub-family constitutes the Semito-Hamitic family. Its three branches are: Egyptian, Libyco-Berber and Kushitic. A grammatical characteristic of these languages is the tri-consonantal (Egyptian and Libyco-Berber) or bi-consonantal (Kushitic, occasionally also Egyptian and Libyco-Berber) word-root.

hammer and anvil: In phonetics, the tongue may be likened to a *hammer* which strikes the *anvil* (the immovable parts of the speech organs) at the various places of articulation.

hamza: The Arabic term for the *glottal stop* (q.v.).

hand: With reference to writing, written letters, etc., this term is usually a synonym of *script* or *writing* (q.v.).

haplography: Omission, in writing, of one of two consecutive identical letters or groups of letters.

haplology: Omission, in speech, of one or two consecutive identical sounds or groups of sounds or syllables.

Harari: An Ethiopic dialect.

hard consonant: A voiceless consonant.

hard sign: In Russian and Bulgarian, the letter Ъ . Whereas in Bulgarian it is pronounced as a short [ʌ] within a word, and is mute when final, in modern Russian orthography it is always mute and used within a word only, between a consonant sign and a vowel sign, to indicate that they are to be pronounced separately. (In modern Russian, it is sometimes replaced by an apostrophe.)

harmony of vowels: See *vowel harmony.*

Harranian: An extinct Eastern Aramaic dialect.

Hausa: An African Negro language, spoken by about 12,000,000 persons in central Sudan and northern Nigeria; a member of the Sudanese-Guinean family of languages.

Hawaiian: The indigenous language of the Hawaiian Islands; a member of the Polynesian sub-family of the Malayo-Polynesian family of languages.

head-word: A term occasionally used by linguists to designate that word which is modified by another word or other words in a sentence.

Hebraism: A word, expression or grammatical or syntactical construction characteristic or reminiscent of the Hebrew language.

Hebrew: A member of the Canaanite subdivision of the Northern branch of the West Semitic group of the Semito-Hamitic family of languages.

Hellenic: Greek.

Hellenism: A word, expression or grammatical or syntactical construction characteristic or reminiscent of the Greek language.

helper verb: A term used by Hogben and Bodmer (*The Loom of Language*) for *auxiliary verbs.*

Hene: An East African Negro language, member of the Bantu family of languages.

Herero: An African Negro language, spoken in Damaraland; member of the Bantu family of languages.

Hernician: An extinct Italic dialect.

hesitation-form: The use in conversation of indeterminate sounds or forms at points of hesitation (e.g., "*er,*" "*who-zis,*" etc.).

heteroclite: In grammatical terminology, said of a word, the declension or conjugation of which differs from the general pattern established for words of the same class.

heterographic spelling: A system of spelling in which the same letter or digraph or group of letters stands for different sounds in different words.

heterography: See *heterographic spelling.*

heteronomous sound change: Conditioned sound change (q.v.).

heteronym: (1) A word identical with another word of the same language as to written form, but different in sound and meaning.—(2) A literal translation of a word from another language.

heterophemy: The mistaken use of a word instead of another word which it very closely resembles in sound or spelling.

heterosyllabic: Belonging, in a given word, to different syllables.

hiatus: The pause or break in sound between two successive vowels. (*Internal hiatus* is such break within a word; *external hiatus* is the break between two successive words, the first one of which ends in a vowel and the second one begins with a vowel.)

Hibernicism: A word, expression or grammatical or syntactical form or construction peculiar to or reminiscent of the English spoken in Ireland, or of the Irish language.

hieroglyph: A pictographic word or syllable sign usually carved on stone.

hieroglyphic writing: A system of writing which utilizes hieroglyphs (q.v.) as symbols; specifically, the writing of ancient Egypt.

High: Prefixed to the name of a language, this adjective is used to designate that version of that language which is current in the highland sections of the country. Occasionally used also to designate the "best" or "literary" form of the language.

high-caste nouns: In Dravidian languages, that group of nouns which includes nouns denoting rational beings. (Cf. *casteless nouns.*)

High German: (1) The southern division of the West Germanic (q.v.) group of languages; also, and more properly, called *High Germanic*, and also *High Teutonic.*—(2) The German language spoken in the southern parts of the German language area. High German, which was affected by the Second or High German sound shift (see *Germanic sound shifts*) is a descendant of a combination of Bavarian, Alemannic and Lombard. Historically, it is customary to distinguish *Old High German* (8th-12th centuries A.D.), *Middle High German* (12th-15th centuries A.D.) and *Modern High German* (since the 15th century A.D.).

High German sound shift: See *Germanic sound shifts*.

High Germanic: See *High German (1)*.

High Teutonic: See *High German (1)*.

high vowel: A vowel produced with the tongue raised toward the roof of the mouth. (Also called *closed vowel*.)

Himalayan: A group within the Tibeto-Himalayan branch of the Tibeto-Burmese sub-family of the Sino-Tibetan family of languages; it includes a number of dialects, the most important ones being: Lepcha or Rong, Gurung and Toto.

Hindi: The collective name of the modern Indic languages Western (Standard) Hindi and Eastern Hindi (qq.v.).

Hindustani: A sub-division of the Indic branch of the Indo-Iranian language group. It includes Hindi and Urdu (qq.v.). Understood and used as a *lingua franca* in most of India.

hiragana: The Japanese syllable writing, derived from cursive Chinese ideographic writing, and employed for general daily use, in newspapers, general literature, and for other non-scientific and popular purposes, also for the phonetic transcriptions of Chinese ideograms in the *kana majiri* system of writing.

Hispanic: A collective term for Spanish, Portuguese and Catalan.

hissing sound: A synonym for *sibilant* (q.v.).

historical grammar: That branch of *explanatory grammar* (q.v.) which traces grammatical, phonetical and syntactical phenomena of a language back to earlier stages of that language. (*Sweet*)

historical linguistics: Diachronic linguistics (q.v.).

historical phonetics: The study and classification of phonetic laws and their effects in the course of linguistic development.

historical present: The present tense used in relating events which occurred in the past.

historical tenses: A term occasionally used to denote all the tenses which indicate that the action took place in the past.

Hittite: An extinct member of the Indo-European family of languages, spoken in Asia Minor between the 19th and 13th centuries B.C. (Cf. Sturtevant, *Comparative Grammar of the Hittite Language*.)

Hobson-Jobson: See *Anglo-Indian*.

holes in the pattern: The English equivalent of the French term *cases vides*, indicating the presence of gaps in one or more series of a phonetic paradigm. (*A. Martinet*)

holophrase: A single word expressing an entire sentence or idea.

holophrasis: The expression of an entire sentence or idea in one word.

holophrastic: Relating to, employing or constituting *holophrasis* (q.v.)

holophrastic language: A language which extensively uses words expressing entire ideas or phrases. Usually employed as a synonym of *polysynthetic language* (q.v.).

homograph: A word identical in written form with another given word of the same language, but entirely different in origin, sound and meaning.

homographic spelling: Any system of writing in which the same sign always represents the same sound, and any given sound can be represented by one and the same sign only.

homography: See *homographic spelling*.

homomorph: A term occasionally used as an alternative of *homophone*.

homonym: A word identical in written form and in sound with another word of the same language, but different in origin and meaning.

homophone: A word identical in sound with another word of the same language, but different from it in written form, origin and meaning.

homophony: Sameness in sound but not in meaning.

homorganic phonemes: Phonemes the utterance of which requires the articulatory action of the same vocal organ.

homorganic sounds: Two or more sounds phonated approximately at the same place of articulation, but differently as to the manner of phonation. (E.g., *t* and *d*.)

honorific: Expressing respect, reverence, high esteem, etc. Most languages use honorific pronouns (e.g., the German *Sie*, the Italian *Lei*) or honorific pronoun-equivalents (e.g., the Portuguese *o Senhor*, the Spanish *Usted*) instead of the second person pronoun, and certain languages (e.g., Japanese) use also honorific nouns, verbs and adjectives when addressing or speaking of a person of superior standing.

hortatory mood: See *cohortative mood*.

Hottentot: See *Nama*.

Hottentot-Bushman: A family of languages, also called *Khoin*, spoken in various areas of southwest Africa, by primitive pygmy tribes, numbering a total of about 300,000. Little is known about these languages, which are divided into *Nama* or *Hottentot* (with four dialects) spoken by about 250,000 persons, and *San* or *Bushman* (with two dialects) spoken by about 50,000 persons. These languages are characterized phonetically by several types of *clicks* (q.v.).

Hozi: The Elamite (q.v.) language in its later period.

Hungarian: A language of the Ugric branch of the Finno-Ugric (or Uralic) sub-family of the Ural-Altaic family of languages, spoken by about 12,000,000 persons in Hungary and neighboring countries.

Hupa: A North American Indian language (Athapascan family), surviving in California.

Huron: A North American Indian language, also called *Wyandot*, member of the Iroquoian family of languages.

Hürq'ili: A Dargva dialect (Eastern branch of the North Caucasian family of languages).

Hurrian: See *Subaraean*.

hushing sound: A palatalized *sibilant* (q.v.)—e.g., the sound represented in English by *sh*.

hybrid language: A language the vocabulary of which contains a great number of borrowed words, terms, etc.

hybrid word: A word composed of elements originating from more than one language. (E.g., *automobile*, composed of the Greek *autos* and the Latin *mobilis*.)

hybridized: Creolized (q.v.).

hyperbaton: A figure of rhetoric or composition, in which words are used in an inverted or transposed order.

hyperbole: In rhetoric, a figure of speech representing an obvious exaggeration.

Hyperborean: A group of languages, spoken by a total of about 50,000 persons in the extreme northeast corner of Asia, consisting of the Chukchi-Kamchadal family (Chukchi, Kamchadal and Koryak), Gilyak and Ainu. Since there exists no demonstrable relationship among these three, the term *Hyperborean* (or its alternative, *Palaeo-Asiatic*) is a geographical rather than linguistic designation.

hyperform: A reconstructed form of a word, mistakenly assumed to be more correct than a correct form which it is intended to replace. (Cf. *hyper-urbanism.*)

hyper-urbanism: The pronunciation of a word in an over-elegant manner, because of its written form. (E.g., "often," with pronunciation of the *t.*)

hyphen: The orthographic mark [-], used between two (or more) words to form a compound word, and also when dividing words at the end of a line.

hypocoristic word, hypocoristic form: A diminutive (q.v.) or a term of endearment (pet name, etc.).

hypotactic clause: A subordinate clause.

hypotaxis: Subordination; the grammatical or syntactical relationship between independent and subordinate elements.

hypothetical clause: In a conditional sentence, the clause which states the condition (hypothesis). Also called *protasis.*

hypothetical conjunction: A conjunction (q.v.) introducing a clause stating a hypothetical or conditional state or relation. (E.g., *if.*)

I

Iberian: The extinct and almost entirely unknown language, or family of languages, of the Iberian Peninsula in pre-Roman times. (Cf. *Aquitanian*.)

Ibero-Basque: A designation of a hypothetical language family, assumed to comprise the extinct and almost completely unknown Iberian and modern Basque.

Ibo: An African Negro language, also called *Bo*, spoken in Southeastern Nigeria; a member of the Sudanese-Guinean family of languages.

Icelandic: A Scandinavian (North Germanic) language, spoken by approximately 150,000 people in Iceland.

identic: A declensional case in certain non-Indo-European languages, denoting identity or sameness.

ideogram: Any graphic character, symbol or figure which suggests the idea of an object without expressing its name, or which symbolizes an abstract idea or quality.

ideograph: See *ideogram*.

ideographic writing; ideography: A system of writing using ideograms (q.v.) instead of letters or syllable signs.

ideophone: In the languages of the Bantu group, a vocable used to qualify a term of the utterance.

idiolect: The individual's personal variety of the community language system.

idiom: (1) Any expression peculiar to a language, conveying a distinct meaning, not necessarily explicable by, occasionally even contrary to, the general accepted grammatical rules.— (2) *The idiom* is a term denoting the general linguistic or grammatical character of a language.

Idiom Neutral: An artificial language created in 1903.

idiomatic: Peculiar to a language.

idiomatic expression: An expression which has a distinct, specific meaning of its own, often incompatible with or even contrary to the individual meanings of the words which compose it.

idiomatic usage: Use of a word or expression with a meaning of its own, often contrary to the principles of grammar or logic.

Ido: An artificial language, created by Louis de Beaufront (1907).

Ijo: An African Negro language, also called *Jo*, spoken in Nigeria; a member of the Sudanese-Guinean family of languages.

Ile-de-France: See *Francien*.

illative: A Finno-Ugric declensional case, having the same denotation as the English preposition *into*.

illeism: Redundant use of the third-person personal pronoun.

Illinois: A North American Indian language (Central Algonquian).

illiterate: Unable to read and/or write.

Illyrian: An extinct member of the Indo-European family of languages, once spoken in the Balkans, and assumed to be related to *Messapic* and *Venetic*, possibly also *Rhaetic*.

Ilocano: A language spoken in the Philippine Islands by about 800,000 native speakers; a member of the Indonesian sub-family of the Malayo-Polynesian family of languages.

imitative word: An onomatopoetic word (q.v.).

immediate constituent: Cf. *constituents*.

immediate future tense: A term occasionally used to denote a tense which expresses that an action or happening is impending.

immigrant language: A language of another country, spoken in communities composed of immigrants from that country, usually with admixtures of words and constructions borrowed from the language of the host-nation.

imperative mood: The mood of a verb used in expressing a command, request, consent, suggestion, entreaty, etc. In certain languages, the imperative mood has a present tense (expressing an order, etc., to be carried out at once) and a future tense (used to express orders, etc., the execution of which is to be delayed or deferred).

imperative sentence: A sentence expressing a command, request, suggestion, consent, entreaty, etc.

imperfect participle: A present participle.

imperfect tense: A verbal tense expressing that the action was continuous or habitual or still in progress or not completed in the past.

imperfective aspect: The verbal aspect which considers the action denoted by the verb in its progress, regardless of its beginning or completion.

impersonal mood: See *infinite form.*

impersonal verb: (1) In Indo-European languages, and in certain other language groups, a verb denoting an action by an unspecified or indefinite agent, and used in the third person singular only (in Indo-European languages which require a subject pronoun, such verbs are used with the neuter third person singular pronoun as subject—with the masculine third person singular pronoun in languages which have discarded the neuter gender.) (The term *monopersonal* or *unipersonal* verb is preferable in this sense).—(2) A verb the conjugational form of which does not express or emphasize whether the agent is the first, second or third person.

implication: The intensional meaning (q.v.) of a term.

implosion: In phonetical terminology, the noise heard as a result of a complete closure of the oral air passage.

improper compound: In the flexional languages, a compound word in which the elements are loosely linked and both (or all) of them are inflected.

improper triphthong: A synonym for *trigraph* (q.v.).

impure language: (1) A hybrid language (q.v.)—(2) Improper or unidiomatic construction or style.

inactive voice: In the grammatical terminology of certain languages which have no passive voice in the strict sense of the term, this designation is used instead of "passive voice."

incapsulating language: A rarely used synonym for *polysynthetic language* (q.v.).

incapsulation: The combination or incorporation of several words or elements into one word.

inceptive aspect; inceptive verb: See *inchoative aspect; inchoative verb.*

inchoative aspect: A verbal aspect in which the action is considered at its start or commencement.

inchoative verb: A verb expressing an action commencing or being started (cf. *inchoative aspect*).

inclination: A term synonymous with *enclisis* (q.v.).

included position: The position had by a word, phrase or other linguistic form (q.v.) when it is a part of a larger form and does not constitute a sentence in itself.

inclusive personal pronoun: One of the plural personal pronouns found in certain languages, meaning "we and you," or "we and they," "you and we," or "you and they," in contradistinction to the *exclusive pronouns* (q.v.).

incomplete verb: (1) A *verb of incomplete predication* (q.v.)— (2) A verb, the conjugation of which does not contain all tenses and forms common to verbs of the same class. (Cf. *defective.*)

incontiguous assimilation: Assimilation (q.v.) when the assimilatory and assimilated phonemes are separated from each other by another phoneme or other phonemes.

incorporating language: An alternative term for *polysynthetic language* (q.v.).

indeclinable: Incapable of being inflected; having only one form and incapable of showing distinctions as to number, person, gender, etc.

indefinite article: A particle inserted before or prefixed to nouns to indicate that the noun is used as a generic term.

indefinite conjugation: See *subjective conjugation.*

indefinite declension: In German grammar, a synonym for the *strong declension* (q.v.) of the adjective.

indefinite pronoun: A pronoun or a word used pronominally, without reference to a specified person, object or thing. (E.g., *whoever.*)

independent clause: A clause which forms a complete sentence in itself.

independent element: Any word or group of words which have no grammatical connection with the rest of the sentence in which they are used. (E.g., an interjection.)

Indian languages: See *American Indian languages;* see also *Indic.*

Indic: The name of a branch of the Indo-Iranian group of the Indo-European family of languages, spoken in India and Ceylon; its most important members are: (1) Classical Sanskrit, (2) the medieval Prakrits (q.v.), and (3) the modern Prakrit vernaculars: Hindustani (including Hindi and Urdu), Bengali, Bihari, Marathi, Punjabi, Rajasthani, Gujarati, Oriya, Sindhi, Pahari, Bhili, Khandesi, Assamese, Sinhalese, Kashmiri, Nepali and Romani, the language of the Gypsies (qq.v.).

indicative mood: The verbal mood which expresses that the action or state denoted by the verb is an actual fact.

indirect discourse: Any form of discourse in which the substance of the words, statements, etc., of another person are related without being quoted verbatim.

indirect object: The substantive denoting the person or object *to, toward* or *for* whom or which the action expressed by the sentence takes place.

indirect question: A question quoted in *indirect discourse* (q.v.).

indirect quotation: The repetition of the substance of the words, statement, etc., of another person, without quoting them verbatim.

indirective aspect: See *benefactive aspect.*

indirectness: Indirect discourse (q.v.).

Indo-Aryan: An alternative name for the *Indic* branch of the Indo-Iranian language group.

Indo-Chinese: An alternative name of the Sino-Tibetan family of languages.

Indo-European: A family of languages, composed of the following languages and language-groups: Albanian, Armenian, Balto-Slavic, Celtic, Germanic (or Teutonic), Greek, Hittite, Illyrian, Indo-Iranian, Italic, Thraco-Phrygian, Tokharian (qq.v.). Originally, all these languages were synthetic and inflected, with a three-gender system, but at the present time many have become analytic, to varying degrees, and have adopted a two-gender or natural gender system.

Indo-Germanic: The designation preferred by German authors and linguists (*indogermanisch*) to *Indo-European*.

Indo-Hittite: A designation intended to express the relationship between Indo-European and Hittite (qq.v.).

Indo-Iranian: A language group, of the Indo-European family of languages, consisting of two branches: the Iranian and the Indo-Aryan languages (qq.v.).

Indonesian: A sub-family (also called *Malayan*) of the Malayo-Polynesian family of languages, spoken in Indonesia, Malaya, Formosa, the Philippine Islands, Madagascar, and a great many islands of the Pacific. It consists of about 200 languages and dialects, the most important of which are: Malay, Javanese, Balinese, Batak, Bicol, Bisaya (Visaya), Bontok, Buginese (Bugi or Bugis), Dayak, Formosan, Ilocano, Macassar, Maduran (Madurese), Malagasy, Sundanese and Tagalog.

inessive: A case in certain languages (e.g., Finno-Ugric) having the same denotation as the English preposition *in* or *within*.

infection: In phonetics, a general term for vowel changes due to the influence of a contiguous or near-by vowel.

infectum: The aspectual category introduced by the Roman grammarian Varro (1st century B.C.), including the present, preterit and simple future tenses.

inferential aspect: See *putative aspect*.

inferior comparison: Downward comparison (q.v.).

infinite form: A collective term for verbal forms which show or imply no distinction as to grammatical person. (Cf. *finite form* and *personal infinitive*.)

infinite mood: See *infinite form*.

infinitive: That form of the verb which expresses action or state without indicating person or number. Certain languages, however, have *personal infinitives* (q.v.) which do indicate a distinction as to grammatical person and number.

infinitive clause: A clause in which an infinitive has predicative function.

infix: A *formative* (q.v.) inserted *within* a word.

inflected language: See *flexional language*.

inflection: The addition of certain *ending*s (q.v.) to the *base* (q.v.) of a word to express certain grammatical relationships and functions and aspects. While this process is common to and characteristic, to a major or minor extent, of the *synthetic languages* (hence called also *inflectional* languages), it is of little or no importance and often non-existent in the *analytic languages*.

inflectional affix: A prefix or suffix without an independent meaning of its own and incapable of being used in itself.

inflexible: Incapable of being inflected; invariable in form.

informant: In linguistic study, a native speaker whose function it is to illustrate the sounds of the language so that his phrases may be recorded or imitated by the students, but not to explain grammar or structure.

ingressive aspect: A verbal aspect which considers the action as limited to its initial stage.

Ingrian: A dialect of the Finnish group of the Finno-Ugric (or Uralic) sub-family of the Ural-Altaic family of languages.

Ingush: A Chechen dialect (Eastern Caucasian group of the North Caucasian family of languages).

Ingweonic: See *Anglo-Frisian*.

initial accent: Accent or stress falling on the first syllable of a word.

initial glide: See *on-glide*.

initial inflection: Inflection by prefixing a letter or a syllable or otherwise modifying the beginning of a word.

initial mutation: The change of the initial consonant of a word, under certain conditions, observed in many languages, and of paramount importance in the Celtic languages where the initial consonants of words change in accordance with the final sound of the preceding word or with the position of the word in question in the sentence; this initial mutation occurs in the form of *aspiration, lenition* or *nasalization* (qq.v.).

initial stress: Stress on the first syllable.

innovation: A change in sound, word form, or word meaning, which begins at a certain geographical location and radiates outward to neighboring areas.

inordinated adjective: That one of two adjectives modifying the same substantive which has a stronger qualifying effect on the substantive and may be considered to form a closer-knit unit with the latter.

inseparable: Incapable of being severed.

inserted clause: A *parenthetical clause* (q.v.).

inspiration: In phonetical terminology, the intake of breath.

instructive: In certain languages (e.g., Finno-Ugric languages), a case having the same denotation as the English *by means of*.

instrumental: A declensional case in which a noun, adjective, pronoun or numeral is used when denoting the agent or means through or by which the action is performed. (In certain languages, also used after certain prepositions and in many idiomatic constructions.)

instrumentative: Another name for the *instrumental* (q.v.) case.

instrumentative verb: A verb which indicates the instrument of the action, too. (E.g., *to pistol-whip*.)

integration: The act or process of organizing parts into a whole or wholes and systematically arranging wholes, usually in the order of their importance.

intension: See *intensional meaning*.

intensional meaning: The qualities or properties the possession of which is implied, suggested or connoted by a word or term. Synonymous with *connotation*. (Often called simply *intension*.)

intensity accent: The distribution of stress over connected sounds.

intensive: In various expressions (e.g., *intensive pronoun*), this term means *emphatic*.

intensive aspect: A verbal aspect expressing that the action or state is being intensified in character.

intensive compound: A compound in which the meaning of one component serves to intensify the meaning of the other one. (E.g., stone-deaf.)

interdental: A sound made with the tip of the tongue between the teeth.

Interglossa: An artificial language proposed by Hogben, based on Greek and Latin roots with a system of syntax resembling that of Chinese.

interjection: An exclamatory word, invariable in form, often derived from some stereotyped phrase, used to express emotion.

interjectional phrase: A phrase or group of words used as an exclamation or interjection.

interjectional theory: That theory which maintains that human speech originated from ejaculations uttered by primitive man under the influence of pain or intense emotions. (Often referred to as the *pooh-pooh theory*.)

interlanguage: A generic term for all languages created or adopted for international communication.

interlingua: (1) An artificial language, consisting of inflectionless Latin (therefore originally named *Latino Sine Flexione*), created by Giuseppe Peano and first used by him in 1908. —(2) An artificial language created more recently by the International Auxiliary Language Association.

interlinguistics: The comparative study of widely-known languages to determine which elements are common to a number of them. The auxiliary language, Interlingua (q.v.—*2*), has recently been devised on the basis of this technique.

intermediate sound: A sound which partakes of the nature or characteristics of two sounds, and represents a transition between those two.

internal flexion: Inflection (q.v.) of words by internal phonemic change or gradation.

internal hiatus: See *hiatus*.

internal punctuation marks: Punctuation marks used within sentences.

International Phonetic Alphabet (I.P.A.): See page 104.

interpreter: A person who explains the meaning of something—specifically, one who translates orally from one language into another.

THE INTERNATIONAL PHONETIC ALPHABET.
(Revised to 1951.)

	Bi-labial	Labio-dental	Dental and Alveolar	Retroflex	Palato-alveolar	Alveolo-palatal	Palatal	Velar	Uvular	Pharyngal	Glottal
Plosive	p b		t d	ʈ ɖ			c ɟ	k g	q ɢ		ʔ
Nasal	m	ɱ	n	ɳ			ɲ	ŋ	N		
Lateral Fricative			ɬ ɮ								
Lateral Non-fricative			l	ɭ			ʎ				
Rolled			r						R		
Flapped			ɾ	ɽ					R		
Fricative	ɸ β	f v	θ ð s z ʃ ʒ	ʂ ʐ	ʃ ʒ	ɕ ʑ	ç ʝ	x ɣ	χ ʁ	ħ ʕ	h ɦ
Frictionless Continuants and Semi-vowels	w ɥ	ʋ	ɹ				j (ɥ)	(w)	ʁ		

Close	(y ʉ u)		Front i y	Central ɨ ʉ	Back ɯ u
Half-close	(ø o)		e ø	ɵ	ɤ o
Half-open	(œ o)		ɛ œ	ə ɞ	ʌ ɔ
Open	(ɒ)		a	ɐ	ɑ ɒ

(Secondary articulations are shown by symbols in brackets.)

OTHER SOUNDS.—Palatalized consonants: ʈ, ɖ, etc.; palatalized ʃ, ʒ : ʆ, ʓ. Velarized or pharyngalized consonants: ɫ, ɖ, ʂ, etc. Ejective consonants (with simultaneous glottal stop): p', t', etc. Implosive voiced consonants: ɓ, ɗ, etc. ɼ fricative trill. σ, ʠ (labialized θ, ð, or s, z). ƪ, ƺ (labialized ʃ, ʒ). ɿ, ʮ, ɹ (clicks, Zulu c, q, x). ɺ (a sound between r and l). ɲ Japanese syllabic nasal. ƫ (combination of x and ʃ). ʍ (voiceless w). ɩ, ɤ, ℧ (lowered varieties of i, y, u). ᴈ (a variety of ə). ɵ (a vowel between ø and o).

Affricates are normally represented by groups of two consonants (ts, tʃ, dʒ, etc.), but, when necessary, ligatures are used (ʦ, ʧ, ʤ, etc.), or the marks ⁀ or ‿ (t͡s or t͜s, etc.). ⁀ ‿ also denote synchronic articulation (m͡ŋ = simultaneous m and ŋ). c, ɟ may occasionally be used in place of tʃ, dʒ, and ʒ, ʒ for ts, dz. Aspirated plosives: ph, th, etc. r-coloured vowels: eɹ, aɹ, oɹ, etc., or eʵ, aʵ, oʵ, etc., or ɛ, a, ɔ, etc.; r-coloured ə : əɹ or əʵ or ɹ or ɑ or ɹ.

LENGTH, STRESS, PITCH.— ː (full length). · (half length). ˈ (stress, placed at beginning of the stressed syllable). ˌ (secondary stress). ˉ (high level pitch); ˍ (low level); ´ (high rising); ˏ (low rising); ` (high falling); ˎ (low falling); ˆ (rise-fall); ˇ (fall-rise).

MODIFIERS.— ˜ nasality. ˳ breath (l̥ = breathed l). ˬ voice (s̬ = z). ʻ slight aspiration following p, t, etc. ˛ labialization (n̫ = labialized n). ˌ dental articulation (t̪ = dental t). ˙ palatalization (z̽ = ʑ). ˳ specially close vowel (e̳ = a very close e). ˷ specially open vowel (e̹ = a rather open e). ˔ tongue raised (e̝ or e̝ = ë). ˕ tongue lowered (e̞ or e̞ = ɛ̈). ˖ tongue advanced (u̟ or ʮ = an advanced u, t̟ = t̪). - or ˗ tongue retracted (i̠ or i = ɨ·, t̠ = alveolar t). ˒ lips more rounded. ˓ lips more spread. Central vowels: ï (= ɨ), ü (= ʉ). ë (= ə·), ö (= ɵ). ɛ̈, ɔ̈. (e.g. n̩) syllabic consonant. ˘ consonantal vowel. ʃ variety of ʃ resembling s, etc.

(*Courtesy of International Phonetic Association, University College, London. W.C.1.*
Reprinted by permission.)

interrogation point: The punctuation mark [?], more commonly called a *question mark*.

interrogative: Indicating, expressing or introducing a direct question.

interrogative sentence: A sentence containing a direct question.

intervocalic: Said of a consonant or group of consonants appearing or sounded between two vowels.

intonation: The modulation of the voice; pitch; tone quality; the musical flow of speech.

intransitive verb: A verb expressing an action or state which does not go beyond the agent, and does not require (and often cannot take) a direct object.

invariable: Having only one form; incapable of inflection or other changes.

inverse spelling: A phenomenon of overcorrection (q.v.) appearing in writing, as when Latin stone-cutters inscribed *diaebus* instead of *diebus* because they were conscious of the fact that they were prone to use *e* for *ae*.

inversion: A reversal or modification of the normal sequence or order, especially of the normal word order.

inverted sound: A *cacuminal* (q.v.).

involution: In grammatical terminology, the use of an involved sentence structure.

Ionian: One of the literary dialects of ancient Greek.

I.P.A.: The *International Phonetic Alphabet* (see page 104).

Iranian: The name of a branch of the Indo-Iranian group of the Indo-European family of languages, spoken in Iran, the Iranian Plateau and in part of the Caucasus. The languages which constitute this branch are: Persian, Kurdish, Pushtu (or Afghan), Ossetic, and Balochi, and probably the extinct Khotanese and Old Sakian.

Irish: A language of the Goidelic branch of the Celtic group of the Indo-European family of languages, the official language of Eire. Frequently referred to by linguists as *Irish Gaelic*. (The designation *Erse* is not used by the inhabitants of Eire themselves). The Irish language between 600 and 1200 A.D. is referred to as *Old Irish,* while the state of the language from 1200 and 1600 A.D. is called *Middle Irish; Modern Irish* is the Irish language since the early 17th century A.D.

Irish Gaelic: See *Irish.*

Irishism: A word or idiomatic expression or construction peculiar to or characteristic of the speech of the Irish.

Iroquoian: A family of North American Indian languages; its surviving members are: Huron (or Wyandot) Iroquois, the languages of the Five Nations (Cayuga, Mohawk, Oneida, Onondaga, Seneca), Cherokee and Tuscarora.

Iroquois: (1) A North American Indian language, member of the Iroquoian family, spoken in Canada, in the Montreal region.— (2) Often used as a designation of the entire Iroquoian family.

irregular: Deviating, in some or several or all features, from the recognized norm or standard.

irrelevant: Said of those articulatory features of a phoneme which are not relevant or distinctive, i.e., *non-phonemic.* Though they play no role in distinguishing the meaning of words, the irrelevant features may be very important in clarifying dialect differences and in determining "foreign accent." (*E. Dorfman*)

Irtysh: An Asiatic language; a member of the Western Turkic group of the Altaic sub-family of the Ural-Altaic family of languages.

Isaurian: An extinct language, of undetermined linguistic affinities, preserved in inscriptions and in glosses recorded by some classical scholars. Classified as *Asianic.*

isogloss: On linguistic maps, a line separating the areas (called *isogloss areas*) in which the language differs with respect to a given feature or features, i.e., a line marking the boundaries within which a given linguistic feature or phenomenon can be observed.

isoglottic line: An *isograph* (q.v.).

isograph: Any line on a linguistic map, indicating a uniformity in the use of sounds, vocabulary, syntax, inflexion, etc. (Cf. *isolexic, isomorphic, isophonic, isosyntagmic, isotonic lines.*)

isolated opposition: The relationship of a set of phonemes whose relevant feature is not shared by other sets; *l:r* as nothing else in English.

isolating language: A language in which all words are invariable and their interrelationship in the sentence is indicated solely by their relative positions and connective words.

isolexic lines: Lines on a linguistic map, indicating the approximate boundaries of the speech-areas in which a uniformity in the vocabulary of the speakers and in their use of words can be observed.

isomorphic lines: Lines on a linguistic map, indicating the approximate boundaries of the speech-areas in which a uniformity in grammatical forms, inflections, etc. can be observed.

isophonic lines: Lines on a linguistic map, indicating the approximate boundaries of phonetically homogeneous speech-areas, i.e., of areas where identical phonetical features prevail in the pronunciation of the language.

isosyntagmic lines: Lines on a linguistic map, indicating the approximate boundaries of the speech-areas in which a uniformity in syntax can be observed.

isotonic lines: Lines on a linguistic map, indicating the approximate boundaries of the speech-areas in which a uniformity can be observed in the use of speech-tones.

Isotype: A system of writing using non-phonetic signs of universal significance, designed as a medium of education. (The word Isotype is the combination of the initials of the full name, *International System Of Typographic Picture Education.*)

Istro-Romanian: The Romanian dialect spoken in parts of Istria. It is ·heavily interlarded with Italian and Slavic words.

Italian: A Romance language, the native tongue of approximately 60,000,000 people in Italy and its colonies.

Italic: A group of the Indo-European family of languages, usually divided into the Latino-Faliscan, Osco-Umbrian and Sabellian (qq.v.) branches.

Italicism: A word, expression, grammatical or idiomatic construction peculiar to, characteristic or reminiscent of the Italian language.

Italo-Celtic: A designation of the hypothetical common parent language of the Italic and Celtic languages.

Itelmic: See *Kamchadal*.

iterative aspect: That verbal aspect which expresses that the action is a repeated or habitual one.

iterative compound: A compound word formed by repetition of a word.

iterative numeral: A numeral which answers the question "How many times?" (Also referred to as *multiplicative numeral*.)

Ivrit: The Hebrew name of the modernized Hebrew which is the official and national language of Israel.

J

Jagatai: See *Chagatai*.

jamming: A term first used by Urban T. Holmes, Jr. for a special case of *syncope* (q.v.) prevalent in Vulgar Latin: the elimination of consonants originally present between vowels. (E.g., the change of *ego* to *eo*, the change of *habeo* to *aio*, etc.)

Japanese: An agglutinating language, without gender and generally without number distinction, using impersonal verbs. The native language of about 85,000,000 persons. Despite similarities to Korean (which have led many linguists to postulate the existence of a Japanese-Korean language family), the opinion at present accepted by most linguists is that Japanese cannot be classified into any known language group or family.

Japhetic: (1) In the terminology of G. W. von Leibnitz (1646-1716), a designation of a language-group which corresponds approximately to the Indo-European family of languages.— (2) A hypothetical language-family, claimed to include North Caucasian, South Caucasian, Sumerian, Elamite, Asianic, Basque, Etruscan and other extinct European languages; this theory, advanced by N. Marr, although for a while favorably regarded by many Russian linguists, is generally rejected.

jargon: The collective term for the words, expressions, technical terms, etc. which are intelligible to the members of a specific group, social circle or profession, but not to the general public.

Jaunsari: A western Pahari (q.v.) dialect, spoken in Jaunsar-Bawar by about 50,000 persons.

Javanese: A language spoken in Java by about 20,000,000 persons; a member of the Indonesian sub-family of the Malayo-Polynesian family of languages.

Jek: A language spoken in the Caucasus; a member of the Samurian branch of the Eastern Caucasian group of the North Caucasian family of languages.

Jew-Tongo: An alternative name of *Bush-Negro English* (q.v.).

Jewish: See *Yiddish*.

Jo: See *Ijo*.

Jobelyn: The underworld cant (q.v.) used by the lower classes of Paris in medieval times; samples of it appear in the writings of François Villon.

journalese: A term applied, often in a derogatory sense, to the style characteristic of newspaper headlines and newspaper articles.

Judaeo-Aramaic: See *Babylonian Judaeo-Aramaic* and *Palestinian Judaeo-Aramaic*.

Judaeo-German: See *Yiddish*.

Judaeo-Romance: See *Ladino*.

Judaeo-Spanish: See *Ladino*.

juncture: The way in which the sounds of a language are joined together; e.g., there is a junctural difference in English between the utterance "a name" and "an aim." (Bloch and Trager)

Junggrammatiker: A school of linguistics of the late 19th century (Brugmann, Hubschmann, Osthoff, Paul, etc.) which taught and believed in the universal and absolute validity of phonetic laws.

jussive mood: A verbal mood (also termed *apocopated* mood) in the Semitic languages, expressing a command with less strong effect than the *imperative* mood.

jussive subjunctive: The subjunctive mood used to express a command, usually in the third person. (E.g., the Latin *exeat*—"let him go out.")

Juwoi: A Great Andamanese language.

juxtaposed compound: A compound consisting of two words placed next to each other but not written as one word.

juxtaposing language: A language which expresses grammatical relations or certain accessory concepts by prefixing *classifiers* (q.v.) to the words which denote the main concepts. (E.g., the Bantu language group.)

juxtaposition: Adjacency; the state of being side by side.

juxtapositional assimilation: Assimilation (q.v.) when the assimilatory and assimilated phonemes are contiguous.

K

K-Celtic: See *Q-Celtic*.

Kabyl: A language of the Berber group of the Hamitic sub-family of the Semito-Hamitic family of languages; a vernacular of mountaineers in Tunisia and Algeria.

Kachin: A Tibeto-Burmese language, also called *Singh-pho;* a member of the Bodo-Naga-Kachin group.

Kaffa: A Kushitic vernacular spoken in Ethiopia.

Kafir: An African Negro language (also called *Xosa* or *Xhosa*), spoken in South-East Africa; a close relation of Zulu, and a member of the Bantu family of languages.

Kalingi: See *Tamil*.

Kalmuk: An Asiatic language which constitutes the Western sub-branch of the Mongol branch of the Altaic sub-family of the Ural-Altaic family of languages.

Kamassin: An alternative name of Sayan or Southern Samoyed.

Kamba: An African Negro language, spoken in British East Africa, member of the Bantu family of languages.

Kamchadal: A language (also called *Itelmic*) spoken by about 10,000 persons in northeastern Asia; a member of the Chukchi-Kamchadal family of languages, classified into the *Hyperborean* or *Palaeo-Asiatic* group.

kana: The Japanese system of syllable writing; specifically, the Japanese syllabaries. (See *hiragana, katakana, kana majiri*.)

kana majiri: The Japanese system of writing employing Chinese ideograms with small *hiragana* (q.v.) characters to the right of each ideogram to indicate its phonetic value.

Kanarese: A language spoken by about 15,000,000 persons in southern India, Mysore and Hyderabad; a member of the Tamil-Kurukh branch of the Dravidian family of languages.

Kanuri: An African Negro language, member of the Sudanese-Guinean family of languages.

Karagas: An Asiatic language; a member of the Eastern Turkic group of the Altaic sub-family of the Ural-Altaic family of languages.

Karasharian: See *Tokharian*.

Karelian: A dialect of the Finnish group of the Finno-Ugric (or Uralic) sub-family of the Ural-Altaic family of languages.

Karen: A Sino-Tibetan language, member of the Tai sub-family; the various Karen dialects are spoken by about 1,000,000 persons in Burma.

K'art'uli'ena: See *South Caucasian*.

K'art'velian: South Caucasian (q.v.).

Kashgar: An Asiatic language; member of the Central Turkic group of the Altaic sub-family of the Ural-Altaic family of languages.

Kashmiri: An Indic language, spoken in Kashmir (northern India) by about 1,000,000 native speakers.

Kashub, Kashubian: See *Kaszub*.

Kassite: See *Cossaean*.

Kaszub: A West Slavic language, spoken by a small speech-community on the Baltic coast. (Also written *Kashub*.)

katakana: The Japanese system of syllable writing, derived from the standard Chinese ideograms, and used mainly in scientific literature and official documents.

Katharévousa: The modern literary Greek, as opposed to the colloquial *Dhēmotikē*.

Kauguru: An East African Negro language, member of the Bantu family of languages.

Kavi: Old Javanese, with written documents dating back to the early ninth century A.D.

Kazikumyk: See *Lak*.

Kechua: See *Quechua*.

Kede: A Great Andamanese language.

Keltic: An alternative spelling of *Celtic* (q.v.).

Kentish: The old Anglo-Saxon dialect of Kent.

Kerewe: An African Negro language, member of the Bantu family of languages.

kernel: That basic part of a word which expresses the principal concept, idea or meaning.

key: An alternative term for *radical* (q.v.) in the Chinese system of writing.

Khajuna: See *Burushaski.*

Khaldic: See *Vannic.*

Khalkha: An Asiatic language, a member of the Eastern group of the Mongol branch of the Altaic sub-family of the Ural-Altaic family of languages.

Khamir: A Kushitic vernacular.

Khamta: A Kushitic vernacular.

Khamti: A Shan dialect, spoken in eastern Assam and in Khamti Long (China).

Khandesi: A modern Indic vernacular.

Khatri: See *Saurashtra.*

Khattian: An extinct language of uncertain linguistic affinities, spoken in Asia Minor in remote antiquity. The earliest written records of this language, classified as *Asianic*, date from before 2000 B.C.

Khmer: A language (also called *Cambodian*) spoken by about 1,500,000 persons in Cambodia (southern Indo-China); a member of the Mon-Khmer branch of the Austro-Asiatic family of languages.

Khotanese: An extinct Iranian language. Its first investigator, E. Leumann, named it *North Aryan* and he considered it a distinct branch of the Indo-European family. It is, however, now genererally classified as a Middle Iranian dialect. (Also called *Middle Sakian.*)

Kichua: See *Quechua.*

Kickapoo: A North American Indian language (Central Algonquian), surviving in the Great Lakes region.

Kikuyu: An African Negro language, spoken in British East Africa, member of the Bantu family of languages.

Kile: A Tungus dialect.

K'inalugh: A language spoken in the Caucasus; a member of the Eastern Caucasian group of the North Caucasian family of languages.

kinemics: The study of units of gestural expression. (*Birdwhistell*)

kinesics: The study of non-vocal bodily movements which play a part in communication.

kinetic consonant: A consonant, the pronunciation of which cannot be prolonged without change in quality. So called in contradistinction to a *static* consonant (q.v.). (Cf. *continuant*.)

King James English: The English of the era of King James of England; more specifically, the language of the Authorized Version of the Bible published in 1611.

King's English: Correct, idiomatic English, as spoken in England.

Kirghiz: An Asiatic language; it belongs to the Western Turkic group of the Altaic sub-family of the Ural-Altaic family of languages.

Kiswaheli: See *Swahili*.

koinê (*or* **koiné**): A branch of a language commonly used by a close-knit group in a self-contained area within a larger linguistic area; usually the result of a compromise among several dialects of a language.

Kol: A Great Andamanese language.

Kolami: A Dravidian language, spoken in Central India, classified in the Gondi group.

Kololo: A South-East African Negro language, member of the Bantu family of languages.

Kongo: See *Congo*.

Konkani: The most important dialect of the Indic language *Marathi;* spoken by over 1,500,000 persons in the Konkan, in Goa, and in neighboring territories.

Kora: A Great Andamanese language.

Korean: An agglutinating language, using impersonal verbs. The native tongue of about 22,000,000 persons. Despite similarities to Japanese which have led many linguists to claim the existence of a Japanese-Korean language family, the opinion at present accepted by most linguists is that Korean cannot be classified as cognate with any other known language group or family.

Koryak: A language, spoken by about 1,000 persons in north-eastern Asia; a member of the Chukchi-Kamchadal family of languages, classified in the *Hyperborean* or *Palaeo-Asiatic* group.

Kottish: See *Cottian.*

Kra: An African Negro language, member of the Sudanese-Guinean family of languages.

Kuchaean: See *Tokharian.*

Kui: A Dravidian language, spoken in the Indian province of Orissa; with the Gondi group, it constitutes the Kui-Gondi branch of the Dravidian family of languages.

Kui-Gondi: A branch of the Dravidian languages, consisting of Kui and of the Gondi group.

Kuki-Chin: A group of dialects (Lai, Lushei, Meithei, Tashon, etc.), constituting a subdivision of the Arakan-Burmese branch of the Tibeto-Burmese sub-family of the Sino-Tibetan family of languages.

Kullo-Walamo: A Kushitic vernacular.

Kului: A western Pahari (q.v.) dialect, spoken in the Kulu valley, Punjab, by about 55,000 persons.

Kumik: A Near-Eastern language; a member of the Southern Turkic group of the Altaic sub-family of the Ural-Altaic family of languages.

Kunama: An African Negro language, member of the Sudanese-Guinean family of languages.

Kunjuti: See *Burushaski.*

Kuo-yü: The new "National Tongue" of China, based on the Pei-ping dialect of North Mandarin; now estimated to be used by about 300,000,000 persons.

Kurdish: A language spoken in Kurdistan and parts of Iran; a member of the Iranian branch of the Indo-Iranian group of the Indo-European family of languages.

K'üri: A language spoken in the Caucasus; a member of the Samurian branch of the Eastern Caucasian group of the North Caucasian family of languages.

Kurukh: A language, also called *Oraon*, spoken in Western Bengal and parts of the Central Provinces of India; the Kurukh dialect spoken in the Rajmahal region of Bengal is called *Malto*. Kurukh is a member of the Tamil-Kurukh branch of the Dravidian family of languages.

Kushitic: A branch of the Hamitic sub-family of the Semito-Hamitic family of languages; it consists of a great many vernaculars, the principal ones being Somali and Galla.

K'varshi: A language spoken in the Caucasus; a member of the Avaro-Andi branch of the Eastern Caucasian branch of the North Caucasian family of languages.

L

labial: In phonetical terminology, a consonant pronounced with the lips.

labialization: (1) Giving a sound the character of a *labial* (q.v.). —(2) Rounding (q.v.).

labio-dental: In phonetical terminology, a consonant pronounced with the lower lip touching the upper front teeth.

labio-velar: In phonetical terminology, a consonant pronounced with the lips rounded and the back part of the tongue arched toward the soft palate.

laboratory phonetics: See *experimental phonetics*.

Laconian: One of the Doric dialects of ancient Greek.

Ladin: See *Rumansch*.

Ladino: A vernacular spoken by Sephardic Jews in Constantinople, Salonika and other areas around the Mediterranean. It is basically 15th century Spanish, with many loan words and elements taken from Turkish, Greek and Hebrew. It is written with a modified version of the Hebrew alphabet. (Also called *Sephardic*, *Judaeo-Romance*, or *Judaeo-Spanish*.)

lag: *Regressive assimilation* (q.v.) of a sound or group of sounds.

Lak: A language, also called *Kazikumyk*, spoken in the Caucasus; a member of the Eastern Caucasian group of the North Caucasian family of languages.

Lala-Lamba: An African Negro language, member of the Bantu family of languages.

lambdaism: Substitution of the phoneme [l] for another phoneme, usually [r].

Lamut: A Tungus dialect.

Landsmål: The modern Norwegian language, representing a consolidation of the various indigenous dialects of Norway.

language: A system of communication by sound, i.e., through the organs of speech and hearing, among human beings of a certain group or community, using vocal symbols possessing arbitrary conventional meanings.

language boundary: An irregular, imaginary line drawn around a given speech-community, usually enclosing a smaller or greater number of small circles indicating various speech-islands.

language family: A group of languages derived from the same parent language.

language of colonization: The language of a politically, economically or culturally superior or strong nation which is imposed upon a conquered or dependent nation, or adopted by the latter, as a language of official dealings, business, and as a cultural medium, parallel with or replacing the native language.

language shift: With reference to individuals, especially to bi-linguals, this term indicates the change from the use of one language as the principal or sole habitual medium of every-day communication to another language.

language strata: The different vocabularies (colloquial usage, professional or trade vocabulary and vocabulary of formal speech or literature) used by an individual. (*Emerson*)

language system: Cf. *langue*.

langue: French for *language*. In linguistics, according to the terminology introduced by F. de Saussure, *langue* (usually translated to English as *tongue*, although *language-system* would be a more appropriate translation) designates a complete and homogeneous grammatical system used and followed by a group or community, in contradistinction to the *parole* (*speech*) which is individual to a given person in a given case.

Langue Bleue: An artificial language, a modified form of Volapük (q.v.), created by Bollack in 1899.

Languedocien: The dialectal variant of Old Provençal spoken in southern France west of the Rhone (the term "Provençal" is indifferently used to cover both the entire southern French area, and the more limited southern French area east of the Rhone).

Lao: A group of vernaculars spoken in Siam and in parts of Burma, classified as Shan dialects. The most important ones are: Thai Lao or Eastern Laotian, Thai Lu, Thai Ya, and Thai Yüan or Western Laotian.

Laotian: See *Lao*.

Lapp: A language, of the Finnish-Lapponic branch of the Finno-Ugric (or Uralic) sub-family of the Ural-Altaic family of languages, spoken by about 30,000 persons in northern Finland, Sweden and Norway.

Lapponic: (1) See *Lapp*.—(2) According to many linguists, a group of the Finnish-Lapponic branch of the Finno-Ugric (or Uralic) sub-family of the Ural-Altaic family of languages, consisting of Lapp, Cheremiss and Mordvin. (Other linguists consider Lapp, Cheremiss and Mordvin to be three distinct branches of the Finno-Ugric sub-family.)

laryngal, laryngeal: See *glottal*.

latent shwa: In Hebrew, the sign of the absence of a vowel sound.

lateral: In phonetical terminology, a consonant pronounced with complete closure in the front of the oral cavity but with incomplete closure at the sides, to permit there the escape of air.

lateral areas: The outer fringes of an imaginary circle surrounding a center of radiation, where innovations have not yet displaced the more archaic forms; also called *marginal areas*.

La-Ti: A language, not related to any known language, spoken by about 500 persons in an isolated speech-community northwest of Hagiang (China).

Latin: A member of the Latino-Faliscan branch of the Italic group of the Indo-European family of languages; extinct as a vernacular or spoken language, but still used as a liturgical language and tongue of communication in the Roman Catholic Church. The parent of the Romance languages (q.v.).

Latinesce: A simplified Latin, proposed as an international auxiliary language by Henderson about 1900.

Latinism: An idiom or construction peculiar to or reminiscent of Latin.

Latino-Faliscan: A branch of the Italic group of the Indo-European family of languages, consisting of the extinct languages Latin, Faliscan, Hernician and Praenestinian (qq.v.).

Latino Sine Flexione: The original name (literally, *Latin without inflection*) of the interlanguage (q.v.) created by Peano and later named *Interlingua*.

lative: A Finno-Ugric declensional case, having the same denotation as the English *as far as*.

Latvian: See *Lettish*.

law: Any statement or formulation of a universally observed regularity.

lax: In phonetics, said of a sound pronounced without much muscular tension in the speech organs or their parts involved in its articulation.

Laz: A language spoken in the Caucasus; a member of the South Caucasian family of languages.

lene, lenis: A laxly articulated consonant.

lenition: In Celtic languages, the phonetic change which consonants undergo when occurring between vowels, as well as the change of the initial consonant of a word under the influence of the final sound of the immediately preceding word. (Cf. *initial mutation*.)

Leonese: One of the dialects of medieval Spain, spoken in the western part of the country, along the Portuguese border; only traces remain of it today.

Lepcha: The language (also called *Rong*) of the state of Sikkim in the eastern Himalayas; a member of the Tibeto-Himalayan branch of the Tibeto-Burmese sub-family of the Sino-Tibetan family of languages.

Lepontine: The language of some ancient inscriptions found near Lake Maggiore, in northern Italy, and supposed to be related to Ligurian.

letter: A written character in an alphabetical system of writing, which represents—alone or in combination with other signs or letters—a phoneme or group of phonemes.

Lettish: A member of the Baltic group of the Indo-European family of languages, the native language of about 1,500,000 persons in Latvia. (Also called *Latvian*.)

levels of articulation: The level of content or meaning (the *morphemes*) and the level of expression (the *phonemes*). (*A. Martinet*)

lexical: Relating to the total stock of linguistic signs or morphemes of a given language.

lexical category: Those classes of signs which express ideas destined to be linked or combined in discourse by grammatical link words or particles. (*Bally*)

lexical form: A linguistic form (q.v.) considered merely in its purely lexical character.

lexical meaning: The meaning of a *lexical form* (q.v.).

lexicalize: To incorporate a word, etc. into the *lexicon* (q.v.) of a language.

lexicography: The definition and description of the various meanings of the words of a language or of a special terminology.

lexicology: The semantic or morphological study of the linguistic stock of a language.

lexicon: The total stock of linguistic signs (words or morphemes) existing in a given language.

liaison: French for *linking* or *ligature;* a term borrowed from French phonetics and grammar, designating the custom of pronouncing an otherwise mute final consonant letter of a word when the immediately following word begins with a vowel, thus pronouncing the two words more or less as one unit.

Liburnian: See *Picenian*.

Libyan: An extinct and little known language of the Libyco-Berber branch of the Hamitic sub-family of the Semito-Hamitic family of languages, known from inscriptions dating from not earlier than the fourth century A.D.

Libyco-Berber: A branch of the Hamitic sub-family of the Semito-Hamitic family of languages, consisting of the extinct and little known Libyan and the Berber group (Tuareg, Shluh, Kabyl, Zenaga, Zenete and the extinct Guanche).

light syllable: An unaccented syllable, obscure in pronunciation.

light vowel: An unaccented vowel, pronounced more or less obscurely or indistinctly.

Ligurian: (1) An extinct language of pre-Roman Italy, of as yet undetermined linguistic affinities; assumed to have been a connecting link between Italic and Celtic.—(2) A Gallo-Italian (q.v.) dialect.

linear phoneme: See *segmental phoneme.*

linear writing: In grammatology, any system of writing which employs signs which are linear designs or other signs not recognizable as pictures of objects.

lingua franca: Originally, the name of the contact vernacular spoken in the ports of the Mediterranean, based on Italian, with admixtures from Arabic, Greek and other languages; by extension, any spontaneously originated or artificially formed language or vernacular combining the vocabularies and elements of two or more languages. (Cf. *contact vernacular.*)

lingua geral brazilica: A contact vernacular (q.v.) used in large areas of Brazil for communication between whites, Negroes and Indians, as well as between Indians speaking different tribal languages. (The designation means *General Brazilian Language.*)

lingua romana rustica: A term used by Charlemagne at the Council of Tours (813 A.D.) to describe the new Romance language of the French portion of his realm, and opposed by him to the *lingua latina,* the traditional Latin language.

linguistic: Relating to language or to the study of language and languages; having the characteristics of language. (For the significance of this adjective in compound terms, see also the terms beginning with the word *speech.*)

linguistic analysis: The analysis of the phonemic and grammatical structure of a given language or group of languages.

linguistic areas: A term introduced by Emerson for the different vocabularies which an individual uses in different periods of his life, as well as for those employed by different social strata.

linguistic comparison: The observation, study and interpretation, in languages of the same family or linguistic group, of similarities or correspondences indicating that they originate from a common parent language.

linguistic form: Any phonetic form which has a meaning.

linguistic geography: That branch of linguistics which studies and classifies the geographic extension and boundaries of linguistic phenomena.

linguistic minority: A group of persons, usually a racial minority, whose native language or language of customary daily communication is different from that of the majority of the country or political subdivision.

linguistic typology: The classification of languages according to their structural features, instead of a genetic classification.

linguistician: A term coined by R. A. Hall, Jr., on the analogy of "mathematician," "mortician," etc., to describe one who works scientifically in language, as distinguished from a *polyglot*, one who speaks several languages.

linguistics: The science of language.

link verb: Copula (q.v.).

link word: Bodmer's term for *conjunction* (q.v.).

linking: (1) Generally, a combination or coordination.—(2) Specifically, see *liaison*.

liquid: In phonetical terminology, the designation of the consonants *l* and *r*.

lisping: The act of pronouncing *s* and *z* as θ and ð either deliberately or because of a speech defect.

literal translation: A word-for-word translation of an utterance or text into another language, without regard for the differences between the two languages as to grammatical structure and idiomatic peculiarities.

literary language: That dialect of a language which is regarded as the best and is used for literary purposes. The formal language of literature, in contradistinction to colloquial language or to the vernacular.

literate: Able to read and write.

litotes: A rhetorical figure in which an assertion is implied by the refutation or negation of its contrary, usually as a form of understatement.

Little Andamanese: A branch of the Andamanese family of languages, consisting of Önge (spoken on Little Andaman) and Yärava (spoken on South Andaman).

Little Russian: See *Ukrainian*.

liturgical language: A language used in religious services and, occasionally, as a means of communication among its religious users. E.g., Latin for Roman Catholics, classical Arabic for Moslems, etc.

living language: A language spoken as a medium of communication by the majority of people within a geographical or national area.

Livonian: A near-extinct dialect of the Finnish group of the Finno-Ugric (or Uralic) sub-family of the Ural-Altaic family of languages.

loan translation: The term recently adopted instead of *translation loan word* (q.v.).

loan-word: A word taken over from another language. (Cf. *translation loan-word.*)

localism: A word, idiom or grammatical or syntactical construction restricted and peculiar to the speech of a certain geographical area or community.

locative: A declensional case used to express geographical or other physical location, i.e., having the same denotation as the English preposition *in*.

locative clause: A clause which indicates the place in, from or to which an action takes place, originates or is directed.

locution: (1) In general, a synonym of *phrase, utterance, expression*, etc.—(2) Specifically, an expression of some idiomatic or structural peculiarity.

logical grammar: The study of the syntactical relations and functions of words.

logogram: A written sign representing one or more words of a given language or several languages.

logography: A system of writing employing mainly or exclusively signs each of which represents one or more words.

logo-syllabic writing: A system of writing employing logograms and syllabic signs.

Logudorese: See *Sardinian*.

Lo-lo (Lolo, Lu-lu): A group of dialects spoken by an estimated total of 1,800,000 persons in the southwestern Chinese provinces of Yün-nan, Si-kang and Sze-chuan. Lo-lo is a member of the Lo-lo-Mo-so language-group, the linguistic classification of which is still not established beyond dispute; it is generally considered a sub-group of the Tibeto-Burmese sub-family of the Sino-Tibetan family of languages, but some authorities place it in the Tai sub-family, and some others in the Chinese sub-family. (*Lo-lo* is a Chinese term; another alternative designation of this group is *T'swan*. However, the indigenous name for the Lo-lo languages is *Ne-su*.)

Lo-lo-Bodo-Naga-Kachin: A branch of the Tibeto-Burmese sub-family of the Sino-Tibetan family of languages, divided into the *Lo-lo-Mo-so* and *Bodo-Naga-Kachin* groups. (These groups are often called also *North Assamese* and *Middle and South Assamese*, respectively, but these designations are not recommended, because they may lead to confusion with the Indic language properly called *Assamese*.) The inclusion of the Lo-lo-Mo-so group in this branch is not a generally accepted fact; some authorities classify it as a group of the Tai sub-family, a few others as a member of the Chinese sub-family.

Lo-lo-Mo-so: A group of languages and dialects, classified generally in the Tibeto-Burmese sub-family of the Sino-Tibetan family of languages (although some authorities put it in the Tai sub-family, and a few others place it in the Chinese sub-family); it consists of Lo-lo and Mo-so, and several minor dialects. The members of this group are also referred to, misleadingly, as *North Assamese* languages.

loose: See *lax*.

Lorrain: A French dialect, spoken in Lorraine; often used as a literary vehicle in the Middle Ages.

low: Prefixed to the name of a language, this adjective designates (1) that version of that language which is spoken in the lowland section of the country (e.g., *Low German*), or (2) the version spoken after the "classical period" or "golden age" of the history of that language (e.g., *Low Latin*).

Low German: (1) A group of West Germanic languages, consisting of Anglo-Frisian (Frisian, Anglo-Saxon and modern English), Old Saxon, Dutch, Flemish and Plattdeutsch. In this sense, the synonyms *Low Germanic*, or *Low Teutonic* are less ambiguous.—(2) The German dialects of the northern parts of the German speech area, which were not affected by the second or High German sound shift (q.v.).

Low Germanic: See *Low German (1)*.

Low Teutonic: See *Low German (1)*.

low vowel: A vowel produced with the tongue in a lowered position. (Also called *open vowel*.)

lower-case letter: In the terminology of printers, editors, etc., a small letter, in contradistinction to a capital (called *upper-case*) letter.

Lower Mesopotamian: See *Sumerian*.

Luba-Lulua: The language of about 3,000,000 persons in the Belgian Congo; a member of the Bantu family of languages.

Ludian: A dialect (also called *Lüdish*) of the Finnish group of the Finno-Ugric (or Uralic) sub-family of the Ural-Altaic family of languages.

Lüdish: See *Ludian*.

Luganda: An African Negro language, also called *Ganda*, spoken in Uganda, East Africa; a member of the Bantu family of languages.

Luian: See *Luvian*.

Lu-lu: See *Lo-lo*.

Lusatian: A West Slavic language, also called *Wend, Sorbian* or *Sorbo-Wendic;* the native tongue of about 100,000 persons forming a linguistic island in Germany (in the Cottbus and Bautzen region).

Luvian: An extinct language (also called *Luian*), little known, but generally regarded a close relation of Hittite, and considered by some linguists to be cognate with Carian and Lycian.

Lycian: An extinct language, spoken in the southwestern part of Asia Minor, preserved in about 150 inscriptions and some coins, dating from the fourth and fifth centuries B.C. The language (the indigenous term for which was *Trmmli* or *Trknmli*) has no known linguistic relationship to any other known language, although various linguists have regarded it as cognate with Hittite, while others have claimed it to be a descendant of Luvian; it has also been called a member of the South Caucasian family of languages. However, the generally accepted opinion is that Lycian was an isolated language. It is classified as *Asianic*.

Lydian: An extinct language, of undetermined linguistic affinities, spoken in antiquity in western Asia Minor, preserved in fifty-three inscriptions. Classified as an *Asianic* language.

M

Macassar: A language spoken by about 300,000 persons in Celebes; a member of the Indonesian sub-family of the Malayo-Polynesian family of languages.

Macedo-Romanian: The Romanian spoken in Macedonia by a linguistic island surrounded by speakers of Greek, Serbian and Albanian.

macron: The diacritic mark [ˉ] placed over a vowel to indicate that it is to be pronounced long.

Maduran, Madurese: A language spoken by about 3,000,000 persons in the Dutch East Indies; a member of the Indonesian sub-family of the Malayo-Polynesian family of languages.

Magahi: A dialect of the Indic language *Bihari;* spoken by about 6,500,000 persons in the Oatna and Gaya regions.

Maghi: See *Burmese.*

Magyar: The Hungarian word for *Hungarian* (q.v.).

Maithili: The most important dialect of the Indic language *Bihari.* Maithili (also called *Tirhutia*) is spoken by over 10,000,000 persons in Tirhut, Champaran, eastern Monghyr, Bhagalpur and western Purnea.

makeshift language: Jespersen's term for *contact vernaculars* (q.v.).

Makua: A South-East African Negro language, member of the Bantu family of languages.

Malagasy: A language spoken on Madagascar by about 3,000,000 persons; a member of the Indonesian sub-family of the Malayo-Polynesian family of languages.

malapropism: Substitution of one word for another which is more or less similar in sound.

Malay: A language, member of the Indonesian sub-family of the Malayo-Polynesian family of languages, the native tongue of about 3,000,000 persons on and near the Malay Peninsula, and used as a *lingua franca* in Thailand, Indo-China, Sumatra, the Straits Settlements, Borneo, Celebes, Timor, parts of Java, and numerous islands, by an estimated 80,000,000 speakers. Now adopted, under the name *Bahasa Indonesia*, as the official tongue of Indonesia. (Cf. *Pasar Malay*.)

Malayalam: A language spoken in southwestern India by an estimated 13,400,000 persons; a member of the Tamil-Kurukh branch of the Dravidian family of languages.

Malayan: An alternative designation of the Indonesian sub-family of the Malayo-Polynesian family of languages.

Malayo-Polynesian: A family of languages (also called *Austronesian*) spoken in the islands of the Pacific and Indian Oceans; its area extends from Formosa in the north to New Zealand in the south, and from Madagascar in the west to Easter Island in the east (but does not include Australia, Tasmania and most of New Guinea). It is divided into four sub-families: *Indonesian* (or *Malayan*), *Melanesian*, *Micronesian*, and *Polynesian*.

malformation: The process or the result of the improper or unapproved formation of words (by prefixes, endings, etc.) from root words by analogical extension.

Malisit: A North American Indian language (Eastern Algonquian), also called *Malesit* and *Maliseet;* surviving in eastern Canada.

Maltese: A North Arabic dialect, with Italian infiltrations, spoken in the Mediterranean island of Malta; written in Roman characters.

Malto: A dialect of the Dravidian language *Kurukh;* spoken in the Rajmahal region of Bengal.

Man: A group of languages (Yao, Miao, etc.) spoken in northern Burma, southwestern China, and parts of Indo-China. Many linguists consider this group an independent family of languages, while other authorities classify it into the Tai sub-family of the Sino-Tibetan family of languages,

Manchu: (1) A language spoken in Manchuria, by an unascertained number of persons; together with Tungus, it forms the Manchu-Tungus branch of the Altaic sub-family of the Ural-Altaic family of languages.—(2) Used by some authors as the designation of the entire Manchu-Tungus branch of the Ural-Altaic family.

Manchu-Tungus: A branch of the Altaic sub-family of the Ural-Altaic family of languages, consisting of Manchu and Tungus. (Some authors refer to this branch as *Manchu*, or *Tungus* or *Tungus-Manchu.*)

Mandaean: An Eastern Aramaic dialect, spoken in the Euphrates Valley from the seventh to the ninth centuries A.D.

Mandarin: A collective name for numerous Chinese vernaculars, the most important of which is *North Mandarin*, on which the new "National Tongue" (*Kuo-yü*) of China is based.

Mandeali: The language of about 150,000 persons in the State of Mandi, India; a dialect of Pahari (q.v.).

Mandingo: An African Negro language, spoken in Sierra Leone, member of the Sudano-Guinean family of languages.

Mangbetu: An African Negro language, member of the Sudanese-Guinean family of languages.

Mangun: A Tungus dialect.

Manipuri: An alternative name of *Meithei* (q.v.).

Manx: A language of the Goidelic branch of the Celtic group of the Indo-European family of languages; the now almost extinct dialect of the Isle of Man.

Maori: The language of the aborigines of New Zealand; a member of the Polynesian sub-family of the Malayo-Polynesian family of languages. According to M. A. Pei (*The Story of Language*), Maori is spoken by about 100,000 persons.

Marathi: An Indic language, spoken in the Bombay region of India by approximately 27,000,000 native speakers. Its most important dialect is called *Konkani* (q.v.).

margin of security: The range within which the variants of a phoneme may move, without encroaching upon the sound range of another phoneme (cf. *A. Martinet*, "Function, Structure and Sound Change").

marginal areas: See *lateral areas*.

Mariandynian: An extinct ancient language, of undetermined linguistic affinities, preserved in inscriptions and glosses recorded by some classical authors. Classified as *Asianic*.

mark: The relevant feature which opposes two phonemes to each other.

mark of correlation: The relevant feature which is present in one *series* (q.v.), absent in the other, holding the two series together in a correlation.

marked member: That member of a *bilateral opposition* (q.v.) characterized by the presence of the relevant feature which marks the opposition; e.g., in *p*in x *b*in, the *b* is marked by the presence of the voice feature, which is absent in *p*, the *unmarked member* of the opposition; if, however, the opposition is seen as tense/lax, the tense *p* is the marked member and the lax *b* the unmarked.

markers: The linguistic signals which mark the grammatical categories; e.g., in English, *-s* added to a noun usually marks plurality, as "hat," "hats"; added to a verb, it usually marks third person singular, present tense, etc., as "I see," "he sees." The word "sheep" has a *zero marker* in the plural, though plurality may easily be marked by means of a numerical adjective or a plural verb form.

Marrucinian: One of the extinct dialects of the Sabellian branch of the Italic group of the Indo-European family of languages.

Marsian: One of the extinct dialects of the Sabellian branch of the Italic group of the Indo-European family of languages.

Masai: An East African Negro language, member of the Sudanese-Guinean family of languages.

masculine: One of the grammatical *genders* (q.v.).

Masoretic points: In Hebrew writing, the signs written after or below the consonant signs to indicate the vowel to be pronounced after (in case of one such sign, before) that consonant sound.

mass-word: Jespersen's term for words denoting concepts, properties or things which ordinarily cannot be separated into distinct component units.

material content: The concept or idea signified by a word, which remains the same regardless of morphological changes. (Cf. *modal content*.)

Matole: A North American Indian language (Athapascan family) surviving in California.

matres lectionis: In the Hebrew system of writing, consonantal signs indicating vowel sounds, thus transforming the *defective writing* into *plene writing* (qq.v.).

Mauritius Creole: A "pidgin-French" contact vernacular (q.v.) originated in the island of Mauritius in the 18th century.

Maya: The language of the ancient civilization of Central America (Guatemala, Honduras and southern Mexico) which flourished until the Spanish conquest of the Western Hemisphere. Maya and its many related dialects form, with *Huastec,* the Mayan family of American Indian languages.

Mayan: A family of Central American Indian languages, including *Huastec* and *Maya* (with about twenty-five known dialects).

meaning: The sense or thought content which a word or expression is intended to convey; the mental image formed in the consciousness of the hearer of an utterance, or of the reader of a written word or phrase.

mechanistic theory: The view that the variability of human speech is the result of complex causes based on the physiological structure of man, particularly the nervous system.

medial accent: Accent or stress falling on a syllable other than the first or the last one of the word.

medial position: The non-initial or non-final position of a sound or sound cluster within a word or word-group unit: e.g., the *e* is in medial position in "bet,"; and so is the *sh-ch* cluster, in "fresh cheese."

mediative case: A declensional case in certain languages (e.g., Basque), expressing the medium through or by which an action is performed. In most languages, this meaning is expressed by the *instrumental case* (q.v.).

Medicalese: Cf. *Gobbledegook.*

Medieval Latin: (1) In one acceptance, the Latin used as a literary language after the appearance of the Romance languages (i.e., from the 9th century A.D. until the Renaissance); (2) in another acceptance, synonymous with *Low Latin* or *Vulgar Latin* (q.v.).

mediopalatal: A sound produced at the middle part of the hard palate.

Meinhof's law: A phonetical law relative to the dissimilation of nasalized consonants in the languages of the Bantu group.

Meithei: A language (also called *Manipuri*) spoken by about 400,000 people in the valley of Manipur in Central Asia; a member of the Kuki-Chin group of the Arakan-Burmese branch of the Tibeto-Burmese sub-family of the Sino-Tibetan family of languages.

Melanesian: A sub-family of the Malayo-Polynesian family of languages, spoken in Fiji, Rotuma and in the Solomon, Banks, New Hebrides, Santa Cruz, Torres and Loyalty Islands. It consists of thirty-five languages, many of which have a *trial* (some even a *quatrial*) number in addition to singular, dual and plural.

Melanesian Pidgin: The form of Pidgin English (q.v.) spoken in the islands of Melanesia, which is sufficiently standardized to be understood over a wide area.

melioration: (1) The semantic shift undergone by certain words, involving and producing an improvement in meaning.—(2) The addition of a meliorative suffix (q.v.).

meliorative suffix: A suffix which gives a word a more favorable or flattering connotation.

Mende: An African Negro language, spoken in Sierra Leone; a member of the Sudanese-Guinean family of languages.

Menomini: A North American Indian language (Central Algonquian) surviving in the Great Lakes region.

mentalistic theory: The view that the variability of human speech is the result of complex causes based on mental processes in individual men.

Mercian: An Anglo-Saxon (Old English) dialect, which became the Midland division of Middle English.

Messapian, Messapic: An extinct Indo-European language, once spoken in southern Italy; variously assumed to have been an Italic dialect, a dialect of Illyrian, etc.

metalanguage: A language used to describe the structure of another language; any language whose symbols refer to the properties of the symbols of another language.

metalinguistics: "The study of what people talk (or write) about and why, and how they react to it" (*Trager* and *Smith*); it covers those aspects of linguistics which deal with the relation of language to the rest of culture.

metanalysis: Jespersen's term for the phenomenon consisting in that certain words or word-groups are analyzed differently than in former ages. (E.g., the words *a napron* were later analyzed into *an apron*, with the result that the word *napron* became *apron*.)—Cf. *numerical metanalysis*.

metaphony: Internal vowel change (cf. *umlaut*).

metaphor: A figure of speech in which one word is employed for another—a method of description which likens one thing to another by referring to it as if it were the other one.

metaphrase: A literal translation from one language to another.

metaplasm: Any change in a standard or accepted linguistic form, whether by the addition or omission of a sound or syllable, by transposition of sounds or groups of sounds, or by any other phonetic or morphological modification.

metathesis: (1) The change of the word order in a sentence.—(2) The transposition of the order of sounds within a word or between two words.

metonymy: The substitution of a word for another word having a closely related meaning.

Miami: A North American Indian language (Central Algonquian).

Miao (Miao-tzu): A Man (q.v.) language, spoken by about 2,000,000 persons in southwestern China and about 500,000 in northern Burma and Indo-China.

Micmac: A North American Indian language (Eastern Algonquian), surviving in northeastern Canada.

microlinguistics: The formal analysis of language structure, which lays the foundation for metalinguistics.

Micronesian: A sub-family of the Malayo-Polynesian family of languages; it consists of eight languages, spoken on the Caroline, Gilbert, Marshall and Marianne Archipelagos and on the island of Yap.

middle: An adjective prefixed to the name of a language to designate its state in the stage intermediary between the oldest known and the most modern forms, or between the *High* and *Low* (qq.v) forms.

Middle and South Assamese: See *Bodo-Naga-Kachin*.

Middle English: The English language, descendant of Old English (Anglo-Saxon), from 1150 to 1400 A.D. Its three main dialect groups were: *Northern* (descendant of Northumbrian), *Midland* (descendant of Mercian) and *Southern* (descendant of West Saxon).

Middle French: The state and period of the French language intermediate between Old French and modern French (roughly, the 14th and 15th centuries A.D.), and typically represented by the language of Villon. (Many Romanists reject the "Middle French" classification.)

Middle German: The basis of modern literary German, descendant of a merging of Middle and Upper Franconian, with an admixture of Thuringian; phonologically midway between High and Low German.

Middle High German: See *High German*.

Middle Irish: The Irish language from the 13th to the 17th century A.D.

Middle Low German: The linguistic ancestor of the modern *Plattdeutsch* dialect of northern Germany.

Middle Sakian: See *Khotanese*.

middle voice: A verbal voice intermediate in denotation between the *active* and the *passive voice*. It expresses that the action denoted by the verb is *dynamic* (performed by the agent for himself) or in general affecting the agent, or *reflexive* (its agent and object are the same).

mid-vowel: A vowel in the phonation of which the tongue is arched toward the middle of the palate.

Midwestern American: See *General American*.

military influence: M. A. Pei's term for "the coming into the language of words having their origin in warfare and soldiers' slang."

mimetic word: A word formed to imitate (1) a natural sound or (2) another word.

Min: A Chinese vernacular, spoken in the Chinese province of Fu-kien by about 30,000,000 persons.

Mingrelian: A language spoken in the Caucasus; a member of the South Caucasian family of languages.

Mitannian: See *Subaraean*.

Mittu: One of the Ubangi (q.v.) dialects.

mixed conjugation: A conjugational scheme which represents a combination of two or more standard conjugational schemes.

mixed declension: A scheme of declension which represents a combination of two or more standard schemes of declension.

mixed language: See *creolized language, hybrid language*.

Mo: See *Mossi*.

Moabite: An extinct language of the Canaanite subdivision of the Northern branch of the West Semitic group of the Semito-Hamitic family of languages.

mobile shwa: In Hebrew, the orthographic sign indicating the neutral vowel [ə].

modal auxiliary: An auxiliary verb indicating mood, i.e., manner or aspect of the action denoted by the verb with which it is used.

modal content: The functional relationship of a word, as indicated by morphological changes. (E.g., the singular form and the plural form of one and the same noun have different modal contents.)

mode: See *mood*.

Modern English: In general, the English language after the early 15th century A.D.

modifier: A word, expression or entire clause which qualifies or limits the meaning of a word.

molecule: See *syntactic molecule*.

momentary aspect: The verbal aspect which considers the action at a given point of its progress or development. More usually called *perfective aspect*.

Mon: A language (also called *Talaing*) spoken by about 225,000 persons in Burma; a member of the Mon-Khmer branch of the Austro-Asiatic family of languages.

Mongol (*or* **Mongolic**): A branch of the Altaic sub-family of the Ural-Altaic family of languages. It is divided into a Western sub-branch (Kalmuk), a Northern sub-branch (Buryat) and an Eastern sub-branch (Khalkha, Tangut and Shara, and according to some linguists, also Yakut). Afghan Mongol, a near-extinct language, is also a member of this branch. The total number of speakers of Mongol languages is estimated at 3,000,000.

mongrel word: A hybrid word (q.v.).

Mon-Khmer: A branch of the Austro-Asiatic family of languages, comprising Mon, Khmer, Cham and a great many minor dialects.

monogenesis theory: The theory, now generally rejected by most linguists, that all the languages of the world originated and descended from one common parent language. (*Trombetti*)

monoglot: A person who speaks, understands and uses one language only.

monograph: A treatise devoted to a single topic or to a single branch or phase of a subject.

Monokoutouba: A contact vernacular (q.v.), also called "*the railway language*," spoken in French Equatorial Africa. It is a combination of various dialects spoken by the native workers who worked on the building of the railroad from Brazzaville to the seacoast.

monopersonal verb: A term preferable to the expression *impersonal verb* to designate verbs used in one person only. (*Unipersonal verb* is an equally good synonym.)

monophone: A single sound or the letter or written sign which represents such a sound.

monophthong: A phoneme pronounced as a single sound, with one emission of sound. (The term is occasionally used also for any combination of two vowel signs which stands for one single vowel sound.)

monophthongization: The change of a diphthong (q.v.) into a simple sound.

monosyllabic: Consisting of one syllable.

monosyllabic language: A language in which all or most of the words consist of one syllable.

monosyllable: A word which consists of one single syllable.

Montagnais: A North American Indian language (Central Algonquian), surviving in the Great Lakes region.

monumental writing: A formal, careful, often ornate form of writing, such as used on monuments and for official purposes.

mood: One of the variations employed in the conjugation of a verb to express the manner or form in which the action or state denoted by the verb is performed or exists. M. H. Weseen (*Crowell's Dictionary of English Grammar*) calls it "the psychological aspect of an assertion."

Mordvin: A Finno-Ugric language, spoken by about 1,000,000 persons in Asiatic Russia. Some linguists consider Mordvin a member of a Lapponic group composed of Lapp, Mordvin and Cheremiss, while others regard these three languages as distinct branches of the Finno-Ugric (or Uralic) sub-family of the Ural-Altaic family of languages.

mora: Particularly in *tone languages* (q.v.), the several parts of the phoneme which may receive divergent tonal treatments: rising-falling, level-rising, etc.

Moro: A language spoken in the Philippine Islands; a member of the Indonesian sub-family of the Malayo-Polynesian family of languages.

morpheme: A distinct linguistic form, semantically different from other phonetically similar or identical linguistic forms, and not divisible or analyzable into smaller forms. The morpheme is the minimal meaningful unit of language; e.g., *boys* consists of two morphemes (*boy* and *s*), *boyishness* consists of three (*boy*, *ish* and *ness*).

morphological assimilation: In syntax, the morphological modification (as to number, gender, case, tense, mood, etc.) of a word, resulting in its deviation from the correct form, under the influence of another word or other words adjacent to it in the sentence.

morphological doublets: Two or more forms of the same word, the use of the proper form being determined by its context or position or function in the sentence. (E.g., the English articles *a* and *an*.)

morphological extension: A variety of *analogical extension* (q.v.), consisting in the formation of a new word or new words by the addition of suffixes or prefixes, or omission of endings, on the analogy of well known existing words.

morphological word: W. L. Graff defines this term (in *Language and Languages*) as meaning "in a wider sense, a word consisting of two or more semanto-phonetic elements consciously interpreted as such; in a narrower sense, a word consisting of two or more semanto-phonetic elements of which at least one does not correspond to an independent word or radical in the system of the language concerned."

morphology: The science and study of the forms and formation of words, i.e., the study of the ways and methods of grouping sounds into sound-complexes, called *words*, of definite, distinct, conventional meanings. According to *Bloomfield*, "by the morphology of a language we mean the constructions in which bound forms appear among the constituents."

morphophoneme: The phonemes which interchange or replace each other in corresponding parts of the various members of a morpheme (Z. S. *Harris*).

morphophonemics: That branch of morphology (q.v.) which deals with the phonemic aspect of the constitution of the morphemes of a language, and with the phonemic variations in morphemes appearing in different grammatical structures.

Mo-so (Moso, Mu-su): A language, consisting of several dialects, spoken east of Upper Burma and in the Yang-tse valley in the southwestern Chinese province of Yün-nan, as well as elsewhere in southwestern China. Mo-so is a member of the Lo-lo-Mo-so group of the Tibeto-Burmese (according to some linguists, of the Tai-Chinese) sub-family of the Sino-Tibetan family of languages. (*Mo-so* is a Chinese designation; the Tibetan term for Mo-so is *Djong*, whereas the indigenous term is *Na-khi* or *Na-shi*.)

Mossi: An African Negro language, also called *Mo*, a member of the Sudanese-Guinean family of languages.

mother tongue: (1) The language first learned by the speaker as a child.—(2) Philologically, the language from which a given language has developed.

Mozarabic: The Romance dialect or dialects used by the Christian populations under Moorish domination in central and southern Spain from the 8th to the 15th century A.D. Though generally unwritten, some samples have come down in *aljimiado* form (i.e., transcribed in Arabic or Hebrew characters).

Mpongwe: An African Negro language, also called *Galoa*, member of the Bantu family of languages.

multilateral opposition: A group of phonemes in a series, having the same relevant feature, e.g., voice aspiration, occlusiveness, etc., as the case may be.

multiplicative numeral: A numeral which answers the question "How many times?" or "How many fold?" (Some authorities classify also the *iterative* numerals as multiplicatives.)

multisyllable: An alternative term for *polysyllable*.

Munda: A language (also called *Kol* or *Kolarian*) constituting a branch of the Austro-Asiatic family of languages, and consisting of a great number of dialects spoken in Central India (Chota-Nagpur) and around the Himalaya Mountains. Accordingly, it is customarily divided into two groups: Chota-Nagpur or Southern Munda, and Himalayan or Northern Munda.

Mundolingue: An artificial language created by Julius Lott in 1890.

Mungu: One of the Ubangi (q.v.) dialects.

Muong: A language spoken, with its numerous related dialects, in South-East Asia; a member of the Annamese-Muong branch of the Austro-Asiatic family of languages.

Murmelvokal: The German term for *murmur-vowel* (q.v.).

murmur-vowel: A whispered or neutral vowel, such as the *e muet* in French (e.g., in *demi*) or the hardly audible *u* in the Japanese *desu*.

Mushkogean. A family of North American Indian languages, spoken in the southern and southwestern United States. Its surviving members include *Creek* (or *Mushkogee*), *Choctaw* and *Seminole*.

Mushkogee: A North American Indian language, also called *Creek*, member of the Mushkogean family; spoken in the southwestern United States.

Musu: See *Mo-so*.

mutation: See *initial mutation, vowel mutation*.

mutative: See *factive*.

mute: See *plosive*.

Mwala: The language of Malayta Island (one of the Solomon Islands); a member of the Melanesian sub-family of the Malayo-Polynesian family of languages.

Mysian: An extinct language, once spoken in Asia Minor, preserved only in a five-line inscription discovered in 1926. A language of undetermined linguistic affinities, classified as *Asianic*.

N

Na-Dene: According to Rivet, a family of North American Indian languages, consisting of the *Athapascan*, *Haida* and *Tlingit* sub-families.

Naga: A Tibeto-Burmese language, having a great many related dialects; a member of the Bodo-Naga-Kachin group.

Naga-Kuki: A Tibeto-Burmese language, having a great many related dialects; a member of the Bodo-Naga-Kachin group.

Nahuatl: See *Aztec*.

Nahuatlan: A family of American Indian languages, a member of which, *Aztec* or *Nahuatl*, was the language of the ancient civilization of Mexico. (According to Rivet, Nahuatlan is a sub-family of Uto-Aztecan, which includes also *Shoshonean* and *Pima-Sonoran*.)

Naiki: A Dravidian language, spoken in Central India, classified in the Gondi group.

Na-khi: See *Mo-so*.

Nam: An extinct Central Asian language, assumed to have belonged to the Tibeto-Burmese sub-family of the Sino-Tibetan languages. (The only record of the existence of this language consists of a few fragmentary manuscripts, discovered by F. W. Thomas, who named this language *Nam*, in 1926.)

Nama: An African language, also called *Hottentot*, with four dialects, spoken by about 250,000 uncivilized pigmies in South-West Africa; a member of the Hottentot-Bushman family of languages. Characterized phonetically by various types of *clicks* (q.v.).

name-word: Sweet's term for a *proper name*.

naming word: A word which denotes or symbolizes a person or thing (substantive), act or happening (verb) or quality (adjective or other modifier).

Nano. See *Umbundu.*

narreme: E. Dorfman's term for "a minimal unit of relevant narrative incident."

Narrinyeri: The language of some Australian aborigines.

Narrow Romic: The original, complex form of Sweet's system of phonetic symbols (*Romic*), which he later simplified in the *Broad Romic.*

narrow transcription: A careful representation of all the identifiable features of a phonetic utterance. (Cf. *broad transcription.*)

narrowed meaning: The more restricted meaning of a word which may in general be used with far wider application; e.g., "doctor" may refer to anyone with a doctor's degree (philosophy, science, letters, etc.) but, usually, is taken to mean "doctor of medicine."

nasal: In phonetical terminology, a sound produced with the uvula lowered, allowing the air to escape through the nose, so that the nasal cavity acts as a resonator.

nasal cavity, nasal chamber: The interior of the nose.

nasal twang: A nasalization characteristic of the pronunciation of vowels in certain regions.

nasalization: The pronunciation of a vowel as a *nasal* (q.v.).

Na-shi: See *Mo-so.*

national accent: A term proposed by Olivet for the sum total of the characteristics of the pronunciation of a certain language.

native language: The first language which a given human being learns to speak.

native speaker: With reference to a given language, any person whose *native language* (q.v.) that language is.

native word: A word which belongs to the original linguistic stock of a given language, i.e., which historical linguistics cannot identify as a loan-word from another language.

nativistic theory: The theory proposed by Max Müller, maintaining that a mystic harmony exists between sound and meaning, and human speech is the result of an instinct of primitive man which made him give a vocal expression to every external impression.

natural gender: Gender distinction based on and corresponding to natural sex, at times to the distinction between animate beings and inanimate objects.

natural gender system: The gender (q.v.) system in which animate beings are classified as masculine or feminine according to their natural sex, and inanimate objects or things usually as neuter.

naturalized word: A word borrowed from another language, but changed in written form or sound so as to be more similar to the words native to the borrowing language.

Navajo: A North American Indian language spoken in Arizona and New Mexico; a member of the Athapascan family.

necessitative aspect: A verbal aspect, also termed *obligatory*, expressing that the action or state denoted by the verb must be performed or exist.

negative aspect: A verbal aspect (e.g., in Turkish), expressing negation of the performance or existence of the action or state denoted by the verb.

negative conjugation: Those forms of a verb which deny the action expressed by the verb itself; negative forms of the verb may be expressed in different languages by negative particles, negative inflexional endings, and by various other means.

negative conjunction: A conjunction (q.v.) with a negative meaning. (E.g., *nor*.)

negative particle: Any word which when used with another word denies or inverts the meaning of the latter.

Negro-African: See *African*.

Negro-English: A creolized language (q.v.) spoken in Dutch Guiana, representing a combination of English, Dutch, Spanish, Portuguese and French elements. Its two varieties are: *Bush-Negro English* and *Ningre Tongo* (qq.v.).

Negroism: In English linguistics, a word, expression or grammatical or syntactical construction peculiar to or characteristic or reminiscent of the speech of the American Negro.

Nenets: See *Samoyed*.

Neo-Aryan: A term occasionally used to designate the modern Indo-Iranian vernaculars, especially the modern Indic dialects.

Neogrammarians: Generally, this term is used as the English translation of the German term *Junggrammatiker* (q.v.). Some authors apply this term at times also to the structural linguists, although not to the *functional and structural* linguists.

Neolinguists: Adherents to the school of linguistics which believes in the primacy of the expressive and esthetic aspects of language and maintains that linguistic change is the result of individual creations which spread and become assimilated on an ever-increasing scale. This school rejects the Neogrammarian theory of sound laws which admit of no exception.

neologism: (1) A newly coined and as yet not generally accepted word or expression.—(2) The coining and the use of new words or the use of established words in a new sense.

Nepali: An Indic language, spoken in Nepal, India, by approximately 6,000,000 native speakers. (Also called *Nepalese* or *Gurkhali*.)

Ne-su: See *Lo-lo*.

neuter: One of the grammatical *genders* (q.v.).

neutral vowel: In the grammar of the Finno-Ugric languages, the vowel [i], which may occur both in words containing back vowels and in words containing front vowels. (Cf. *vowel harmony*.)

neutralization: The temporary suspension of an otherwise functioning *opposition* (q.v.) (*t*ie x *d*ie, but for many speakers of American English, we*t*ting-we*dd*ing, articulated in identical fashion). Since the *t* and *d*, normally in *opposition*, do not oppose each other here, we have an *actualization* (q.v.) of the archiphoneme.

New Akkadian: See *Akkadian*.

new word: See *neologism (1)*.

nexus: Jespersen's term for a group of words, one of which is a verb, forming a sentence.

nigori mark: In Japanese syllable writing (*kana*), the superscript ["] which indicates that the consonant in the syllable is voiced.

Ningre Tongo: A creolized form of English spoken in Suriname (Dutch Guiana). (Also called *taki-taki*.)

noa word: A word that may not be uttered because of its profane meaning. (Cf. *taboo*.)

noeme: The meaning of a *glosseme* (q.v.).

nomenclature: The set of names used in relation to a specific subject or field of science or study.

nominal definition: The definition which explains the meaning of a word which names a thing. (Cf. *real definition*.)

nominal language: See *noun language*.

nominal sentence: A sentence in which the principal part (Graff calls it "pivotal part") is a noun or nominal form.

nominative: That case-form in which a noun, pronoun, adjective, etc., is used when standing alone and without any syntactical context or relationship, or when used as the grammatical subject of a sentence.

non-compound flexion: In Irish grammar, the conjugation of the simple verbs.

non-distinctive: Cf. *acoustic features*.

non-objective conjugation: See *subjective conjugation*.

non-phonemic: See *irrelevant*.

non-sentence: A group of words which does not express a complete thought in itself and therefore does not constitute a sentence.

non-standard: The use of speech sounds or forms in a given language, which differ markedly from the so-called *standard* language, and are frequently labeled "vulgar" and "incorrect"; also called *sub-standard*.

non-syllabic: In a syllable, any sound other than the *syllabic* (q.v.).

nonce word: A word coined for a special occasion.

Nootka: A language of Vancouver Island.

Norman: A French dialect, spoken in Normandy, and often used as a literary vehicle in the Middle Ages.

normative grammar: See *prescriptive grammar*.

Norse: See *Old Norse*.

North Arabic: A Southern West Semitic language, the sacred tongue of Islam and the common literary language of the Mohammedan countries; spoken, in a great number of dialects or vernaculars, by approximately 37,000,000 native speakers. Usually referred to simply as *Arabic*.

North Aryan: See *Khotanese*.

North Assamese: See *Lo-lo-Mo-so*.

North Caucasian: A family of languages spoken by about 1,000,-000 persons in the Caucasus area in Asia. These languages, characterized phonetically by a great variety of consonants (including many lateral affricates and labialized consonants) are divided in two groups: Eastern Caucasian or Checheno-Lesghian and Western Caucasian or Abasgo-Kerketian.

North Chinese vernacular: One of the Mandarin dialects of China, spoken by about 250,000,000 people.

North Germanic: A branch of the Germanic group of the Indo-European family of languages; it comprises Icelandic, Swedish, Danish, Norwegian, Faroese and Gotlandic (or Gutnian). Also called *Scandinavian*.

North Italian: A term used by some Romance linguists as a collective designation of the *Gallo-Italian* and *Venetian* dialect groups (qq.v.).

Northern Mongol: See *Buryat*.

Northern West Semitic: A subdivision of the Semitic group of the Semito-Hamitic family of languages, comprising two subgroups: Canaanite (Old Canaanite, Hebrew, Phoenician and Moabite) and Aramaic (Eastern and Western Aramaic).

Northumbrian: An Old English (Anglo-Saxon) dialect, which was the parent of the Northern division of Middle English.

Norwegian: A Scandinavian (North Germanic) language, spoken by about 3,000,000 native speakers. (Cf. *Landsmål* and *Riksmål*.)

noun: A word designating or naming a person, living being, object, thing, etc. A *proper noun* is the name of one specific entity, whereas a *common noun* designates an entire class, category or group or any member thereof.

noun-equivalent: A word (pronoun, participle, adjective) or group of words used in the sense and function of a noun.

noun language: A language which uses mainly or solely *nominal sentences* (q.v.).

noun numeral: A numeral used as a noun.

noun sentence: See *nominal sentence*.

noun-word: A term used by Sweet collectively for nouns and other words used in a noun function.

Novial: An artificial language created by Otto Jespersen in 1928.

Nubian: An African Negro language, spoken by about 300,000 persons in the Nile valley and the Anglo-Egyptian Sudan; a member of the Sudanese-Guinean family of languages.

nucleus: See *kernel*.

number: The grammatical distinction, common to the majority of the principal families or groups of languages, based on a morphological differentiation according as the speaker intends to designate one object, thing, etc., or more than one. The form designating *one* is called the *singular*, that designating *more than one* is the *plural*. Some languages have also distinct forms to designate *two* (*dual*), some even forms to designate *three* (*trial*) and even *four* (*quatrial*). On the other hand, certain languages attach no importance to number distinction and indicate number, by special linguistic devices, only when especially emphasized or absolutely necessary for the proper interpretation of the utterance.

number concord: The grammatical agreement, as to number, of those words in a sentence which are syntactically interrelated.

numeral: A word indicating number or quantity and relationship as to number and quantity. Numerals answer the question "How many?" (*cardinals*), "Which one in sequence?" (*ordinals*), "How many times?" (*iteratives*), "How many fold?" (*multiplicatives*), "What fraction?" (*partitives*), etc.

numeral classifier: See *auxiliary numerals*.

numeral pronoun: A term occasionally used for a word which denotes an indefinite number of persons or things.

numerative classifiers: Various words which in Japanese, in Chinese, and in other languages are inserted between a numeral and the substantive to which the numeral refers, also between a demonstrative and a noun.

numerical metanalysis: Jespersen's term for the change which causes a word which was originally singular to be regarded now as plural, or vice-versa.

nunation: In Arabic, the suffixation, in certain cases, of the letter *nun* [n] to words ending in a short vowel.

Nyamwezi: An East African Negro language, member of the Bantu family of languages.

Nyanja: An African Negro language (also called *Nyanza, Nyasa, Nyassa,* etc.) spoken, in various dialects, by about 1,500,000 persons in Nyasaland in eastern Central Africa; a member of the Bantu family of languages.

Nyaturu: An East African Negro language, member of the Bantu family of languages.

Nyoro: An African Negro language, member of the Bantu family of languages.

O

Ob-Ugrian: A language group (consisting of Ostyak and Vogul) which with Hungarian constitutes the Ugric branch of the Finno-Ugric (or Uralic) sub-family of the Ural-Altaic family of languages.

Oberi Okaime: A newly created African language, having its own script, employed by a sect founded about 1928 in the village of Ikpa, near Iyere in the Calabar Province of Nigeria. R. G. Adams, who first reported on this language (African Journal, 1947) states that even new speech-sounds were introduced by the speakers of this tongue.

object: The word or word-group or phrase designating the person or thing at which the action expressed in the sentence is directed. (Cf. *direct object, indirect object.*)

object-language: That language the structure of which is described in terms of a *meta-language* (q.v.).

object of reference: A term occasionally used as a synonym for *indirect object* (q.v.).

objectal: Relating to the grammatical object of a sentence.

objectal conjugation: See *objective conjugation.*

objectival: Relating to the grammatical object of a sentence.

objective conjugation: In the Finno-Ugric languages, that form of conjugation (q.v.) which indicates a definite object of the action. (Also called *definite conjugation.*)

obligatory aspect: See *necessitative aspect.*

oblique case: A collective term for all declensional cases other than the nominative and vocative. (In Old French and Old Provençal, the oblique case appears as a single form, opposed to the nominative.)

oblique question: An indirect question (q.v.).

obsolescent: In the process of becoming obsolete.

obsolete: No longer in general, current use.

obviative: The form of pronouns used in some languages, when non-identical third persons are referred to; e.g., "He took *his* (own) pipe," simple possession; "He took *his* (someone else's) pipe," obviative.

Occidental: An artificial language, created by de Wahl.

occlusive: See *plosive*.

Odri: See *Oriya*.

Odshi: See *Twi*.

off-glide: In phonetics, the final phase of the articulation of a phoneme, in which the vocal organs return to their normal, neutral position or assume a position preparatory to forming another sound. (Also called *final glide*.)

Officialese: See *Gobbledegook*.

Oghams: The symbols of the script of the early Celtic population of the British Isles.

Oji: See *Twi*.

Ojibway: A North American Indian language (Central Algonquian), surviving in the Great Lakes region. (Also called *Ojibwa* and *Chippewa*.)

Old Akkadian: See *Akkadian*.

Old Aramaic: An early variant of Western Aramaic, preserved in Palmyrene, Nabataean and Sinaitic inscriptions (eighth century B.C. to fourth century A.D.).

Old Armenian: See *Grabar*.

Old Bulgarian: See *Church Slavonic*.

Old Canaanite: An extinct language of the Canaanite subdivision of the Northern West Semitic branch of the Semito-Hamitic family of languages.

Old Church Slavonic: See *Church Slavonic*.

Old Dutch: See *Old Low Franconian*.

Old English: The Anglo-Saxon language—the English language from the middle of the 5th to the beginning of the 12th century A.D.

Old French: The period of the French language from the Oaths of Strasbourg (842 A.D.) to, roughly, the 14th century: characterized by a two-case flectional system for masculine nouns and adjectives.

Old Frisian: A Low German language spoken in the area between the Scheldt and the Weser Rivers from the 7th to the 12th century A.D.; it was closely akin to Anglo-Saxon.

Old High German: See *High German*.

Old Iranian: A collective term for Zend (or Avestan) and Old Persian.

Old Irish: The Irish language from the 7th to the 13th century A.D.

Old Kuki: A group of various dialects (Khami, Khyang, etc.); a member of the Arakan-Burmese branch of the Tibeto-Burmese sub-family of the Sino-Tibetan family of languages.

Old Low Franconian: The West Germanic dialect also known as Old Dutch, ancestor of modern Dutch and Flemish.

Old Norse: The extinct ancestor of the North Germanic (q.v.) languages. (Also called *Old Scandinavian*.)

Old Persian: The language spoken in the southwestern part of the Iranian plateau between the 6th and the 4th centuries B.C.

Old Provençal: The literary language of southern France from the 10th to the 13th century A.D. Though fairly well standardized for literary purposes, it evidently represents a compromise among the spoken dialects of Provençal proper (east of the Rhone) and Languedocien (west of the Rhone).

Old Prussian: An extinct language, a member of the Baltic group of the Indo-European family of languages.

Old Sakian: An extinct Iranian language, considered by some linguists to have been the ancestor of *Ossetic*.

Old Saxon: A West Germanic language, spoken from the 9th to the 12th century A.D., when it was absorbed into Middle Low German; it survives today in the Saxon vernaculars of northeast Germany.

Old Scandinavian: See *Old Norse*.

Old Slavonic: See *Church Slavonic*.

Olonetzian: A member of the Finnish group of the Finno-Ugric (or Uralic) sub-family of the Ural-Altaic family of languages.

Önge: A Little Andamanese language.

on-glide: The initial phase of the articulation of a phoneme, in which the vocal organs occupy the position necessary for the formation of that sound. (Also called *initial glide*.)

onomasiology: The study of the meanings of names.

onomastics: See *onomasiology, onomatology*.

onomatology: The study of names, their origin and meaning.

onomatopoeia: The formation of words imitating natural sounds.

onomatopoeic theory: That theory which maintains that human speech originated as an imitation of the sounds produced by animals and other natural sounds. (Often referred to as the *bow-wow theory*.)

onomatopoetic (onomatopoeic) word: A word which imitates, reproduces or represents a natural sound.

onset: The movement of the speech organs from a state of rest to the positions necessary for the articulation of a given speech sound.

open stress: Sweet's term for the stress when the consonant is heard just as the intensity of the vowel has begun to decrease.

open syllable: A syllable ending in a vowel. Also called *free syllable*.

open vowel: A vowel pronounced with the mouth opened more than in the pronunciation of another vowel sound.

operator: In the terminology of Basic English (q.v.), the designation of the verbal forms, prepositions, particles, etc. (totalling altogether 100) included in the system.

opposition: Every phoneme in a language is opposed to every other, since a change from one phoneme to another in a chain of speech should give either a new form or an unintelligible one. Oppositions can be classified as *bilateral, multilateral, disjunctive, isolated, proportional* or *binary* (qq.v.). (Cf. *contrast*.)

optative mood: The verbal mood, existing as a distinct, independent mood in several languages, used to express a wish or desire. (In other languages, this mood has absorbed or has been absorbed into the *subjunctive* or the *imperative* mood.)

optional variants: A synonym for *free variants* (q.v.).

oral cavity, oral chamber: The interior of the mouth.

order: In phonology, the vertical listing of a row of phonemes according to the place of articulation. E.g., *labial order* ([p], [b], [m]), etc.

ordinal numeral: A numeral expressing the position or order of a member or element in a series. (E.g., *first.*)

Oriya: An Indic language (also called *Odri*) spoken in Orissa, Bihar, Bengal, the eastern regions of the Central Provinces and in the northern part of the Madras Presidency, by a total of about 13,000,000 native speakers.

Orochon: A Tungus dialect.

Oroq: A Tungus dialect.

orthoepic: Pertaining to or characteristic of *orthoepy* (q.v.).

orthoepist: A student of or a person skilled in *orthoepy* (q.v.).

orthoepy: The art and the study of correct pronunciation.

orthographic: Relating to orthography; conformable with the rules of orthography.

orthography: The art and rules of spelling according to the accepted standards, i.e., the use of the written characters of a language for forming words and sentences in conformity with the rules conventionally recognized as correct.

orthophonic: Relating to *orthophony* (q.v.); conformable with the standard or accepted rules of pronunciation.

orthophony: Correct pronunciation or articulation.

Oscan: An extinct Italic dialect spoken in southern Italy in the second half of the first millennium B.C. (Oscan inscriptions have been found on walls in Pompei.)

Osco-Umbrian: A branch of the Italic group of the Indo-European family of languages, consisting of the extinct Oscan and Umbrian dialects.

Osmanli: See *Turkish (1)*.

Ossetic: A language of the Iranian branch of the Indo-Iranian group of the Indo-European family of languages, spoken in the Caucasus by approximately 225,000 native speakers.

Osthoff's law: A phonetic law, propounded by Osthoff, concerning the shortening of vowels in Greek when followed by [i], [u], a nasal or liquid sound plus a consonant.

Ostyak: A language, belonging to the Ob-Ugrian group of the Ugric branch of the Finno-Ugric (or Uralic) sub-family of the Ural-Altaic family of languages; spoken by about 18,000 persons in Asiatic Russia. (Not related to *Yenisei-Ostyak*.)

Ottoman: See *Turkish (1)*.

overcorrection: In speech or writing, the error induced by the fear of falling into the opposite error: e.g., "between you and I," caused by the desire to avoid the use of the accusative for the nominative in such expressions as "You and me are going to do it."

oxytone: A word in which the last syllable bears the main accent. (Cf. *paroxytone* and *pro-paroxytone*.)

oxytonic language: A language in which the majority of the words bear the main accent on the last syllable.

P

P-Celtic: A designation sometimes applied to the Brythonic branch of the Celtic family of languages.

Paelignian: One of the extinct dialects of the Sabellian branch of the Italic group of the Indo-European family of languages.

Pahari: A modern Indic vernacular, the various dialects of which are spoken by about 2,500,000 persons on the lower ranges of the Himalayas from Nepal as far as Bhadrawal. The most important of these dialects are: Jaunsari, Kului, Chambiali, Mandcali, Sukcti, Sirmauri.

Pahlavi: See *Pehlevi*.

Palaeo-Asiatic: See *Hyperborean*.

Palaian: See *Palawi*.

palatal: In phonetical terminology, a consonant pronounced with the surface of the tongue arching toward or held near or against the hard palate. (E.g., [ĵ], [ç].)

palatal law: A phonetic law formulated by V. Thomsen, in 1875, although discovered by various linguists more or less independently. This law states that in Sanskrit a Proto-Indo-European velar or guttural ([k] or [g]) preceding the vowel [a] become the palatalized Sanskrit ç and j when the Sanskrit [a] corresponds to Greek or Latin [e], but the [k] and [g] preceding [a] remains unchanged when the Sanskrit [a] corresponds to Greek or Latin [a] or [o]. This law proved that, contrary to the view held up to 1875, Proto-Indo-European had the front vowel [e].

palatal vowel: A synonym of *front vowel* (q.v.).

palatalization: The change of a sound which is ordinarily not a palatal into a palatal sound.

Palawi: An extinct and almost completely unknown Near-Eastern language of remote antiquity, classified as *Asianic*. (Alternative names of Palawi are: *Palaian* and *Balaian*.)

paleography: The study of ancient ways, methods and forms of writing, including the deciphering and interpretation of ancient texts painted or traced with ink, colors, etc. on paper, parchment, fabrics, and other soft materials. (Cf. *epigraphy*.)

Palestinian Judaeo-Aramaic: A Western Aramaic dialect, the language of the Palestinian Talmud (fourth to fifth centuries A.D.).

Pali: One of the Prakrit (q.v.) vernaculars of India, no longer a spoken language; it was used in southern India as a literary language, and it is the language in which the Buddhist scriptures (*Tripitaka*) are written.

Pampangan: A language spoken in the Philippine Islands by about 350,000 persons; a member of the Indonesian sub-family of the Malayo-Polynesian family of languages.

Pamphylian: An extinct language, of undetermined linguistic affinities, spoken in southwestern Asia Minor until the first century A.D. Classified as *Asianic*.

Pangasinan: A language spoken in the Philippine Islands by almost 400,000 persons; a member of the Indonesian sub-family of the Malayo-Polynesian family of languages.

Panjabi: See *Punjabi*.

Paphlagonian: An extinct language, of undetermined linguistic affinities, preserved in some inscriptions and in some glosses recorded by classical authors. Classified as *Asianic*.

Papiamento: A creolized (q.v.) Spanish, spoken by the natives of Curaçao.

Papuan: A family of 132 little known languages, spoken in most of New Guinea, parts of New Britain and Bougainville, in Halmahera, and Tolo, Ran, Tidore and Ternate Islands.

paradigm: (1) A complete set of all the various forms of a word (conjugation, declension).—(2) A model, pattern, or example.

paradigmatic: Relating to or constituting a paradigm (q.v.)—In phonemics, the most important use of this adjective can be summed up as follows: The listing of all the phonemes of a language, in series, orders (qq.v.) and isolated elements forms a paradigm, from which the individual phonemes are selected as needed for the chain of speech. (Cf. *syntagmatic*.)

paragoge: The addition of a sound, letter, or syllable to the end of a word, without any etymological justification, often for euphony or ease in pronunciation, without changing or affecting the meaning of the word.

paragogic, paragogical: Relating to, constituting or producing a *paragoge* (q.v.).

paragogic sound, phoneme, syllable: A sound, phoneme or syllable added to a word, for euphony or ease in pronunciation.

paraphrase: The statement of the contents of a passage, text, etc., in the same or another language, without following the original text verbatim.

paraplasm: Replacement of an established form by a newly coined form.

paraplastic form: A form replacing an old, established form.

parasynthesis: Formation of words using both composition and derivation.

parasynthetic: Relating to or produced by *parasynthesis* (q.v.).

parasyntheton: A word formed by *parasynthesis* (q.v.) (The plural form is *parasyntheta*.)

paratactic: (1) Relating to, based on or constituting a *parataxis*.— (2) Coordinated, especially syntactically.

parataxis: The coordination or juxtaposition of two or more phrases of equal significance or rank.

parent language: The language from which another language or other languages developed is said to be the parent language of the latter.

parenthesis: (1) A word or expression interpolated in a sentence (between commas, dashes, etc.) without being essential or necessary for the grammatical completeness of the sentence; also called *parenthetical expression* or *phrase*.—(2) A *parenthesis mark* (q.v.).

parenthesis marks: The punctuation marks [(] and [)], used to inclose *parenthetical words* or *phrases* (see *parenthesis*).

parenthetical clause: See *parenthesis (1)*.

parenthetical words and phrases: See *parenthesis (1)*.

parisyllabic: Consisting of an equal number of syllables.

parlance: Mode of speech; special usage of words; cf. *jargon*.

parole: French for *word*. According to the linguistic terminology introduced by F. de Saussure, *parole* (usually translated into English as *speech*) consists in the use of a language by a given individual in a given case, in contradistinction to the *langue* (*language* or *tongue*) which is characterized by a complete and homogeneous grammatical system observed and followed by a group or community.

paronym: A word derived from the same primary word as a given word. Paronyms are similar in form but differ in meaning.

paronymous: Constituting a *paronym* (q.v.).

paroxytone: A word bearing the main accent on the penultimate syllable.

paroxytonic language: A language in which the majority of the words are *paroxytonic* (q.v.).

parse: To analyze a word grammatically as to form and function in a sentence; to analyze a sentence grammatically as to elements and their interrelationships.

Parthian: A synonym for *Pehlevi* (q.v.).

participial: Belonging or relating to or having the nature of a *participle* (q.v.).

participial noun: A term occasionally applied to gerunds or verbal nouns.

participial phrase: A group of words built around a *participle* (q.v.).

participialization: The act or process of transforming into a *participle* (q.v.).

participle: A verbal adjective, i.e., a verbal form which has the characteristics both of verbs and adjectives, and may be used as an adjective.

particle: A word, usually uninflected and invariable, used to indicate syntactical relationships.

partitive: A case in certain Finno-Ugric languages, having the same denotation as conveyed in English by the use of the word *some* before the noun, or in French by the use of the partitive article (q.v.).

partitive: (*adj.*): Denoting division or the result of a division.

partitive article: In certain languages, a particle used before nouns to indicate that the noun is used to designate a part of the totality of the concept or object meant by it. (E.g., the *de l'* in the French *de l'eau*, meaning "some water.")

partitive numeral: A numeral which answers the question "What fraction?"

parts of speech: The categories into which the words of a given language can be classified, either according to their functions in sentence construction (nouns, pronouns, verbs, adjectives, adverbs, prepositions, conjunctions and interjections) or according to their forms, mode of inflection, etc.

Pasar Malay: A creolized (q.v.) form of Malay, representing a blend of various Malayo-Polynesian dialects, used as a trade language or "contact vernacular" all over British Malaya and the Dutch East Indies, and understood even in the Philippine Islands. (Also called *Bazaar Malay*.)

Pashto: See *Pushtu.*

pasigraphy: A system of writing using signs of universal significance.

pasimology: The art of communicating by means of gestures, as practised by some American Indian tribes, by the deaf-mutes, etc.

Passamaquoddy: A North American Indian language (Eastern Algonquian).

passive case: See *patient case.*

passive voice: The conjugational category expressing that the action denoted by the verb is performed upon the grammatical subject, i.e., the grammatical subject is actually the direct object, target or recipient of the action.

past: A general term for all verbal tenses which indicate that the action took place prior to the utterance.

past anterior: In the Romance languages, a form of the pluperfect tense, composed of the preterite of the auxiliary verb and the past participle of the main verb (whereas the regular pluperfect is a compound of the imperfect of the auxiliary verb and the past participle of the main verb). The past anterior is used generally in temporal clauses when the verb of the main clause is in the preterite.

past infinitive: An infinitive referring to past time.

past perfect tense: That tense which indicates that the action was completed by the time another action occurred; the tense which designates a past state which was the result or outcome of a previous action.

past tense: In general, a tense which expresses that the action took place in the past.

Patanuli: See *Saurashtra.*

patient case: In certain Caucasian languages, a declensional case which designates the subject of an intransitive verb or the logical complement of a transitive verb. (*Marouzeau*)

patois: Popular speech, mainly that of the illiterate classes, specifically a local dialect of the lower social strata.

patronymic: A name describing the paternity of the bearer. E.g., *Johnson,* from *John's son.*

pattern: The paradigm of all the phonemes of a language. Also, the phonemic system of a language.

Paulista: The dialectal variant of Portuguese used in the State of São Paulo, Brazil.

pause-pitch: A rise of pitch before a pause within a sentence.

Pedageese: See *Gobbledegook.*

pedigree theory: The theory (*Stammbaumtheorie*) formulated by August Schleicher in 1866, according to which a parent language split into two branch languages, each of which again bifurcated into two languages, etc., as branches grow from the trunk of a tree, to produce smaller branches, twigs, etc.

Pehlevi: (1) The intermediary stage of the Persian language between Old Persian and Modern Persian.—(2) The alphabet created in Persia about 200 B.C.

pejoration: (1) The semantic shift undergone by certain words, involving and producing a lowering in meaning.—(2) The addition of pejorative suffixes (q.v.).

pejorative suffix: A suffix which gives a word a deprecatory connotation. (E.g., the Italian *-accio*.)

Pelasgian: An extinct language of southern Europe, variously described as Mediterranean or Japhetic, and said to have been linked with Caucasian, Basque and Etruscan. (*N. Marr*)

pendent: Said of a grammatically incomplete construction.

Pennsylvania Dutch: A variety of German, originally from the Palatinate, used in parts of Pennsylvania (notably York and Lancaster counties); though it is heavily interlarded with English, its German origin is clearly perceptible. "Dutch" is a misnomer in this expression, and many prefer "Pennsylvania German."

Pennsylvania German: An alternative designation of *Pennsylvania Dutch* (q.v.).

Penobscot: A North American Indian language (Eastern Algonquian).

penult: The syllable next to the last in a word.

penultimate: Next to the last.

peregrinism: Foreignism (q.v.).

perfect: A collective term applied to all verbal forms which designate an action or a state which is the result or outcome of an action performed in the past.

perfect infinitive: The past infinitive (q.v.).

perfect tense: A verbal tense expressing that the action has been completed, or designating a present state which is the result or outcome of an action in the past.

perfectivation: The transformation of an imperfective (q.v.) verb into a perfective (q.v.) one by a morphological change, such as the addition of a prefix or suffix, internal vowel change, etc.

perfective aspect: A verbal aspect expressing a non-habitual or one-time action, or an action considered from the point of view of its completion.

perfectum: The aspectual category introduced by the Roman grammarian Varro (first century B.C.), including the perfect, past perfect and future perfect tenses.

period: (1) The punctuation mark [.] used at the end of a declarative sentence.—(2) Occasionally used as a synonym for *periodic sentence* (q.v.).

periodic sentence: In rhetoric, a sentence in which the most significant element or part occupies the final position.

peripheral language: A language which shows characteristics or features typical of another language group or family, supposedly acquired as a result of an early separation from its own parent speech-community and contact with that other group or family. (*Meillet*)

periphrasis: Circumlocution; the use of superfluous words.

periphrastic: Using several words for what could be expressed by fewer words.

periphrastic conjugation: Conjugation with the aid of an auxiliary or auxiliaries, instead of inflections.

periphrastic declension: Declension with the aid of prepositions or other independent particles.

periphrastic form: With reference to verbs, a form in which the principal verb is combined with an auxiliary or some other particle; with reference to substantives, a case formed with the aid of a preposition or other particle.

periphrastic tense: A verbal tense formed with the aid of an auxiliary.

perissologic, perissological: Redundant (q.v.).

perissology: Redundancy (q.v.).

permansive aspect: A verbal aspect in Semitic languages, which considers the action from the point of view of its permanency.

Permian: A branch of the Finno-Ugric (or Uralic) sub-family of the Ural-Altaic family of languages; it consists of Votyak and Zyrien (or Syryen).

permissive mood: The verbal mood indicating permission or liberty to perform the action.

Persian: A member of the Iranian branch of the Indo-Iranian group of the Indo-European family of languages, spoken by approximately 10,000,000 native speakers.

person: The grammatical distinction between the speaker, listener and subject of an utterance. Defined by M. H. Weseen (*Crowell's Dictionary of English Grammar*) as "the grammatical property of substantives and verbs indicating the relations of the persons or things concerned." The *first person* refers to the speaker, the *second person* to the person addressed, and the *third person* to the person, concept or thing spoken of. The distinction may be made by morphological variations of the verb or by appropriate subject pronouns or other particles. (Certain languages, e.g., Japanese, may express this differentiation by the use of entirely different verbs or nouns.)

person concord: The agreement as to person of syntactically related words in a sentence.

personal endings: The inflectional endings or suffixes which indicate person (and, usually, number).

personal infinitive: An infinitive with a personal ending (q.v.) which indicates distinction as to grammatical person and number. This form is found in various, unrelated languages (e.g., in Portuguese, which is a language of the Romance group of the Indo-European family; in Hungarian, which is a Finno-Ugric language; etc.).

personal pronoun: A pronoun used to indicate or refer to the speaker or speakers (*first person*), the person or persons addressed (*second person*) and the person or persons, etc. spoken of (*third person*).

personal suffix: See *personal ending*.

personal verb: (1) A verb which can be used in all three persons, in contradistinction to *impersonal verbs,* used in the third person singular only.—(2) A verb which has different forms for the three grammatical persons.—(3) A verb which shows difference in person by different conjugational suffixes (*personal endings*).

Petit Nègre: A creolized (q.v.) version of French, used as a "contact vernacular" in French West Africa.

petitionary sentence: A variety of the imperative sentence, expressing a request or supplication.

petroglyph: A primitive pictogram carved into rocks.

petrogram: A primitive pictogram painted or drawn on rocks.

Peul: See *Fula*.

phantom word: A word that came into being through an error of a lexicographer or printer.

pharyngal: In phonetical terminology, a consonant phonated at the pharynx.

phememe: A rarely used cover term for the smallest lexical and/or grammatical unit. Lexically, it is the *phoneme*, grammatically the *taxeme* (qq.v.).

phenomenon word: A word, usually an adjective, expressing a non-permanent attribute or property.

philology: The science and scientific study of language, words and linguistic laws. According to one accepted interpretation of the term, also literature (in particular the older texts of a language) is included, and the study of language is regarded as a means to other ends. Another interpretation of the term makes *philology* practically synonymous with *linguistics*.

philosophical grammar: The study of language and languages in general, and of the basic principles behind the grammatical phenomena of all languages, without confining itself to any particular language.

Phoenician: An extinct member of the Canaanite subdivision of the northern branch of the West Semitic group of the Semito-Hamitic family of languages.

phonation: The process or act of producing speech-sounds, i.e., the act or process of uttering phonemes by conscious and deliberate use of the vocal organs in a desired manner.

phonatory: Causing or producing vocal sounds.

phone: A rudimentary vocal sound.

phoneme: A single speech-sound or a group of similar or related speech-sounds which function analogously in a given language and are usually represented in writing by the same letter (with or without diacritic marks to indicate the differences). Bloomfield calls the phoneme "a minimum unit of distinctive sound-feature." It may be defined also as "a minimal bundle of relevant sound features."

phonemic analysis: See *phonemics.*

phonemic transcription: The representation of the phonemes in an utterance, carefully excluding all the irrelevant (q.v.) features.

phonemicist: One who makes or specializes in a phonemic analysis of a language.

phonemics: The study, analysis and classification of phonemes (q.v.), their relationships and changes.

phonetic (*noun*): In Chinese writing, the symbol within a compound ideograph, which gives a clue to the pronunciation of the spoken word represented by the ideograph.

phonetic, phonetical (*adj.*): Pertaining to, derived from, according to, or based on sound or sounds.

phonetic alphabet: See *International Phonetic Alphabet.*

phonetic change: A general term for the modifications of a phoneme in the course of the history of the development of a language.

phonetic complement: In logographic or ideographic systems of writing, a non-semantic phonetic element added to the logogram or pictogram to indicate the proper pronunciation and significance of the sign in the context.

phonetic indicator: See *phonetic complement.*

phonetic law: Any systematic formulation of the rules and principles behind sound shifts and other phonetic changes. According to Jespersen (*Language, Its Nature, Development and Origin,* p. 269), "a 'phonetic law' is not an explanation, but something to be explained; it is nothing but a mere statement of facts, a formula of correspondence, which says nothing about the cause of change. . . ."

phonetic spelling: See *phonetic writing*.

phonetic symbols: See *International Phonetic Alphabet*.

phonetic transcription: The representation of a phoneme, sound or utterance in the phonetic alphabet or in the conventional script of another language. (Cf. *broad transcription, narrow transcription*.)

phonetic writing: (1) In general, a method of writing using signs representing individual sounds (*alphabetic writing*) or individual syllables (*syllabic writing*) in contradistinction to *ideographic writing* (q.v.).—(2) Specifically, a system of writing in which each written sign represents one spoken sound only, and each spoken sound is represented by one written sign only.

phonetician: Phoneticist (q.v.).

phoneticist: A person who studies or is skilled in *phonetics* (q.v.).

phoneticization: (1) The act or process of making something phonetic; (2) representation of articulate sounds phonetically; (3) phonetic transcription (q.v.).

phonetics: The science, study, analysis and classification of sounds, including the study of their production, transmission and perception. (Cf. *acoustic phonetics, articulatory phonetics, experimental phonetics, genemmic phonetics, genetic phonetics, physiological phonetics*.) Many authors use the terms *phonetics* and *phonology* (q.v.) indiscriminately and interchangeably.

phonetist: Phoneticist (q.v.).

phonic: Relating to or characteristic of sound.

phonics: The science of spoken sounds, more commonly called *phonetics* (q.v.).

phonogram: (1) A written sign representing a spoken sound.— (2) A graph obtained by the aid of a laboratory apparatus for the study of spoken phonemes.

phonology: The study of the changes, transformations, modifications, etc. of speech-sounds during the history and development of a language or a given dialect, considering each phoneme in the light of the part which it plays in the structure of speech-forms, accepting it as a unit without considering its acoustic nature. (Many authors use the term *phonetics* indiscriminately for *phonology*, too; others use the term *phonology* as a synonym for *historical* or *diachronic phonetics*).

phrasal compound: A compound word consisting of words distinguishable as such and having independent meanings of their own when used alone.

phrasal tense: A periphrastic tense (q.v.).

phrase: A group of words not containing a subject or predicate.

phrase-whole: A group of words in a grammatical pattern, taken or learned as a unit.

phraseology: The choice and arrangement of words.

Phrygian: An extinct Indo-European language, once spoken in Asia Minor; preserved in a few inscriptions, dating from the seventh and sixth centuries B.C.

physical phonetics: The study of the sound waves produced when sounds are uttered. A branch of *experimental* or *laboratory phonetics*.

physiological phonetics: The study of the production of sounds and of the movements in the body which produce sounds. A branch of *experimental* or *laboratory phonetics*.

Picard: A French dialect, spoken in Picardy (France). During the Middle Ages, Picard was a flourishing literary medium, rivalling Francien.

Picenian: An extinct language, once spoken in Italy, of undetermined linguistic affinities. (Also called *Liburnian* and *Pre-Sabellian*.)

pictogram: A written symbol which denotes a definite object, of which it is a complete or simplified picture.

pictograph: See *pictogram*.

pictography: A system of writing by semantic representation using *pictograms* (q.v.). as symbols. (See also *pictorial writing*.)

pictorial writing: The system of using pictures for written communication.

pidgin: See *Pidgin English*.

Pidgin English: A creolized (q.v.) version of the English language, used by traders for communication with the Chinese and other

Orientals. The word *pidgin* (a corruption of the English word *business*) is often used popularly as an adjective to designate hybrid forms of other languages, too, for which the designation of Bodmer and Hogben, *contact vernacular*, is a better and more descriptive term.

Pidgin Malay: See *Pasar Malay*.

Pima-Sonoran: A family of American Indian languages, spoken in the southern United States and in Mexico; its surviving members are: Pima, Papago, Yaqui (or Kahita), Sinaloa, Tarahumare and Huichol. According to Rivet, this family is a sub-family of *Uto-Aztecan* which includes also *Shoshonean* and *Nahuatlan*.

Pisidian: An extinct, almost unknown ancient Near-Eastern language, classified as *Asianic*.

pitch: The highness or lowness of tone. Defined in laboratory phonetics as the frequency of vibration in the musical sound of the voice.

pitch accent: A variation of pitch within a single phrase or word.

Plattdeutsch: A Low Germanic dialect, spoken in northern Germany.

plene writing: A Hebrew system of consonantal writing, indicating vowel sounds by means of consonantal signs called *matres lectionis*. (Cf. *defective writing*.)

pleonasm: The use of superfluous words.

pleonastic: Redundant, superfluous.

plosive: In phonetical terminology, a consonant produced by completely closing the nasal and oral air-passages (*implosion*), resulting in a retention of air, and then suddenly opening the closure (*explosion*). Variously termed also *explosive, mute, occlusive,* and *stop.*

pluperfect: The past perfect tense (q.v.).

plural: The grammatical number denoting *more than one.* (In languages having *dual* forms, the plural denotes *more than two.*)

plural (*adj.*): Multiple; more than one; several.

plural of approximation: Jespersen's term for the plural of numerals referring to decades in the lives of individuals or in centuries (e.g., "in the *nineties* of the past century").

plurative: An adjective used, very rarely, as a synonym for the adjective *plural*.

plurilingual: A synonym for *polylingual* (q.v.).

Pochismo: A "contact vernacular," spoken along the American-Mexican border, and consisting of Spanish heavily interlarded with English words and expressions.

poetry: A composition in rhythmical and metrical form, with or without rhymes.

pointer words: A term for *demonstratives* (used by Hogben and Bodmer in *The Loom of Language*).

Polabian: A West Slavic language, extinct since the eighteenth century.

Polish: A West Slavic language, the native tongue of about 25,000,000 people.

polyglot: (1) As an adjective, this word means containing or combining several languages.—(2) As a noun (rarely used), it means a person mastering or using several languages.

polylingual: (1) With reference to a text: written in several languages.—(2) With reference to persons: speaking several languages.

Polynesian: A sub-family of the Malayo-Polynesian family of languages, spoken east and west of the Melanesian area, viz., in Samoa, New Zealand, Tahiti, Hawaii, Easter Island, the Hervey, Society, Mangareva, Chatham, Marquesas, etc. Islands. It consists of twenty languages (characterized phonetically by a strong tendency to eliminate consonants and by the lack of consonant clusters and closed final syllables), the most important of which are: Hawaiian, Samoan, Tahitian and Maori.

polyphone: A written sign or combination of written signs which represents different sounds in different words or contexts.

polyphony: The property or characteristic of a written letter, syllable or word sign or other visible sign, of standing for more than one phoneme or sound or group of phonemes or sounds.

polysemantic: Having several, often quite different, meanings, all derived from the basic idea or concept.

polysemous: See *polysemantic*.

polysemy: The possession of several different meanings.

polysyllabic: Consisting of several syllables.

polysyllable: A word consisting of several syllables.

polysynthesis: The combination of several words into one word.

polysynthetic language: A language in which various words are combined (usually merged into the equivalent of a verb), with the resulting composite word representing an entire sentence, statement or idea.

polytonic language: See *tone language*.

Pontic: An extinct language, of undetermined linguistic affinities, preserved in inscriptions and in glosses recorded by some classical authors. Classified as *Asianic*.

pooh-pooh theory: See *interjectional theory*.

popular etymology: See *folk etymology*.

portmanteau word: A word coined by combining the first part of one word with the second part of another.

Portuguese: A Romance language, the native tongue of approximately 60,000,000 people in Portugal, its colonies and in Brazil.

Portuguese Creole: A creolized (q.v.) Portuguese spoken in the Cape Verde Islands.

positional variants: Variants (q.v.) due to position in the environment. (Also called *combinatory*, *conditional* or *contextual* variants.)

positive conjunction: A term occasionally applied to conjunctions (q.v.) introducing a clause which expresses an actual, existing state or relation. (E.g., *because*.)

positive degree: That form of an adjective or adverb which merely expresses the presence of a quality or condition, without comparing or indicating its degree.

possessive: Expressing or signifying possession.

possessive case: The grammatical case which indicates possession; in Indo-European languages, the *genitive* case.

possessive compound: A compound in which one of the components designates a quality possessed by the other one.

post-dental: See *alveolar*.

postfix: A rarely used synonym for *suffix* (q.v.).

postposition: A particle or word placed after a word to indicate its grammatical or syntactical relationship to the other words in the sentence.

post-velar: In phonetical terminology, a consonant pronounced with the tongue farther back than the *velar* (q.v.) position.

Potawatomi: A North American Indian language (Central Algonquian), surviving in Kansas.

potential mood: A term occasionally applied to verbal forms expressing ability, possibility, freedom for action, also obligation or necessity.

Praenestinian: An extinct dialect of the Latino-Faliscan branch of the Italic group of languages.

Prakrit: Any of the non-Sanskrit vernaculars and literary languages of ancient India. The Prakrits developed into the *Apabhramsa* vernaculars on which the modern Indic vernaculars are based. Some Indian authorities list as many as thirty-eight Prakrits.

pre-adjective: Sweet's designation for an adjective which precedes the noun which it modifies.

precative mood: In certain languages, a distinct verbal mood used in utterances expressing a request or entreaty.

precisionist: One who observes and insists on strict, often exaggerated, care and precision in the forms and rules of speech and expression.

pre-dental: In phonetical terminology, a consonant pronounced with the front part of the tongue held near or touching the upper teeth.

predicate: The word or group of words which states or negates a property, condition, etc. of the subject of the sentence. (Cf. *complete predicate; compound predicate; simple predicate.*)

predicate adjective: An adjective or adjective phrase which modifies a noun or noun-equivalent indirectly, through a *copula* (q.v.), thus completing the meaning of the latter. In languages which use no copula, the predicate adjective functions as the predicate (q.v.) of the sentence.

predicate noun: A noun used in the sentence to describe, identify, etc. the subject, to which it is linked through a *copulative verb* (q.v.).

predicate verb: A verb used as the predicate of a sentence, or the verb part of a *complete predicate* (q.v.).

predicating word: Any finite verb form, so called because it can be used as predicate in a sentence.

predication: A statement or assertion.

predicative: Having the characteristics of a predicate or predication (qq.v.).

predictive future; predictive tense: Terms occasionally used to denote the future tense used to indicate what will happen.

prefix: A *formative* (q.v.), consisting of a letter, syllable or syllables, placed before and fused with a word, so as to form one unit with the latter and change or alter its meaning. (*To prefix* means to fuse a letter, syllable or syllables to the beginning of a word.)

preposition: In general, a word or particle placed before a substantive to show the syntactical or grammatical relation of the latter in the sentence. (Unlike prefixes, prepositions do not fuse with the word which they modify.)

preposition-group: A synonym for *prepositional phrase* (q.v.).

prepositional: In the Slavic languages, a declensional case which is used after certain prepositions only. (Many Slavic grammars call this case *locative*.)

prepositional phrase: A substantive (with or without modifiers) preceded by a preposition showing the grammatical or syntactical function of the substantive.

Pre-Sabellian: See *Picenian*.

prescriptive: A synonym for *jussive*. (Cf. *jussive mood*.)

prescriptive grammar: The presentation of grammar as a set of rules which must be obeyed by those who wish to be considered as employing the "standard language." Also called *normative grammar*.

present tense: The verbal tense indicating that the action or state denoted by the verb is contemporarily occurring or existing.

presentational affix: A word capable of being used as a prefix or suffix or as a separate word with a distinct independent meaning of its own.

presentive word: A word which directly conveys an idea, a concept, the picture or notion of an object to the mind of the listener.

preter-: A prefix formerly used in grammatical terminology to form names of certain verbal tenses, viz.: *preterimperfect* (now customarily called *imperfect tense*), *preterperfect* (now customarily called *perfect tense*) and *preterpluperfect* (now customarily called *past perfect tense*).

preterit, preterite: A verbal tense expressing that the action occurred in the past.

preterit future: An obsolete name of the verbal tense now usually called *future perfect*.

primary accent: The main stress in the pronunciation of a given word.

primary compound: A compound word consisting of two simple words.

primary derivative: (1) A word derived from another word which itself is not a derived word.—(2) A word derived from another word by vowel mutation.

primary language: A term often used to designate the spoken language, in contradistinction to the written form of the language (called *secondary language*).

primary phoneme: (1) A simple, non-compound phoneme.—(2) A speech feature or element, any change in which has a direct bearing on the meaning of the word or utterance.

primary tense: A designation often applied to the *present, simple past* and *future* tenses (also called *simple tenses*).

primary word: In general, a word not derived from another word. (Jespersen uses this term in the sense of *substantive*.)

prime word: A word which cannot be shown to be composed of other words or linguistic elements.

primitive: The adjective customarily employed in the designation of the unrecorded parent languages of language groups or families (e.g., Primitive Germanic, Primitive Indo-European, etc.).

principal clause: An independent clause (q.v.).

principal word: This term is used by Jespersen in the meaning of *substantive*.

privative: A generic term for suffixes, prefixes, and other elements of word-formation which indicate lack, absence, etc. (E.g., the English *non-*, *un-*, *-less*, etc.)

proclitic: Said of a word which bears no accent of its own, but is pronounced as forming a phonetic unit with the accented word following it.

productive suffix: A term introduced by Jespersen for suffixes which still can and are used to form new derivatives.

progressive: (1) With reference to changes (phonetical, grammatical, etc.), this adjective indicates that the change occurs under the effect or influence of a preceding element.—(2) See *progressive tense*.

progressive assimilation: Assimilation (q.v.) of a phoneme which follows the assimilatory phoneme responsible for this phenomenon.

progressive dissimilation: Dissimilation (q.v.) of a phoneme under the influence of a preceding phoneme.

progressive tense: A verbal form, usually periphrastic, expressing that the action is, was or will be in progress at the time indicated.

prohibitive: Expressing a prohibition.

prolative: A declensional case in certain languages (e.g., Finno-Ugric), having the same denotation as conveyed in English by the preposition *along*.

prolepsis: Anticipative use of a word in the sentence construction.

promissive future; promissive tense: Terms occasionally used to denote the future tense used to express a promise, assurance, etc., in contradistinction to the expression of what is expected or bound to happen (the latter is called *predictive tense*).

pronominal: Relating to or characteristic of a pronoun (q.v.); having the characteristics of a pronoun.

pronoun: A word used to replace a proper name or a noun, or to refer to the person, object, idea, etc. designated by a noun.

prop-word: A term occasionally used for a word used to replace a substantive. (Cf. *anaphoric word*.)

proparoxytone: A word bearing the main accent on the syllable immediately preceding the penultimate.

proparoxytonic language: A language in which the majority or a great many of the words are *proparoxytones* (q.v.).

proper compound: In flexional languages, a compound word in which the members are so intimately linked or fused that only the last member is inflected.

proper noun: The name of a specific individual person, object, place, etc.

proper triphthong: See *triphthong*.

propiate noun: A noun designating a state or condition or occupation or vocation.

proportional analogy: A rarely used synonym for *analogical creation* (q.v.).

proportional opposition: The relationship of sets of phonemes to each other: $p:b = t:d = k:g; f:v = \theta:\eth = s:z = \int:\mathit{3}$ etc., where more than one set has the same relevant feature.

proposition: A declarative sentence; in general, any complete utterance or assertion. Also, the content of meaning of such a sentence, utterance or assertion.

prose: Language as used in writing and speaking, without observance of rhythm, meter, stanzaic pattern and the other distinctive features of poetry.

prosecutive: A declensional case in certain languages (e.g., in Yukagir), having the same denotation as conveyed in English by the preposition *along*.

prosodeme: The minimal unit of prosodic feature serving a phonemic purpose. Also called *supra-segmental phoneme*, and *secondary phoneme*.

prosodic features: Those phonemic features which are tied, not to individual phonemes, but to larger units (the syllable) or to smaller units (the *mora*—q.v.).

prosody: The science and art of versification and of the rhythmic structure of sound in speech, especially in poetry.

prosthesis, prosthetic: See *prothesis, prothetic*.

protasis: See *hypothetical clause*.

prothesis: The prefixing of a prothetic (q.v.) vowel or syllable to a word.

prothetic phoneme, prothetic vowel: A sound prefixed to a word for easier pronunciation or other phonetical or linguistic reasons.

proto-: When prefixed to the name of a language, this term serves to designate the earliest known, at times the earliest artificially reconstructed, form of that language.

prototype: A primitive form; the original or model after which other words or forms are patterned.

Provençal: A Romance language, formerly used throughout southern France as a unified literary language, today a series of local dialects. An attempt to reconstitute a literary Provençal was made by Mistral about 1900.

provincialism: A word or phrase or construction peculiar to or characteristic of a local dialect or manner of speech.

Prussian: See *Old Prussian*.

psycholinguistics: The study of linguistics as connected with human behavior.

Puchikvar: A Great Andamanese language.

punctuation: The use of conventional marks (*punctuation marks*) in order to separate certain parts or elements of a written text, for the purpose of assuring and improving the clarity of its meaning.

punctuation mark: Cf. *punctuation*.

punctuation words: Particles used in certain languages (e.g., Malay) which serve to indicate a point of division between units of meaning, thus being the spoken equivalents of written or printed punctuation marks.

Punjabi: An Indic language, spoken in the Punjab region of northern India by approximately 17,000,000 native speakers. (Also called *Panjabi*.)

pure language: A language free of hybridization, admixture of foreign linguistic features, borrowed words and forms, etc.

purism: The tendency or effort to preserve a language "pure" from the use of foreign terms; exaggerated care and precision in the observance of the rules of grammar and speech.

purist: One who believes in and practices purism (q.v.).

Pushto: See *Pushtu.*

Pushtu: A language, of the Iranian branch of the Indo-Iranian group of the Indo-European family of languages, spoken in Afghanistan by an estimated 4-5,000,000 native speakers. This language is also called *Pushto, Pashto* or *Afghan.*

putative aspect: A verbal aspect, also termed *inferential*, expressing that the action or state denoted by the verb is reported as an inference or as an item of information gained from someone else's statement.

Pyu: A language once spoken in Burma, extinct since the 14th century A.D. Hardly anything is known about this language, the only known records of which consist of a few inscriptions. The language is tentatively classified as Tibeto-Burmese.

Q

Q-Celtic: A designation sometimes applied to the Goidelic branch of the Celtic group of languages.

Qabardi: A language spoken in the Caucasus; a member of the Adyghe group of the Western Caucasian branch of the North Caucasian family of languages.

Qaputsi: A language spoken in the Caucasus; a member of the Eastern Caucasian branch of the North Caucasian family of languages.

quadrisyllabic: Consisting of four syllables.

quadrisyllable: A word consisting of four syllables.

quadruplets: Four words of the same language, any of which represents a doublet (q.v.) with any of the other three.

qualifier: A word which qualifies, limits or modifies the meaning of another word.

qualitative accent: Stress and pitch (qq.v.).

qualitative gradation: Vowel gradation (q.v.).

quantifier: A term occasionally applied to a numeral or another word denoting quantity when used as a modifier of another word.

quantitative gradation: The lengthening or shortening or suppression of a vowel.

quantitative accent: Duration (q.v.).

quantity: In phonetics, a term synonymous with *duration*—the relative length of time during which the vocal organs remain in the position required for the articulation of a given sound.

quantity mark: A mark placed over a vowel or diphthong to indicate that it is to be pronounced long or short. The *macron* [¯] indicates a long sound, the *breve* [˘] indicates a short sound.

Quara: A Kushitic vernacular.

Quechua: A family of South American Indian languages, also called *Kechua* or *Kichua*. Its principal dialects are: Ayacucho, Bolivian, Chinchaya (or Chinchasuyu), Tucumano or Argentine, Cuzqueño, Huancaya, Lamaño (or Lamista), and Quiteño, spoken by an estimated total of 4,000,000 Indians in central South America. Quechua was the language of the ancient Inca civilization.

Queen's English: The same as King's English (q.v.).

question mark: The punctuation mark [?] used in most Indo-European, and many other languages, at the end of a direct question.

questione della lingua: The discussion originated by Dante as to the true nature of the literary Italian language; whether it is based on Florentine Tuscan pure and simple, or represents a compromise or merger of the various dialectal forms of northern, southern and central Italy.

quinquesyllabic: Consisting of five syllables.

quinquesyllable: A word consisting of five syllables.

quotation marks: The punctuation marks used to inclose direct quotations. (The quotation marks commonly used in English are ["..."], whereas in the other European languages the marks [„..."] and [«...»] are customary.)

R

radiation: The spread of a new sound or form from a center to out-lying regions in ever-widening circles.

radical (*noun*): (1) In linguistics, that part of a derived word which is phonetically and semantically the vehicle of the basic meaning, i.e., one or more sounds or syllables common to all words relating to or signifying the same idea or concept, and thus capable of being regarded as the semantic vehicle of that idea or concept in a given language. (Cf. *root.*)—(2) In Chinese writing, any one of the 214 elementary ideographs.

radical (*adjective*): In etymological, phonetic, etc. analysis, this designation is applied to an element which is a part of the *root* (q.v.), in contradistinction to the flexional endings, formatives, etc.

radical flexion: Inflection (q.v.) in which the endings are attached directly to the *root* (q.v.) of the word (*root base*).

radical language: Any language in which all words are or behave like *radicals* (q.v.—*1*) and their grammatical relationships and syntactical functions are indicated solely or mainly by the word order.

Raetic, Raetian: See *Rhaetic.*

Raeto-Romanic: See *Rumansch.*

Ragusan: One of the two dialects of Dalmatian, extinct since the 15th century A.D.

railway language: See *Monokoutouba.*

Rajasthani: An Indic language, spoken in northwestern India by approximately 14,000,000 native speakers.

ramification: Division into branches; a branch or subdivision.

ramified: Possessing or divided into various branches or subdivisions.

Rarotonga: A language spoken on the Cook Islands; a member of the Polynesian sub-family of the Malayo-Polynesian family of languages.

real condition: The statement of a fact (e.g., "he knows the answer"). (Cf. *unreal condition.*)

real definition: A definition which explains the nature of a thing, not its etymological meaning. (Cf. *nominal definition.*)

realization: See *actualization.*

reciprocal assimilation: The assimilation (q.v.) of two phonemes under the influence of each other.

reciprocal pronoun: A pronoun expressing or implying mutual action (e.g., *each other*).

reciprocal verb: A term often used for verbs expressing mutual action by and on two or more agents.

rection: A synonym for *government* (q.v.).

reduction: Shortening (q.v.).

redundancy: The use of unnecessary words.

redundant: (1) With reference to words: superfluous, constituting a repetition.—(2) With reference to grammatical or syntactical forms or constructions: including unnecessary or superfluous words or forms.

reduplication: The complete or partial repetition of an element or elements. In some Indo-European languages (e.g., Greek), the reduplication of the initial consonant or syllable of a verb root is a method of tense formation. In various other languages, repetition is a device for forming the plural of a noun (e.g., Malay), for indicating emphasis or intensity, etc.

reduplicative expression (*or* **phrase**): An expression or phrase consisting of two words which are synonyms or near-synonyms for the same idea connected by a conjunction such as *and;* the two words are usually alliterative or rhyming or both alliterative and rhyming.

reduplicative words: Words of recurring sound and meaning (e.g., *chit-chat*).

reference: (1) In grammar, the indication of the relationship between words in the same sentence.—(2) The semantic meaning of a word, expression, etc., i.e., the mental content which is thought of by the speaker when using a word or expression as a semantic symbol, and/or is called forth in the mind of the listener.

referend: In semantics, the vehicle or instrument of an act of reference.

referent: In semantics, the object or concept denoted by a word, expression or judgment; the thing, notion, etc., to which *reference* (q.v.) is made.

reflective: See *reflexive*.

reflexive pronoun: A personal pronoun indicating that the object of the action is identical with the agent.

reflexive verb: A verb which indicates an action of which the subject or agent and the object are identical. In many languages, all verbs used with reflexive pronouns (q.v.) are considered reflexive verbs, while the grammars of other languages consider only those verbs reflexive the action of which is directed back ("reflected") toward the agent.

regimen: See *government*.

regionalism: See *provincialism*.

regressive: With reference to changes (phonetical, grammatical, etc.), this adjective indicates that the change occurs under the effect or influence of a following element.

regressive assimilation: The assimilation (q.v.) of a phoneme which precedes the assimilatory phoneme responsible for this phenomenon.

regressive dissimilation: Dissimilation (q.v.) of a phoneme under the influence of a following phoneme.

regular: In grammar, a word is considered regular if its declensional or conjugational pattern, comparison, etc. follows the paradigm accepted for that particular class of words.

related languages: Languages which have developed from the same *parent language* (q.v.).

relating words: Prepositions, conjunctions, and other words the function of which in a sentence or phrase is to show the relationship between other words.

relational words: A general term for words which serve to express grammatical or syntactical relationships between *naming words* (q.v.).

relative adverb: According to the Joint Committee on Grammatical Nomenclature, this term is recommended for denoting an adverb which introduces a subordinate clause and serves both as an adverb and a conjunction.

relative clause: Any subordinate clause introduced by a relative pronoun or relative adverb.

relative degree: An alternative term for the *comparative degree* (q.v.).

relative pronoun: Any pronoun which is used to connect a dependent clause to a main clause and refers to a substantive in that main clause.

relative superlative: The superlative degree of an adjective used to indicate the highest degree of a quality, characteristic or property in comparison to other persons or objects possessing the same characteristic, etc. to a lesser degree.

release: In phonology, the movement of the speech organs from the positions of articulation to a state of rest.

relevant: Distinctive; having a function in a given system.

relic form: A linguistic form which shows or suggests an obsolete linguistic feature of the language under consideration.

representational: Currently used (Troubetzkoy, and others) as the third of the three important aspects of language—that denoting the subject of discourse. (Cf. *expressive* and *appellative*.)

resonance: The effect produced by the vibration of the vocal cords in pronouncing voiced consonants. It may also involve the joining of the oral and nasal cavities, resulting in *nasal resonance*.

restrictive clause: A dependent clause that defines or limits a word in the main clause, and is therefore an essential part of the latter with respect to the meaning thereof.

restrictive phrase: A phrase that defines or limits a word in the sentence and is essential to the meaning of the latter.

restrictive relative pronoun: A relative pronoun introducing a restrictive clause (q.v.).

retracted: In phonology, said of a sound pronounced with the tongue drawn back from a given position. (Also called *velarized*.)

retroflex: In phonetical terminology, a synonym of *cacuminal* (q.v.).

retrogressive: See *regressive*.

Rhaetian: See *Rhaetic*.

Rhaetic: An extinct language, once spoken in the eastern part of present-day Switzerland and the western part of present-day Austria; little known, and variously assumed to have been an Italic dialect, a dialect of Illyrian, an offshoot of Etruscan, etc.

Rhaeto-Romanic: See *Rumansch*.

Rhetian: See *Rumansch*.

rhetoric: The art of discourse.

rhotacism: The use of the phoneme [r] instead of another phoneme, usually [l] or [s].

rhotacize: To practice *rhotacism* (q.v.).

rhyme: In general, the use of an identical sound or syllable at the ends of adjacent words or words placed at definite intervals.

rhyme-word: (1) A word which has undergone a semantic shift because rhymed with other words of related connotations; (2) a word which has undergone a change in form so as to rhyme with a word or words of related meaning.

rhythm: A harmonical succession of sounds, consisting in a regular periodicity in a series of phonemes, constituting or contributing to the measured movement or musical flow of language.

Riksmål: That form of the Norwegian language based on the literary form of Danish, in general use in Norway until recent times. (The Danish spelling of the term is *Riksmaal*.)

rising diphthong: A diphthong in which the non-syllabic element precedes the syllabic one.

Ritwan: A branch of the Algonquian family of North American Indian languages.

rolled: In phonetical terminology, said of a consonant pronounced by a rapid tapping of the front part of the tongue against the teeth, or of the uvula against the back part of the tongue.

Romanal: An artificial language, created by Michaux.

Romance languages: The modern descendants of Latin, viz.: Italian, French, Provençal, Spanish, Portuguese, Catalan, Romanian, Rumansch (also called Rhetian or Raeto-Romanic or Ladin), Sardinian, and the extinct Dalmatian.

Romani: The Indic language spoken by Gypsies, in several dialects.

Romanian: A Romance language, the national tongue of Romania, and the native language of approximately 15,000,000 people. The three main divisions of this language are: *Daco-Romanian* (the language as spoken in Romania proper), *Istro-Romanian* (the variant spoken in parts of Istria), and *Macedo-Romanian* (the variant spoken in Macedonia).—Also written as *Roumanian* or *Rumanian*.

Romanization: (1) The changing of a non-Roman alphabetic script to the Roman alphabet, as in the case of Turkish under Kemal Atatürk, or the attempt to get the Japanese to replace their ideographs and syllabic characters with Roman script; (2) transcription into Roman script, as when Chinese is represented in Roman characters.

Romic: Sweet's system of phonetic transcription. He called the original, more complex form of this system of notation *Narrow Romic*, to distinguish it from the simplified form, the *Broad Romic*.

Rong: See *Lepcha*.

Ronga: A South-East African Negro language, also called *Thonga*, a member of the Bantu family of languages.

root: The ultimate constituent element common to all cognate words, i.e., that element of a word which remains after the removal of all flexional endings, formatives (q.v.), etc. The root is usually present in all members of a group of words relating to the same idea, and is thus capable of being considered as the ultimate semantic vehicle of a given idea or concept in a given language.

root base: The *root* or *radical* (qq.v.) of a word. In flexional languages, the flexional endings are appended to this form.

root inflexion: The modification of the meanings of words by internal vowel changes (cf. *vowel gradation, vowel mutation*) without the use of suffixes or prefixes.

Roumanian: See *Romanian.*

rounded: Said of phonemes pronounced with rounded lips.

rounding: The process of pronouncing a sound with the lips arched or forming a near-circle.

Ruanda: An African Negro language, spoken northeast of Tanganyika, member of the Bantu family of languages.

Rumanian: See *Romanian.*

Rumansch: A series of related Romance languages and dialects (also called Rhetian, Raeto-Romanic and Ladin), spoken by about 50,000 persons in Switzerland and approximately 1,000,-000 in northeastern Italy.

Rundi: An African Negro language, spoken north-east of Tanganyika, member of the Bantu family of languages.

rune: A character of the script of the early Germanic (Teutonic) tribes.

runiform: resembling runes (q.v.).

Russian: An East Slavic language, the native tongue of over 100,000,000 persons. (Also called *Great Russian,* to distinguish it from Little Russian and White Russian.)

Ruthenian: A Ukrainian dialect spoken in the former Czechoslovak province of Carpatho-Russia. (Also called *Carpatho-Russian.*)

Rutul: A language spoken in the Caucasus; a member of the Samurian branch of the Eastern Caucasian group of the North Caucasian family of languages.

S

Sabellian: A branch of the Italic group of the Indo-European family of languages; it includes Aequian, Marrucinian, Marsian, Paelignian, Sabine, Vestinian and Volscian.

Sabine: One of the extinct dialects of the Sabellian branch of the Italic group of the Indo-European family of languages.

Sabir: A mixture of French, Italian, Spanish, Greek and Arabic, containing also Catalan and Provençal elements, used as a "contact vernacular" (q.v.) in Mediterranean ports.

Sakian: See *Khotanese, Old Sakian.*

Samaritan: A Western Aramaic dialect, used in the translations of and commentaries on the Pentateuch in the third and fourth centuries A.D.

Samoan: A language spoken in the Samoan Islands; a member of the Polynesian sub-family of the Malayo-Polynesian family of languages.

Samoyed: A language or dialect group (Yenisei-Samoyed, Ostyak Samoyed and Sayan or Southern Samoyed, also called Kamassin), spoken in Asiatic Russia by about 10,000 persons; a member of the Samoyedic branch of the Finno-Ugric (or Uralic) sub-family of the Ural-Altaic family of languages. The speakers of this language call it *Nenets* and consider the designation *Samoyed* (Russian for "cannibal") deprecatory.

Samoyedic: A branch of the Finno-Ugric (or Uralic) sub-family of the Ural-Altaic family of languages; it consists of Samoyed, called *Nenets* by the speakers themselves (with various local dialects), Yurak, Kamassin and Tagvy, with an estimated total of 20,000 native speakers in Siberia.

Samurian: A branch of the Eastern group of the North Caucasian family of languages. It comprises Aghul, Buduk, Ch'ak'ur, Jek, K'üri, Rut'ul and Tabarasan.

San: An African Negro language, also called *Bushman*, with two dialects, spoken by about 50,000 uncivilized pigmies in South-West Africa; a member of the Hottentot-Bushman family of languages. Characterized phonetically by various types of *clicks* (q.v.).

Sandalwood English: See *Beach-la-mar*.

sandhi: A term of Sanskrit origin (literally meaning *linking*), designating the phonetic changes of a word according to its function or position in a sentence, i.e., the various changes in words as a result of their mutual influence on each other when used in conjunction.

sandhi-form: A form of a word or word-group used in *included positions* (q.v.), i.e., as linked up with other elements in an utterance.

Sanskrit: Old Indic, the conventionalized literary language considered to be the parent of most modern Indic languages. Sanskrit was derived from an unknown old Indic dialect, closely related to the *Vedic* language (the language of the Vedas) and became the literary language and the language of the educated in India about the fourth century B.C.

Sara: An African language, member of the Sudanese-Guinean family of languages.

Sarakolle: An African Negro language, member of the Sudanese-Guinean family of languages.

Sardinian: A collective name for the indigenous Romance dialects spoken in Sardinia. The most important of these dialects are: Campidanese (Campidanesian) and Logudorese (Logudoresian), spoken in the southern and central parts of the island. The northern speech forms of Sardinia (Gallurese and Sassarese) are linked with Corsican and with the Central Italian dialects.

Sart: An Asiatic language; member of the Central Turkic group of the Altaic sub-family of the Ural-Altaic family of languages.

satem languages: Those Indo-European languages in which the Proto-Indo-European guttural [k] sound has changed into the sibilant [s]. (Balto-Slavic, Albanian, Armenian, Indo-Iranian.)

Sauk: A North American Indian language (Central Algonquian), surviving in the Great Lakes region.

Saurashtra: An Indo-European language, also called *Saurashthra, Patanuli* and *Khatri*, spoken by over 100,000 persons chiefly in Madras. The *Linguistic Survey of India* (Vol. IX, Part II, [1908]) calls this language "ordinary Gujarati with . . . a slight addition of local words to its vocabulary." However, some linguists consider Saurashtra a distinct branch of Indo-Iranian.

Sayan Samoyed: The Southern Samoyed dialect.

Scandinavian languages: The customary designation of the North Germanic (q.v.) languages.

schema: A graphic representation of relationships.

Schwytzer Tütsch: See *Schwyztütsch.*

Schwyztütsch: A standardized form of the High German dialects of the German-speaking cantons of Switzerland, advocated by some of its speakers as a national language. (Also called *Schwyzer Tütsch.*)

Scots Gaelic: A language of the Goidelic (Gaelic) branch of the Celtic group of the Indo-European languages, spoken by approximately 100,000 persons in the Scottish Highlands.

Scotticism: A word, expression or grammatical or syntactical construction characteristic of or confined to the English language as spoken in Scotland.

script: See *writing.*

scriptio continua: Latin for *continuous script* or *continuous writing* (q.v.).

scriptio defectiva: Latin for *defective writing* (q.v.).

scriptio plena: Latin for *plene writing* (q.v.).

second German sound shift: See *Germanic sound shifts.*

second person: The person addressed.

secondary accent: A weaker stress than the primary accent (q.v.) falling upon a different syllable of a given word.

secondary compound: A compound word consisting of a simple word and a compound word, or of two compound words.

secondary derivative: (1) a word derived from a word which is itself a derivative—(2) A word derived from another word by the addition of a prefix or a suffix.

secondary language: (1) A term used by linguists and semanticists to designate the written form of language, in contradistinction to the spoken language (called *primary language*).— (2) A *cultural language* (q.v.).

secondary phoneme: Any variation in the utterance of a sound or word, such as a difference in tone, pitch or stress or duration, etc., to express or imply different shades of meaning. A speech-feature which is regarded a secondary phoneme in a given language is often considered a primary phoneme in another language. E.g., variations in pitch are secondary phonemes in English, but primary phonemes in the *tone languages*, such as Chinese. (Cf. *prosodeme*.)

secondary tenses: In the Indo-European languages, the *imperfect* and *preterit* tenses, and in general any other tense than the *primary tenses* (q.v.).

secondary word: Jespersen's term for *adjunct words* (q.v.).

secretion: Jespersen's term for the phenomenon consisting in that a part of an indivisible word acquires a new grammatical signification and so comes to be regarded as a suffix or prefix or compounding element.

segmental phonemes: Phonemes arranged in sequence in the *spoken chain* (q.v.). Also called *linear phonemes*.

semanteme: The ultimate, smallest irreducible element or unit of meaning, such as a *base* or *root* which contains and represents the general meaning of a word or group of derivatives. Bally calls the semanteme "a symbol expressing a purely lexical idea —whether simple or complex, whether a root or inflected form or a compound word."

semantic, semantical: Relating to meaning or sense or to *semantics* (q.v.).

semantic change: A general term for the changes in the meanings of words.

semantic complement: In ideographic writing, a *determinative* (q.v.).

semantic contagion: The transference of a semantic connotation or characteristic of a word or speech-element to another customarily associated with the former.

semantic extension. (1) See *extensional meaning.*—(2) The modification or amplification of the meaning of a word or expression on the basis of analogy with existing and generally used patterns.

semantic indicator: In ideographic writing, a *determinative* (q.v.).

semantic shift: A synonym for *semantic change* (q.v.).

semantics: A science dealing with the relations between *referents* and *referends*—linguistic symbols (words, expressions, phrases) and the objects or concepts to which they refer—and with the history and changes in the meanings of words.

semasiography: A term (literally, *meaning-writing*) used by I. J. Gelb to designate all pictorial, ideographic and logographic systems of writing in general.

semasiology: An alternative name for *semantics* (q.v.).

sematology: The science of meaning—an alternative term for *semantics* (q.v.).

semeiology: See *semiology.*

sememe: Any one particular element of the semantic significance of a given word; the meaning of a *morpheme* (q.v.).

semicolon: The punctuation mark [;].

semiconsonant: See *semivowel.*

semideponent verb: In Latin grammar, a verb which is *deponent* (q.v.) in the compound tenses only.

semiology: The English equivalent of the French term *sémiologie*, introduced by F. de Saussure as the designation of the science and study of signs in general, of which linguistics, as the science and study of linguistic signs, is regarded by him as a mere subdivision.

semiotic: Pertaining to the general theory of signs and their applications.

semiotics: According to Victor Kraft, "semiotics comprises the analysis of language along three dimensions: with regard to the *use* of the language, i.e., from the pragmatic point of view, then with regard to the *meanings* of linguistic signs, from the semantic point of view, and with regard to the relations between signs *without* reference to their meanings, from the syntactic point of view."

semi-plosive: See *affricate*.

Semitic: A language group which with the Hamitic group forms the Semito-Hamitic family of languages. The two branches of Semitic are: East Semitic (its only known member being the extinct Akkadian) and West Semitic (in turn divided into Northern West Semitic and Southern West Semitic—qq.v.). The Semitic languages have a two-gender system and are characterized by three-consonantal (in some languages also two-consonantal) word-roots.

Semito-Hamitic: A family of languages, composed of two groups: Semitic and Hamitic (qq.v.).

semi-syntactic compound: A compound word, in which the relation to each other of the members conforms in general with the syntactical rules of the sentence, except for slight deviations.

semivowel: A sound intermediate between a vowel and a consonant, or partaking of the nature of both. (E.g., the sounds represented in English by the letters *w* and *y*.)

Senga: An African Negro language, member of the Bantu family of languages.

sense: See *meaning*.

sentence: A number of words arranged grammatically and syntactically so as to constitute a grammatically complete sense unit.

sentence phonetics: The study of phonetical changes resulting from the position or function of a word in a sentence.

sentence stress: The stress within a sentence as a whole; often serving to express emphasis on a certain constituent of the sentence, a certain shade of meaning, etc.

sentence-word: A single word expressing a complete thought and used as a complete grammatical unit.

Senufu: An African Negro language, member of the Sudanese-Guinean family of languages.

separable prefix: A prefix which can also be used as a separate word.

separable suffix: A suffix which is a word with a meaning of its own when used separately.

Sephardic: See *Ladino*.

sequence of tenses: In many languages, the use of certain verbal tenses in subordinate clauses, depending on the tense in which the verb of the main clause is used.

sequence utterance: See *situation and sequence utterances*.

Serbian: See *Serbo-Croatian*.

Serbo-Croatian: A South Slavic language, spoken by about 12,000,000 persons in Yugoslavia. *Serbian* is the designation of the language as spoken in Serbia and written with Cyrillic characters, whereas *Croatian* is the language as spoken in Croatia and written with Roman letters.

Serer: An African Negro language, member of the Sudanese-Guinean family of languages.

series: In phonology, the horizontal listing of a row of phonemes on the basis of their relevant feature. E.g., *voiceless series* ([p], [t], [k]), *voiced series* ([b], [d], [g]), etc.

sermo familiaris: Expressions appearing in the writings of some Latin authors, and interpreted by many Latinists as indicating the existence of clear-cut social or local levels in the speech of ancient Rome and the Roman Empire. (Also referred to as *sermo plebeius* and *sermo rusticus*.)

Sesotho: See *Sotho*.

Setälä's law: K. Wessely's term for a law relating to a consonant shift (or gradation) in Finnish.

Shambala: An African Negro language, spoken in Mozambique; a member of the Bantu family of languages.

Shan: See *Siamese*.

Shara: An Asiatic language, a member of the Eastern group of the Mongol branch of the Altaic sub-family of the Ural-Altaic family of languages.

Shawnee: A North American Indian language (Central Algonquian), surviving in Oklahoma.

shibboleth: A linguistic device whereby it is possible to tell the nationality or linguistic affiliation of the speaker (e.g., the inability to pronounce a certain phoneme in a certain manner).

shift-signs: Signs appended to vowel signs of the phonetic alphabet to indicate differences in the articulation of the corresponding vowel sound.

Shilh: See *Shluh.*

Shiluk: An African Negro language, member of the Sudanese-Guinean family of languages.

Shluh: A language of the Berber group of the Hamitic sub-family of the Semito-Hamitic family of languages; a vernacular of southern Morocco. (Also called *Shilh.*)

shortening: (1) With respect to a phoneme, the reduction of the time normally required for uttering it.—(2) With respect to a word, omission of a part in speech or writing.

Shoshonean: A family of North American Indian languages, spoken in the southern United States and northern Mexico. Its surviving members are: Shoshon, Comanche, Pueblo, Ute, etc. According to Rivet, Shoshonean is a sub-family of *Uto-Aztecan,* which includes also *Pima-Sonoran* and *Nahuatlan.*

shwa: A term borrowed from Hebrew phonetics, designating an indistinct vowel (also called *neutral vowel*), usually indicated in phonetic script by an inverted *e*—[ə]. (In Hebrew, distinction is made between the *mobile shwa,* which stands for this [ə] sound, and the *latent shwa,* which indicates the absolute absence of all vowel sound.)

Siamese: The official language of Thailand (Siam), which with its various dialects constitutes the native tongue of about 10,000,000 persons; a member of the Tai sub-family of the Sino-Tibetan family of languages.

sibilant: In phonetical terminology, a fricative consonant produced on the hard palate.

Sicel: An extinct dialect, once spoken in Italy and Sicily, variously claimed to have been an Italic or Ligurian dialect.

Sicilian: The collective term applied to the dialects spoken in

Sicily. Also, the name given to the more or less standardized literary form used by Sicilian dialectal writers.

Siculan: An extinct Indo-European language spoken in pre-Roman times in Sicily.

sigmate: To add or insert the letter or sound *s*.

sigmatic: Characterized by the presence of the letter or sound *s*.

sigmation: The addition or interpolation of the letter or sound *s*.

sign: (1) A visible symbol of an idea; specifically, a written letter, syllable or word symbol.—(2) A word considered as a symbol of the *signified* (q.v.).—According to F. de Saussure, a *sign* is a lexical unit, consisting of a *signifier* and a *signified* (qq.v).

sign language: A system of human communication by gestures.

signals: A synonym for *markers* (q.v.).

significance: Meaning, sense.

significant (*noun*): The complex of sounds by which a speaker gives expression to the *signified* (q.v.).

significian: A student or practitioner of significs (q.v.).

significs: The science of meaning, i.e., the scientific analysis of significance.

signified (*noun*): The concept in the mind of a speaker which he intends to convey to the listener.

signifier: The spoken or written expression which calls up a specific *signified* (q.v.).

similative: A declensional case in certain non-Indo-European languages, denoting resemblance. (Also termed *conformative*.)

simple predicate: A verb or verb-phrase used as predicate of a sentence.

simple tense: Any verbal tense formed without an auxiliary.

simple word: A word the uninflected form of which cannot be divided or analyzed into component units.

Sindhi: An Indic language, spoken in Sindh (western India) by approximately 3,000,000 native speakers.

Singhalese: See *Sinhalese*.

Singh-pho: See *Kachin*.

sing-song theory: The theory that language originated from inarticulate chants of primitive man.

singular: The grammatical category or variant of a word which designates *one* person, object, idea, etc., in contradistinction to the *dual, trial* and *plural* (qq.v.).

singulative: In Slavic languages, a grammatical form which expresses that an individual is singled out of a group.

Sinhala: Modern vernacular Sinhalese, mixed with foreign words.

Sinhalese: An Indic language, also called *Singhalese*, spoken in Ceylon by 4-5,000,000 native speakers. The literary language is called *Elu,* while the modern Sinhalese vernacular is termed *Sinhala.*

Sinitic: A generic term, designating the unified written language and the various dialects spoken in China.

Sino-Japanese: A term applied to Chinese loan-words in the Japanese language, the spoken form of which is different from the form or forms occurring in any of the spoken Chinese vernaculars.

Sino-Siamese: See *Tai-Chinese.*

Sino-Tibetan: A family of languages (also called *Indo-Chinese*) spoken in China, Tibet, Burma, Thailand, Indo-China and Manchukuo by almost 500,000,000 persons. This family is divided into the *Chinese, Tai* and *Tibeto-Burmese* sub-families, although many linguists classify Chinese and Tai into one Tai-Chinese or Sino-Siamese sub-family. Some linguists are of the opinion that *Yenisei-Ostyak* and the extinct *Cottian* or *Kottish* constitute another sub-family of Sino-Tibetan, but these two languages are generally considered to form an isolated family. The Sino-Tibetan languages are *tone languages* (q.v.), analytic in structure, consisting of invariable monosyllabic words and relying on word order to express grammatical relationship and syntactical function, although the Tibeto-Burmese sub-family shows certain agglutinative features.

Sioux: A family of North American Indian languages (also called *Siouan*) spoken in the Minnesota-Nebraska-Dakota region. Its surviving members are: Assiniboin, Biloxi, Crow, Dakota, Iowa, Kansas, Katawba, Mandan, Missouri, Ogalala, Omaha, Osage, Oto, Ponka, Teton, Wahpeton, Winnebago, Yankton.

Sirmauri: A Pahari (q.v.) dialect spoken by about 125,000 persons in Sirmaur (Punjab), also Jubbal and Ambala.

situation and sequence utterances: The situation utterance is one which may begin a conversation, without depending on previous information for intelligibility; generally called a "complete sentence." The sequence utterance is one which must be linked up with something previously mentioned, in which case it may be considered a complete answer, if not a complete sentence. Thus, "By all means" may be considered a "sequence sentence" in response to a "situation sentence" like: "Will you be sure to do it?" (*C. C. Fries*)

slang: A type of language in fairly common use, produced by popular adaptation and extension of the meaning of existing words and by coining new words with disregard for scholastic standards and linguistic principles of the formation of words; generally peculiar to certain classes and social or age groups.

Slavic: A language group, of the Indo-European family of languages, customarily classified with the Baltic group into the Balto-Slavic sub-family. It is divided into three branches: *East Slavic*, *West Slavic* and *North Slavic* (qq.v.).

Slavonic: (1) A synonym for *Slavic* (q.v.)—(2) See *Church Slavonic*.

slender consonant: In Irish phonetics, a consonant immediately following or preceding a *slender vowel* (q.v.) in the same word.

slender vowel: This term is used, especially in Irish phonology, for a *front vowel* (q.v.).

slit-spirant: In phonology, a sound produced with a relatively flat opening between the tongue and roof of the mouth.

Slovak: A West Slavic language, spoken by about 3,000,000 native speakers, mainly in Slovakia.

Slovan: A proposed international language for Slavic speakers, based on a combination, compromise or merger of the principal Slavic languages.

Slovene: A South Slavic language, spoken by 1,500,000 persons in Yugoslavia.

sociative: That declensional case (also called unitive) frequently described as "the case of the accompanying circumstances." In those Indo-European languages which still retain the declensional scheme, this case has been absorbed in the *instrumental*.

soft consonant: A voiced consonant.

soft sign: In Russian, Ukrainian and Bulgarian, the letter Ь which is a mute sign and merely indicates the palatalization of the consonant which immediately precedes it.

solecism: An instance of incorrect use of words or a violation of the rules of grammar or syntax.

solid compound: A compound word consisting of two components written as one word and having a meaning which often is quite different from the meaning of the individual components.

Somali: A member of the Kushitic branch of the Hamitic subfamily of the Semito-Hamitic family of languages, spoken in Somaliland in Africa.

sonant: (1) A voiced consonant.—(2) A syllabic.—(3) A semivowel.

Songoi: An African Negro language, spoken in French West Africa, member of the Sudanese-Guinean family of languages.

sonorization: See *voicing*.

sonorousness: The amount of sound in the pronunciation of a speech-sound.

Sorbian: See *Lusatian*.

Sorbo-Wendic: See *Lusatian*.

Sotho: An African Negro language, also called *Suto* and *Sesotho*, spoken in Bechuanaland; member of the Bantu family of languages.

sound: Generally, the sensation experienced through the organs of hearing.

sound change: Any change in a speech sound or phoneme, whether due to its internal character (*functional* or *spontaneous* or *autonomous sound change*) or to the influence of adjacent or near-by phonetic elements (*conditioned sound change*).

sound shift: Any change in phonemes observed as regularly recurrent in the development of a language.

sound spectrograph: A machine used in experimental or laboratory phonetics, to measure variations in vowel qualities, to ascertain the range of phonetic variation for a given phoneme, and to record sound frequencies in general.

sound types: The types or classes into which the sounds of a language may usually be divided, viz.: *consonants, sonants* or *semivowels,* and *vowels.* These may be further subdivided into *stops, continuants, aspirates, voiced, unvoiced,* etc., as appropriate.

South Arabic: A Southern West Semitic language, known in its ancient form from inscriptions which range from the ninth century B.C. to the sixth century A.D., and spoken as a modern vernacular in several dialects on the southern coast of Arabia (Mahri and Qarawi) and on the island of Sokotra (Soqothri).

South Caucasian: A family of languages (also called *K'art'velian* or *K'art'uli'ena*), spoken by about 2,000,000 persons in the Caucasus region in Asia. It includes Georgian (or Grusinian), Laz, Mingrelian and Svanian (or Svanetian).

South Slavic languages: A branch of the Slavic group of the Indo-European family of languages, comprising Bulgarian, Serbo-Croatian, Slovene, and also Church Slavonic (Old Slavonic or Old Bulgarian) which is extinct as a vernacular but exists as a liturgical language.

Southern American English: The dialectal variant of American English used, generally, south of the Mason-Dixon line and as far west as Texas.

Southern Turkic: A language-group, a subdivision of the Turkic branch of the Altaic (or Turco-Tartaric) sub-family of the Ural-Altaic family of languages. It comprises Osmanli (Turkish), Azerbaidjani, Anatolian, Balkar, Kumik and Turkoman.

Southern West Semitic: A subdivision of the West Semitic branch of the Semitic group of the Semito-Hamitic family of languages, consisting of the North Arabic, South Arabic and Ethiopic languages.

Soyonian: An Asiatic language; a member of the Eastern Turkic group of the Altaic sub-family of the Ural-Altaic family of languages.

Spanish: A Romance language, the native tongue of approximately 110,000,000 persons in Spain, Central and South America, Mexico, Cuba, Puerto Rico, Santo Domingo, etc.

specialization of meaning: A semantic change whereby a word formerly endowed with a broader range of meaning, or a variety of meanings, is restricted to a single meaning-function.

specialized meaning: An unexpected or unusual meaning, as when a form like "cloth" has a regular plural, "cloths," with normal meaning, and an *irregular plural*, "clothes," with the specialized meaning of "garments."

speech: (1) Verbal expression of thoughts.—(2) The faculty of uttering articulate sounds.—(3) Cf. *parole*.

speech-center: A town, community or small geographic area, the local dialect of which becomes the accepted standard for the speech of the surrounding area or areas.

speech-community: A group of people using the same system of speech-signs.

speech-island: A relatively small speech-community (q.v.) surrounded by a much larger area occupied by people speaking another language or other languages.

speech mechanism: The entire apparatus involving all the organs of speech.

speech stretcher: A machine used in experimental and laboratory phonetics; it permits the experimenter to play a record at different speeds, without altering the original pitch of the recorded utterances.

Spelin: An artificial language, a modified form of Volapük (q.v.), created by Bauer in 1888.

spelling: The conventional way of representing, also the conventional representation, in writing, of a spoken word. (The term *spelling* is used with reference to alphabetic writing only.)

spelling pronunciation: Cf. *hyper-urbanism*.

spirant: In phonetical terminology, a synonym of *fricative* (q.v.); a sound produced with some constriction, but with some degree of aperture at the place of articulation. (Cf. *groove-spirant,* *slit-spirant.*)

spoken chain: The chain or flow of speech in a given situation.

spontaneous sound change: A sound change, assumed or likely to have been caused by the character of the sound itself, independently from any influence of its phonetic environment. While it is true that many scholars still believe in the "spontaneous" sound change, important recent developments indicate that both kinds of sound change are "conditioned"; one is the result of pressures in the phonemic system on a *paradigmatic* (q.v.) basis; the other is the result of *syntagmatic* (q.v.) pressures in the flow of speech. (Cf. *André Martinet,* "Function, Structure and Sound Change," WORD, 8 [1953], pp. 1-32). (Cf. *functional change.*)

spoonerism: The interchange of initial sounds or syllables of two or more words, either deliberately or accidentally. (E.g., "I fool so feelish" instead of "I feel so foolish.")

sporadic: Occurring now and then, occasionally, accidentally, or on separate and unconnected occasions.

standard language: That dialect of a language which has gained literary and cultural supremacy over the other dialects and is accepted by the speakers of the other dialects as the most proper form of that language.

starred form: A word or word-form to which an asterisk [*] is prefixed to indicate that it is a hypothetical form or one reconstructed on the basis of known data and linguistic laws.

static consonant: A synonym of *continuant* (q.v.). (Cf. *kinetic consonant.*)

static linguistics: A term, introduced by F. de Saussure (*linguistique statique*); synonymous with *synchronic linguistics* (q.v.).

statics: Jespersen's term for descriptive grammar which considers grammatical phenomena as isolated and grammatical rules as arbitrary regulations.

statistics: (1) Any systematic collection and tabulation of meaningful, related facts and data. (2) the systematic study and interpretation of such collection and tabulation of facts and data.

stem: The root (q.v.) of a word plus a *thematic morpheme* (q.v.).

stem base: A rarely used synonym for *stem*.

stem-compound: A compound word (q.v.) in which one of the components appears in the stem form.

steno-sonograph: A machine, perfected by Dreyfus-Graff, reported to translate spoken sounds into a graphic record, using distinct characters.

stereotyped: Inflexible; rigidly adhering to a fixed pattern.

stød: The Danish term for *glottal stop* (q.v.), often used by phoneticians for other languages, too.

stop: See *plosive*.

stress: Special emphasis on a sound or sound-group. Defined in laboratory phonetics as the result of a greater amplitude of sound-waves. (Cf. *fixed stress* and *free stress*.)

stress accent: The variation of loudness within a word or within a single utterance.

stress group: In a sentence or in a longer utterance, a group of syllables, one of which bears a stronger stress than the others.

stress-unit: In prosody, a recently introduced synonym for *foot*.

strong: (1) This adjective is applied, in the grammars of many languages (notably the Germanic languages), to verbs or nouns which undergo an internal vowel change in their conjugation or declension.—(2) In phonemics, this term is applied also to those *oppositions* (q.v.) in which it is difficult to determine which of two possible relevant features really is operative. Thus in English, the mid vowels in *met* and *mate* ([ɛ] and [e]) are different because: the first is *lax* and *lower*, the second is *tense* and *higher*; since it is probably impossible to tell whether the *tension* or the *height* is the functional element, the first vowel is considered a *weak phoneme*, the second a *strong phoneme*. (Cf. *phonetic law*.)

strong conjugation: In Germanic languages, the conjugation of the *strong verbs* (q.v.).

strong declension: In Germanic languages, (1) the declension of *strong nouns* (q.v.), (2) the inflection of an adjective when it is not preceded by a definite article or by a pronoun of the same function or force.

strong noun: In Germanic languages, a noun which is capable of an internal vowel change (*umlaut*) in its declension.

strong phoneme: Cf. *strong (2)*.

strong verb: In Germanic languages, a verb which undergoes an internal vowel change in its conjugation.

structural linguistics: Linguistic study in which each language is viewed as a coherent, homogeneous entity.

stylistic: The study and art of the selection among linguistic forms.

Subaraean: The collective name of *Mitannian* and *Hurrian,* two extinct languages spoken in ancient Northern Mesopotamia (in those days called Subartu). These two languages were extremely similar to each other, and probably were dialects of a common language.

Subiya: An African Negro language, member of the Bantu family of languages.

subject: The agent performing the action expressed by the verb in an active sentence or by a reflexive verb, or on whom or which the action of a passive sentence is performed.

subject word: A term occasionally applied to any word grammatically capable of being used as the subject of a sentence.

subjective: Relating to the subject as the agent of the action expressed in an utterance.

subjective conjugation: In the Finno-Ugric languages, that form of conjugation (q.v.) which indicates an indefinite object or no object at all. (Also called *indefinite conjugation.*)

subjunct: Jespersen's term for modifiers of adjuncts (or secondary words).

subjunctive mood: The verbal mood indicating that the action or state denoted by the verb is regarded as hypothetical or subject to another action or state.

sublative: In certain languages (notably, languages of the Finno-Ugric family), a declensional case having the same denotation as in English the use of the construction *from below* before a substantive.

subordinate clause: A clause which does not constitute a complete sentence in itself, but must be connected with or attached to an independent clause.

subordinating conjunction: A conjunction (q.v.) connecting two words or word-groups or clauses and indicating that one of these connected elements is dependent on the other.

subordinating language: A language in which the determinative particles or elements, expressing grammatical or semantic relationships, are grouped about the elements expressing the principal idea, as though subordinated to the latter.

substantival adjunct: A noun used as an adjective, without a suffix or other change.

substantive: Any noun, as well as any other word or group of words used as a noun or instead of a noun, in contradistinction to *adjectives*.

substantive verb: A designation occasionally applied to the verb *to be* and its equivalents.

substantivized: Used as a noun or noun-equivalent.

substratum: A language displaced, as dominant tongue, by another language, e.g., by the language of a conquering military power, of a colonizing nation, etc. Many linguists consider the linguistic substratum responsible for linguistic changes in the language which suppresses or replaces it. (Cf. *substratum theory*.)

substratum theory: The theory which regards the linguistic substratum (q.v.) as the cause of linguistic or phonological changes in the replacing or superimposed language. According to the adherents of this theory, as the speakers of socially, politically, economically or otherwise subordinate languages adopted the language of their conquerors or a language of colonization, or in general the language of a culturally or economically more advanced nation, difficulties in pronunciation caused words, even grammatical forms and constructions, to be affected by under-surface speech habits.

Sudanese: See *Sudanese-Guinean*.

Sudanese-Guinean: A family of African Negro languages, spoken by an estimated total of 50,000,000 persons. The many languages and dialects of this family have been variously classified —e.g., Drexel lists 171 distinct Sudanese-Guinean languages (in *Die Gliederung der afrikanischen Sprachen*, 1921-1925), whereas Delafosse (in *Les Langues du Monde*, 1924), distinguishes 435. The most important Sudanese-Guinean languages are: Ewe, Efik, Hausa, Mandingo, Mende, Masai, Nubian, Twi, and Yoruba. (Some linguists consider Sudanese and Guinean as two independent families; others, notably Delafosse, consider Sudano-Guinean and Bantu to be members of a larger linguistic unit.)

suffix: A *formative* (q.v.), consisting of a letter, syllable or syllables, added to the end of a word to modify its meaning or to form a new derivative.

Suk: An African language, member of the Sudanese-Guinean family of languages.

Suketi: The language of about 55,000 persons in Suket, India; a dialect of Pahari (q.v.).

Sumerian: An extinct language, classified as *Asianic*, without any demonstrable linguistic affiliation with any known language; it was spoken in Mesopotamia, from Babylon to the Gulf of Persia, from at least 4000 B.C. till the third century B.C.

Sundanese: A language spoken by about 6,500,000 persons in Indonesia; a member of the Indonesian sub-family of the Malayo-Polynesian family of languages.

superessive: In certain languages (notably, languages of the Finno-Ugric family), a declensional case, having the same denotation as the English preposition *on* or *upon*.

superior comparison: Upward comparison (q.v.).

superlative degree: That form of an adjective or adverb which expresses that a certain thing possesses a certain quality to a greater extent than any other thing.

superstratum: The language of a culturally, economically, politically superior nation, or of a military conqueror, introduced into a foreign national or geographical territory and affecting or even supplanting the native language of the latter (See *substratum*).

supine: A verbal noun, usually incapable of complete inflection.

suppletive form: A form used to replace a missing form in a defective (q.v.) conjugation or declension, and derived from another basic word than the existing forms in the scheme.

suppositive conjunction: A synonym for *hypothetical conjunction* (q.v.)

supra-segmental phoneme: See *prosodeme* and *secondary phoneme*.

Surinam Negro-English: See *Negro-English*.

survival: An archaic word or construction which has remained in current use at a later stage of the linguistic development of the language.

Susian: See *Elamite*.

suspension-pitch: See *pause-pitch*.

Suto: See *Sotho*.

Svanetian: See *Svanian*.

Svanian: A language (also called *Svanetian*), spoken in the Caucasus; a member of the South Caucasian family of languages.

svarabhakti sound: A term, based on an ancient Sanskrit phonological expression, meaning an *anaptyctic vowel* or *glide* (qq.v.).

Swahili: An African Negro language (also called *Kiswaheli*), the *lingua franca* of East Africa, spoken by an estimated 8,000,000 persons; a member of the Bantu family of languages.

Swedish: A Scandinavian (North Germanic) language, spoken by about 6,500,000 native speakers.

syllabary: A collection of the written syllable signs of a language, arranged in a conventional order.

syllabation: See *syllabication*.

syllabic: The sound which has the maximum degree of sonority in a given syllable.

syllabic peak: With reference to a syllable (q.v.), the vowel or continuant within it.

syllabic sign: See *syllable sign*.

syllabic stress: The stress within a syllable.

syllabic writing: See *syllable writing*.

syllabication: The division of words or a word into syllables.

syllabification: See *syllabication*.

syllable: A group of phonemes, consisting of a vowel or a continuant, alone or in combination with a consonant or consonants, which represents a complete articulation or complex of articulations constituting a unit of word-formation. A syllable ending in a vowel is called *open*, one ending in a consonant is called *closed*.

syllable sign: A written sign representing an entire syllable or a single vowel capable of forming a syllable in itself.

syllable writing: A method of writing by using written characters representing spoken syllables or individual vowels which can constitute independent syllables.

syllabogram: A *syllable sign* (q.v.).

syllepsis: In general, irregular or unusual grammatical agreement; specifically, improper or awkward use of a word in two senses or for two purposes, in a literal as well as in a metaphorical sense, in the sentence.

symbol: In semantics, a word or expression.

synchronic: For the meaning of this adjective, cf. *synchronic grammar*, *synchronic linguistics* and *synchronic phonemics*.

synchronic grammar: Grammar limited to recording and studying a given stage of a language.

synchronic linguistics: Linguistic study limited to the recording and analysis of a given linguistic state or stage.

synchronic phonemics, synchronic phonetics: Phonetics confined to the recording and classification of phonemes and their combinations, in general or in a given language, at a given date or at a given stage of linguistic development.

synchysis: A disorderly placing of words in a sentence, to indicate or create confusion of thought.

syncopation: See *syncope*.

syncope: The loss of a medial sound, letter or syllable, resulting in a contraction of the word.

syncretic case: A declensional case which has absorbed the function of another, now obsolete, declensional case and is used both in its original proper sense and in constructions where formerly that other case was required.

syncretic form: A grammatical form which has absorbed the meaning and function of another, now obsolete, form and is used not only in its proper, original function but also in constructions where formerly that other form was required. (E.g., *syncretic case*—q.v.; analogously: *syncretic tense, synchretic aspect,* etc.)

syncretism: The use of one grammatical form to fulfill the functions of another form or other forms as well. (Cf. *syncretic case.*)

syndesis: Coordination of elements and their linking by a connecting particle or connecting particles.

syndetic: Linked by a connecting particle.

syndetic word: A connecting or conjunctive word or particle.

syndeton: A phrase or construction in which the elements are linked together by connecting particles.

synecdoche: Using a word designating or denoting a part or a quality of a thing as the name of the entire thing.

synenclitic: The second of two adjacent *enclitic* (q.v.) words.

syneresis: In phonetics, the fusion of two vowel sounds into one. (Occasionally, this term is used to denote also any contraction of a word or words by omitting a vowel sound.)

synesis: A syntactical construction in which grammatical concord follows the sense of a word rather than its grammatical form. (E.g., the use of a plural verb with a collective noun, even though the latter is singular in form.)

synizesis: A synonym for *syneresis* (q.v.).

synonymous: Having the same meaning.

synonyms: Two or more words of the same language having the same meaning.

synonymy: Identity of meaning.

syntactic, syntactical: Relating to *syntax* (q.v.); pertaining to construction in accordance with grammatical rules.

syntactic category: A classification of a word according to its grammatical function and relationship to other words in the sentence.

syntactic compound: A compound word, the members of which show the same grammatical relationship to each other as individual words in a phrase.

syntactic construction: The grouping and combining of words in a sentence, and their resulting relationship to each other.

syntactic molecule: Bally's term (*molécule syntaxique*) for any combination of a semanteme (q.v.) and one or more grammatical signs, form-words, link words, etc., required for its being able to function in a phrase.

syntactic order: In certain languages, especially in those lacking a full-fledged inflectional system, the word-order in a sentence as a means of indicating the grammatical or syntactical relationships and functions of the words.

syntactic regimen: See *government*.

syntagmatic: Relating to or constituting a *syntagme* (q.v.). The most important use of this term in linguistics is in connection with characterizing the ordered arrangement of *phonemes*, *morphemes* (qq.v.), etc., in the flow of speech. (Cf. *paradigmatic*.)

syntagme: The term used by F. de Saussure to designate the fusion of two or more linguistic signs or elements in a word, phrase, idiomatic expression, etc.

syntax: The study and rules of the relation of words to one another as expressions of ideas and as parts of the structures of sentences; the study and science of sentence construction.

syntax-language: The language by means of which the syntactic structure of another language (the *object-language*) is described; the syntax-language need not be a separate language, or a meta-language (q.v.), but may be a part of the object-language.

synthesis: The act or process of combining two or more elements to form a new unit or complex. Specifically, the process or act of combining several concepts in a single word by the use of suffixes.

synthetic, synthetical: Pertaining to or constituting a *synthesis* (q.v.).

synthetic compound: A compound word in which one member is used in an inflectional form which it could not assume when used alone.

synthetic language: A language in which grammatical relationships of words are expressed principally by means of inflections.

Syriac: An Eastern Aramaic language, spoken by about 100,000 persons in Iraq, Turkey and Iran.

Syryen: See *Zyrien*.

T

Tabarasan: A language spoken in the Caucasus; a member of the Samurian branch of the Eastern Caucasian group of the North Caucasian family of languages.

taboo: The avoidance of the use of certain words, and their replacement by euphemistic expressions, for superstitious, moral, social, etc., reasons.

tabu: See *taboo*.

tachygraphy: The use of shorthand or other conventional signs, for speedy writing.

tactic form: A grammatical arrangement consisting of *taxemes* (q.v.).

Tagalog: A language spoken in the Philippine Islands by about 1,800,000 native speakers; a member of the Indonesian sub-family of the Malayo-Polynesian family of languages. Tagalog was recently decreed to be the "national language" of the Philippine Islands.

tagmeme: The smallest meaningful unit of grammatical form. (*Bloomfield*)

Tagvy: A language, spoken by a few thousand people in Siberia; a member of the Samoyedic branch of the Finno-Ugric (or Uralic) sub-family of the Ural-Altaic languages.

Tahitian: The language of the Tahiti Islands; a member of the Polynesian sub-family of the Malayo-Polynesian family of languages.

Tai (Thai). (1) A sub-family of the Sino-Tibetan family of languages, comprising Siamese and the Shan (or Siamese) dialects (Khamti, Lao, Lü, Khün, the extinct Ahom, etc.), (Cf. *Tai-Chinese*.)—(2) An alternative term for *Siamese*.

Tai-Chinese: A hypothetical sub-family (also called *Sino-Siamese*) of the Sino-Tibetan family of languages, claimed by certain linguists to comprise the Chinese and Tai sub-families.

taki-taki: An alternative name for *Ningre-Tongo* (q.v.).

Talaing: See *Mon.*

Tamashek: A member of the Hamitic group of the Semito-Hamitic family of languages, spoken by Bedouins in the Sahara.

Tamil: A language, also called *Kalingi,* spoken by about 26,500,000 persons in southern India and northern Ceylon; a member of the Tamil-Kurukh branch of the Dravidian family of languages.

Tamil-Kurukh: A branch of the Dravidian family of languages, spoken in southern India and northern Ceylon; it comprises Tamil (or Kalingi), Malayalam, Kanarese, Kurukh, and Tulu.

Tangut: An Asiatic language, a member of the Eastern group of the Mongol branch of the Altaic sub-family of the Ural-Altaic family of languages.

tap: In phonology, the single articulatory movement, several of which make up a *trill* (q.v.). (E.g., the Spanish *pero* is pronounced with a *tap r,* but *perro* with a *trill r.*)

Taranchi: An Asiatic language; member of the Central Turkic group of the Altaic sub-family of the Ural-Altaic family of languages.

Tasmanian: A group of five extinct languages, once spoken in Tasmania; very little is known about these languages, but they are assumed to have constituted an independent, isolated language-family.

tautological compound: A compound which is formed by the mere juxtaposition of two or more synonyms.

tautology: A redundant construction consisting of two or more words, each of which expresses the same idea.

tautophony: The contiguous use of rhyming or similar-sounding words.

tautosyllabic: Belonging, in a given word, to the same syllable.

taxeme: An individual grammatical feature. Bloomfield calls it "the smallest unit of form in grammar."

Tebele: An African Negro language, considered a dialect or close cognate of Zulu.

technical term: (1) A word or expression restricted to a given field or branch of study or endeavor; (2) a word or expression employed in a given field or branch of study or endeavor with a restricted denotation, although having a wider connotation in general usage.

telescope word: A word formed by combining parts of two or more words. (Also called *telescoped word.*)

telescoped expression: A combination of parts of two or more expressions.

Telugu: A Dravidian language, spoken in eastern and southeastern India by about 33,000,000 persons.

temporal: Relating to time or to tenses.

temporal clause: An adverbial clause, introduced by an adverb of time and indicating the time when a certain action or event is, was or will be taking place.

temporal conjunction: A conjunction (q.v.) introducing a clause expressing a temporal relationship. (E.g., *until.*)

tense (*noun*): The grammatical modification expressing, by inflexional or other changes, the time (relative to the time of the utterance) of an action or of the existence of a state or condition. In Indo-European languages, the category of tense is restricted to verbs, but, e.g., in Japanese also adjectives show tense inflexion; in the Sudanese language Mende, personal pronouns are inflected to show tense differences.

tense (*adj.*): In phonetics, said of a sound pronounced with great muscular tension in those parts of the speech organs involved in its articulation.

tense-phrase: A *periphrastic tense* (q.v.).

tense sequence: See *sequence of tenses.*

tenuis: A *devoiced plosive* (q.v.).

term: In general, a synonym for *word;* specifically, a word or word-group constituting a syntactical unit.

terminal stress: Stress on the last syllable.

termination: (1) The final letter or syllable of a word; (2) usually a declensional, conjugational, etc., suffix.

terminative: In certain languages, a declensional case used to designate the goal or purpose toward which an action tends.

terminative aspect: A verbal aspect in which the action denoted by the verb is considered with respect or in relation to its goal or purpose.

terminology: The special terms or vocabulary customarily used by those engaged in a specific activity or field of endeavor.

ternary: Consisting of or involving three elements, aspects, etc.

tetraphthong: A combination of four vowel sounds.

Teutonic: An alternative designation of the Germanic (q.v.) group of the Indo-European family of languages. (For all terms beginning with "Teutonic," see the corresponding terms beginning with "Germanic.")

Teutonicism: An idiomatic expression or construction characteristic of or peculiar to the speakers of Germanic ("Teutonic") languages. (Often used as a synonym for *Germanism*——q.v.)

Thai: See also *Tai*.

Thai Lao: A Lao (q.v.) dialect, spoken in Eastern Thailand and French Laos. (Also called *Eastern Laotian*.)

Thai Lu: A Lao (q.v.) dialect, spoken in western Indo-China, eastern Burma and southern Yün-nan by an estimated 500,000 persons.

Thai Ya: A Lao (q.v.) dialect spoken in southwestern China.

Thai Yüan: A Lao (q.v.) dialect, also called *Western Laotian*, spoken in northern Thailand.

thematic: Relating to, attached to or constituting a *stem* (q.v.).

thematic flexion: Inflection (q.v.) in which a *thematic morpheme* (q.v.) appears between the *root* (q.v.) and the *inflectional affixes* (q.v.).

thematic morpheme: A morpheme (q.v.), usually a single vowel (*thematic vowel*) attached to the root of a word to form the inflectional *stem*.

theme: See *stem*.

third person: The person or thing spoken of.

Thonga: See *Ronga*.

thought mood: A rarely used synonym for *subjunctive mood* (q.v.).

thought stress: Deliberate emphasis on certain words in the spoken language.

Thracian: An extinct Indo-European language, once spoken in the western part of the Balkans.

Thraco-Phrygian: A group of Indo-European languages, composed of Thracian, Old and New Phrygian. Some linguists include also *Bithynian* (q.v.) in this group.

Tibetan: (1) A group (also called *Bhotian*) within the Tibeto-Himalayan branch of the Tibeto-Burmese sub-family of the Sino-Tibetan family of languages; it includes Balti, the standard literary language of Tibet, and several dialects.—(2) The dialect spoken in Central Tibet, in the provinces Ü and Tzang, and employed as a *lingua franca* all over Tibet.

Tibeto-Burmese (Tibetan-Burman). A sub-family of the Sino-Tibetan family of languages, divided into four branches; (1) *Tibeto-Himalayan*, (2) *Arakan-Burmese*, and (3) *Lo-Lo-Bodo-Naga-Kachin*, often, but misleadingly called also *Assamese* (qq.v.). The extinct *Pyu* (q.v.) language is also classified tentatively in this sub-family.

Tibeto-Chinese: See *Sino-Tibetan*.

Tibeto-Himalayan: A branch of the Tibeto-Burmese sub-family of the Sino-Tibetan family of languages, consisting of Tibetan, or Bhotian (the standard literary language Balti, and various dialects), and Himalayan (Lepcha, or Rong, Gurung, Toto, etc.).

Tigray: An alternative name for *Tigriña* (q.v.).

Tigre: A language belonging to the Ethiopic sub-group of the Southern West Semitic languages, spoken on the East Coast of Africa.

Tigriña: The modern descendant of the Southern West Semitic language Ge'ez (q.v.); used as a literary and official language in Eritrea. (Also called *Tigray*.)

til: See *tilde*.

tilde: the diacritic mark [~] placed over certain letters to indicate the proper sound in pronunciation. Its significance varies in the various languages which employ it. (*Tilde* is the Spanish name of this diacritic mark. Its Portuguese name is *til*.)

Tirhutia: See *Maithili*.

Tlingit: See *Na-Dene*.

tmesis: The interpolation of a word between the parts of a compound word or expression.

Toaripi: A Papuan language spoken in New Guinea.

Tokharian: An extinct member of the Indo-European family of languages, assumed to have been spoken in Chinese Turkestan; divided into two dialects, called *Tokharian A* (also called *Agnean, Karasharian, Turfarian*, and called *East Tokharian* by W. Krause) and *Tokharian B* (also called *Kuchaean*, and called *West Tokharian* by W. Krause).

tone language: A language characterized by variations in pitch or tone which distinguish the meanings of words of the same or very similar written form or of the same vowel sound or sounds.

toneme: A stress or tonal element which distinguishes two otherwise identical words or forms.

Tongatabu: A language spoken in the Tonga Islands; a member of the Polynesian sub-family of the Malayo-Polynesian family of languages.

tongue: A synonym for *language*, seldom used in linguistics. (Occasionally used as the English equivalent of the French term *langue*—q.v.)

tonic accent: Musical speech and its modulation in speaking.

toponomasiology, toponomastics, toponomatology: The study and analysis of place-names within a geographical area or within a given language.

Tosk: One of the two predominant dialects of Albanian, spoken in southern Albania, with speech islands in Greece, Italy and Sicily.

Toto: A Himalayan dialect (Tibeto-Himalayan branch of the

Tibeto-Burmese sub-family of the Sino-Tibetan family of languages).

trade language: (1) A language used as a medium of communication among speakers of various languages. (Cf. *cultural language*)—(2) See *contact vernacular, Pidgin English*.

tradition: The conventions, forms and habits of expression handed down from the past.

traditionalism: Adherence to and insistence on forms and patterns handed down from the past.

transcription: Short for *phonetic transcription* (q.v.).

transferred meaning: The metaphorical use of a word (e.g., when a man is described as a "fox" or a "wolf," or a woman as an "angel" or a "peach," etc.).

transition: Change from one stage or state to another.

transitional: Connecting; intermediate; constituting, representing or relating to a *transition* (q.v.).

transitional writing, transitional script: A system of writing using *pictographs* as well as *ideographs* (qq.v.) and phonetic symbols.

transitive verb: A verb expressing an action which does not end with or is not confined to the agent; transitive verbs are capable of governing a direct object.

translate: To render a word or text written in one language into another language, retaining the full and correct meaning of the word or text in the other language.

translation: The rendition of anything said or written in one language into another language.

translation loan-word: Jespersen's term for words modelled, more or less closely, after foreign words, but consisting of the speech material of the language in which they are created.

translative: See *factive*.

translator: A person skilled in rendering the true and correct meaning of a written text in another language.

transliteration: The representation of a sound, phoneme or word or utterance in the conventional symbols of another language or system of writing.

transmutation: A term occasionally used by grammarians for the use of a word, without any change in form, in syntactic functions assigned to different parts of speech. (E.g., in English, Chinese, etc., a great many words can be used as verbs, adjectives, nouns, etc.)—Also called *functional change*.

transposition: The act, process or result of exchanging the relative positions of two elements, substituting one for the other.

tree-stem theory: See *pedigree theory*.

trema: The diacritic mark [¨] more commonly called *diaeresis* (q.v.).

trial: The grammatical number designating *three*, used by certain languages (e.g., Melanesian vernaculars) as distinct from the *singular, dual* and *plural* (q.v.).

trigraph: A combination of three vowel letters which represents one single vowel sound. (Cf. *consonantal trigraph*.)

triliteral root: The predominant type of word roots in the Semitic languages, consisting of three consonants.

trill: In phonetical terminology, a vibration of the tongue, lips or uvula, produced by the expulsion of the breath. (Cf. *tap*.)

triphthong: A combination of three vowel sounds, functioning as a single unit. Often called *proper triphthong*, in contradistinction to the term *improper triphthong* which is a synonym for *trigraph* (q.v.).

triplets: Three words of the same language, any of which represents a doublet (q.v.) with either of the other two.

triptote: In certain languages, this term is applied to designate substantives which have defective declensions, consisting of only three cases.

trisyllabic: Consisting of three syllables.

trisyllable: A word consisting of three syllables.

Trknmli: See *Lycian*.

Trmmli. See *Lycian*.

trope: In general, a *figure of speech* (q.v.).

Tsaconian: A modern Greek dialect, spoken along the Gulf of Nauplia; it is a direct descendant of ancient Laconian.

Tshi: See *Twi*.

T'swan: See *Lo-lo*.

Tuareg: A member of the Berber group of the Hamitic subfamily of the Semito-Hamitic family of languages; the vernacular of Bedouins in the Sahara.

Tubu: An African Negro language, member of the Sudanese-Guinean family of languages.

Tulu: A language spoken on the west coast of India; a member of the Tamil-Kurukh branch of the Dravidian family of languages.

Tumeli: An African language, member of the Sudanese-Guinean family of languages.

Tungus: (1) A language, divided into a great many dialects (the most important ones being Chapogir, Kile, Lamut, Mangum, Orochon and Orop), spoken by about 70,000 persons in the Yenisei River region of Siberia. Together with Manchu, it forms the Manchu-Tungus branch of the Altaic sub-family of the Ural-Altaic family of languages.—(2) Used by some authors as the designation of the entire Manchu-Tungus branch of the Ural-Altaic family.

Tupi: A South American Indian language, member of the Tupi-Guaraní family; spoken as a *lingua franca* by Indians in Brazil, especially in the Amazon Basin and the coastal region.

Tupi-Guaraní: A family of 68 South American Indian languages, of which 14 are extinct; the surviving 54 languages of this family are spoken in Paraguay and Brazil, and also in parts of Argentina. The two most important members of this family are *Tupi* (spoken as a *lingua franca* by Indians in Brazil, especially in the Amazon Basin and the coastal region), and *Guaraní*, the vernacular used in Paraguay.

Turanian: An alternative name of the *Ural-Altaic* family of languages. (Some linguists have used the term *Turanian* as the name of a hypothetical linguistic family including Ural-Altaic, Japanese and Korean. The existence of this "super-family" has, however, been generally denied.)

Turfanian: See *Tokharian*.

Turkic: A branch of the Altaic sub-family of the Ural-Altaic family of languages. It consists of four groups: Eastern (or Altaic proper), Western, Central and Southern (qq.v.). According to some linguists, Yakut is also a Turkic language, while others consider it a member of the Mongol branch of the Altaic sub-family. The speakers of the various Turkic languages and dialects number altogether about 40,000,000.

Turkish: (1) The national language of Turkey, spoken by about 18,000,000 people; a member of the Southern Turkic group of the Altaic sub-family of the Ural-Altaic family of languages. Also called *Osmanli* or *Ottoman*.—(2) An alternative but not recommended designation of the Altaic family of languages.— (3) Often, incorrectly, used instead of the term *Turkic* (q.v.).

Turkoman: A Near-Eastern language; it belongs to the Southern Turkic group of the Altaic sub-family of the Ural-Altaic family of languages.

turn: A term used by Jespersen instead of *voice* (e.g., *active turn* instead of *active voice*).

Tuscan: The collective name given to the Central Italian dialects of Tuscany (Florentine, Pisan, Senese, etc.). Tuscan, particularly in its Florentine variety, forms the backbone of the literary Italian language.

Tuscarora: A North American Indian language, member of the Iroquoian family.

T'ush: A Chechen dialect (Eastern Caucasian group of the North Caucasian family of languages). (Also called *Bats*.)

twang: See *nasal twang*.

Twi: An African Negro language spoken by about 100,000 persons in the Gold Coast Colony and a part of the French Ivory Coast Colony; a member of the Sudanese-Guinean family of languages. (This language is variously called also *Amina, Asante, Ashanti, Chwee, Odshi, Oji, Tshi, Tyi*.)

Tyi: See *Twi*.

U

Ubangi: A group of African Negro languages (including Banda, Mittu, Zande, etc.); a member of the Sudanese-Guinean family of languages.

Ubyk: A language spoken in the Caucasus; a member of the Western branch of the North Caucasian family of languages.

Udi: A language spoken in the Caucasus; a member of the Eastern group of the North Caucasian family of languages.

Uea: A language spoken in the Loyalty Islands; a member of the Polynesian sub-family of the Malayo-Polynesian family of languages.

Ugaritic: An extinct language, known only from clay tablets (dating from at least the fourteenth century B.C.) bearing inscriptions in a cuneiform alphabet of 32 letters, discovered at Ras Shamrah, on the Syrian coast, in 1929. The exact linguistic position and classification of this language has not been decided as yet, although many linguists consider it a Canaanite (q.v.) dialect. (The name *Ugaritic* is derived from *Ugarit*, the ancient name of Ras Shamrah.)

Ugric: A branch of the Finno-Ugric (or Uralic) sub-family of the Ural-Altaic family of languages, consisting of Hungarian and the Ob-Ugrian group (Ostyak and Vogul).

Uighur: An Asiatic language; member of the Eastern Turkic group of the Altaic sub-family of the Ural-Altaic family of languages.

Ukrainian: An East Slavic language, also called *Little Russian*, the native tongue of about 40,000,000 persons. The Western dialect of the language is called *Ruthenian* or *Carpatho-Russian*.

ultimate constituent: Cf. *constituents*.

Umbrian: An extinct Italic dialect.

Umbundu: An African Negro language, also called *Nano*, a member of the Bantu family of languages.

Umgangssprache: A German term meaning (1) vernacular, (2) colloquial language, (3) the language customarily and principally used by an individual as daily means of communication.

umlaut: (1) An internal vowel change, usually caused by a vowel in the following syllable, sometimes also by a semi-vowel or even a consonant.—(2) The diacritic mark ['] placed over a vowel to indicate such change.

underlying form: The free morpheme in a complex form; e.g., *man* in *manliness*.

unfinite verb forms: A term introduced by Sweet for verbal nouns and verbal adjectives.

unipersonal verb: A term preferable to the designation *impersonal verb* in referring to verbs used in one person only. (*Monopersonal verb* is an equally good synonym.)

unitive: See *sociative*.

universal: General or generalizing.

universal grammar: The study of languages in general, and the general principles basic to the grammatical phenomena of all languages, without confining itself to any particular language.

Universal-Sprache: An artificial language, created as an interlanguage by Pirro in 1863.

unmarked member: Cf. *marked member*.

unproductive suffix: A term introduced by Jespersen for suffixes which are no longer used to form new derivatives.

unreal condition: The statement of a hypothetical situation, which is contrary to actual facts (e.g., "if he knew the answer. . . .").

unrounding: The process of changing a sound pronounced with rounded lips into one pronounced without rounding the lips.

unstable: Prone to changes or variations; said in particular with reference to phonemes.

unvoicing: The change of a voiced (q.v.) consonant to the unvoiced (q.v.) pronunciation.

upper-case letter: In the terminology of printers, editors, etc., a capital letter, in contradistinction to small letters (called *lower-case* letters).

Upper German: See *High German (1)*.

upward comparison: Comparison of adjectives or adverbs to denote an increase in the degree of the characteristic or quality expressed.

Ural-Altaic: A family of languages, consisting of the Finno-Ugric (or Uralic) and Altaic (or Turco-Tartar or Turkish) subfamilies. (The unity of these two groups is generally recognized by Hungarian and Finnish linguists, but is disputed by many others.)

Uralic: An alternative name of the Finno-Ugric (q.v.) sub-family of the Ural-Altaic family of languages.

Urartaean: See *Vannic*.

urbanism: A word, grammatical form or construction characteristic of or restricted in use to the inhabitants of a city or cities in general, in contradistinction to the speech of the rural population.

Urdu: An Indic language, the official tongue of Pakistan, usually classified as a variant of Hindustani; the number of its native speakers is estimated at 70,000,000.

Uto-Aztecan: A family of North American Indian languages, consisting, according to Rivet, of the *Shoshonean, Pima-Sonoran* and *Nahuatlan* sub-families, spoken in the southern and southeastern United States and in Mexico.

utterance: In general, any self-sufficient unit of spoken language. (Defined by Z. S. Harris as "any stretch of speech by a person, preceded and followed by silence by that person.")

Uvea: See *Uea*.

uvular: In phonetical terminology, a consonant sound produced by raising the back part of the tongue near the soft palate (uvula). (E.g., [q].)

Uzbeg: An Asiatic language; member of the Central Turkic group of the Altaic sub-family of the Ural-Altaic family of languages. (Also called *Uzbek*.)

V

Vai: An African Negro language, member of the Sudanese-Guinean family of languages.

Valdensian: See *Vaudois*.

Vandal, Vandalic: An extinct East-Germanic language.

Vannic: An extinct language (also called *Khaldic* or *Urartaean*) of uncertain linguistic affinities, spoken in the Ararat region of the Near East between 900 and 600 B.C. Classified as *Asianic*.

variant: (1) A related but not identical form. (The difference may be phonetical, morphological, a matter of meaning or of written appearance.)—(2) An alternative form. —(3) Often used instead of the term *allophone* (q.v.).

Vaudois: A Romance dialect (also called *Valdensian*), spoken in northwestern Italy and southeastern France. (A colony of Vaudois speakers was founded in Valdese, N.C., in 1892.)

Vedic: The Old Indic language of the Brahmin scriptures, the Vedas. Regarded by some as an early form, by others as a collateral relation, of Sanskrit.

Veglian: One of the two Dalmatian dialects, extinct since 1898.

velar: In phonetical terminology, a consonant pronounced with the back part of the tongue raised toward the soft palate (*velum*). (E.g., [g], [k].) Also called *guttural*.

velar vowel: A synonym of *back vowel* (q.v.).

Veltparl: An artificial language, a modified form of Volapük, created by von Arnim in 1896.

Venetian: (1) The dialect of the city of Venice; (2) a group of North Italian dialects, spoken in Venetia, Alto Adige and Julian Venetia (Trieste, Gorizia, Pola, etc.), as well as in some cities of Dalmatia. These dialects are generally characterized by Central Italian vocalism and Gallo-Italian consonantism.

Venetic: An extinct Indo-European language, once spoken around the Adriatic; variously assumed to have been an Italic dialect, a dialect of Illyrian, etc.

Vepsian: A member of the Finnish group of the Finno-Ugric (or Uralic) sub-family of the Ural-Altaic family of languages.

verb: That part of speech which expresses an action, a process, state or condition or mode of being.

verb-adjective: See *verbal adjective*.

verb husk: A term occasionally used to refer to verbal forms which no longer have verbal functions.

verb language: A language which uses mainly or solely *verb sentences* (q.v.).

verb-noun: See *verbal noun*.

verb of complete predication: A verb which has a complete meaning when used as a predicate without any complement. (Usually an intransitive verb.)

verb of incomplete predication: A verb without a complete meaning when used by itself, and which when used as predicate requires some complement. (Usually a transitive verb.)

verb-phrase: According to the Joint Committee on Grammatical Nomenclature, "an auxiliary with another verb-form is to be called a verb-phrase."

verb sentence: A sentence in which a finite verb is the main part (Graff calls it "pivotal part").

verbal (*noun*): A collective term for those words which have the nature of a verb as well as that of a noun (*verbal noun*) or adjective (*verbal adjective*)—i.e., infinitives, participles, gerunds, gerundives and supines.

verbal (*adj.*): Pertaining to or characteristic of verbs; derived from a verb.

verbal adjective: A participle—so called because it is an adjective but has verbal qualities.

verbal aspects: See *aspect*.

verbal preposition: A participle used in a prepositional sense.

vernacular: The current spoken daily language of a people or of a geographical area, as distinguished from the literary language used primarily in schools and in literature.

Verner's Law: The philological law formulated by Karl Verner in 1875, stating that the Teutonic medial voiceless spirants f, θ, h, hw, s became v, $\eth$, g, gw, z, respectively, and final s became z, when in contact with voiced consonants, unless the original Indo-European accent was on the preceding vowel.

Vestinian: One of the extinct dialects of the Sabellian branch of the Italic group of the Indo-European family of languages.

vetative: Expressing a prohibition.

Vietnamese: The name recently adopted for *Annamese* (q.v.).

Visaya: An alternative name of the *Bisaya* language.

Visible Speech: The system of phonetic transcription originated by A. M. Bell, indicating the part played by the speech organs in the production of each phoneme.

vocable: A word considered as a combination of spoken sounds or written signs, and not as a semantic symbol.

vocabulary: (1) The *lexicon* (q.v.) of a given language.—(2) The total stock of words at the command of a given individual. —(3) A dictionary.

vocalic consonants: In phonetical terminology, those consonants which may occasionally function as vowels, i.e.: the liquids l and r, and the nasals m and n.

vocalism: The scientific study, historical or descriptive, of the vowel system of a language or dialect.

vocalization: (1) The change of a consonant to a vowel. (2) In Hebrew writing, the indication of vowel sounds by the diacritic marks called *Masoretic points*.

vocative: A declensional case, still surviving in some Indo-European languages, used for the form of direct address.

Vogul: A language, belonging to the Ob-Ugrian group of the Ugric branch of the Finno-Ugric (or Uralic) sub-family of the Ural-Altaic family of languages; spoken by about 5,000 persons in Asiatic Russia.

voice: (I) Grammatically, the verbal category expressing whether the subject of the verb is the agent of the action or exists in the condition or state denoted by the verb (*active voice*), or is the recipient or target of the action (*passive voice*). Many languages have also a *middle voice* (q.v.). —(2) Phonemically, one of the possible relevant features of a phoneme.

voiced: In phonetical terminology, said of a consonant pronounced with a vibration of the vocal cords.

voiceless: In phonetical terminology, said of a consonant pronounced without any vibration of the vocal cords.

voicing: The change of a consonant from the voiceless (q.v.) to the voiced (q.v.) pronunciation.

Volapük: An artificial language created by Johann Martin Schleyer in 1880.

volitive: A designation of the verbal form or mood used in expressing an intention, wish, etc.

Volscian: One of the extinct dialects of the Sabellian branch of the Italic group of the Indo-European family of languages.

voluntative: A synonym for *volitive* (q.v.).

Votian: A member of the Finnish group of the Finno-Ugric (or Uralic) sub-family of the Ural-Altaic family of languages.

Votyak: A member of the Permian branch of the Finno-Ugric (or Uralic) sub-family of the Ural-Altaic family of languages; the native tongue of about 425,000 persons in Asiatic Russia.

vowel: (1) A sound produced with a vibration of the vocal cords, by the unobstructed passage of air through the oral cavity.— (2) A letter representing such a sound.

vowel fracture: The diphthongization of a simple vowel under the influence of a neighboring sound or sounds. (The German term is *Brechung*.)

vowel gradation: A change in internal vowels of a word to indicate distinctions in meaning (e.g., different tenses in a verb). Vowel gradation may be *qualitative* (change to a different vowel) or *quantitative* (lengthening, shortening or suppression of the vowel). [The German term is *Ablaut*.]

vowel harmony: The phonetic rule observed, more or less strictly and universally, in the Finno-Ugric languages, also in Turkish, Manchu, etc., according to which any given word may contain only back vowels or only front vowels, but a back vowel and a front vowel may not occur in the same word. In these languages, this principle is of paramount importance in the selection of the proper suffixes or case-endings. (The *middle vowel* [*i*] may occur in combination with back vowels as well as with front vowels.)

vowel mutation: A vowel change caused by the presence of a vowel (sometimes a semivowel or even a consonant) in the following syllable. Customarily referred to, with the German term, as *umlaut*.

vowel quality: That characteristic property in producing an acoustic effect which distinguishes a vowel from another vowel or other vowels.

vox nihili: A synonym for *phantom word* or *ghost word* (q.v.).

vulgar: When prefixed to the name of a language, this adjective designates that form of the language which is used by the great masses, in contradistinction to the literary form.

Vulgar Latin: The Latin vernacular spoken in Rome and all over the Roman Empire, in contradistinction to classical literary Latin. It was the successor of the *sermo familiaris* (q.v.) and survived the Roman Empire of the West.

vulgarism: A word or form of expression which violates the purity of diction; a debased form of colloquialism.

W

Walloon: A Romance dialect, closely related to French, spoken in southern Belgium and northeastern France.

wave theory: The theory (*Wellentheorie*) formulated by Johannes Schmidt in 1872, according to which related languages originated from a common center, the parent language, and spread from that center in all directions, like waves around a stone dropped into the water.

weak: This adjective is applied in the grammars of many languages (notably the Germanic languages) to those verbs the past tense of which is formed by the addition of suffixes and without internal vowel change, as well as to those nouns which undergo no vowel change in their declension and form their oblique cases and plural forms by taking on the suffix *-n* or *-en*.

weak conjugation: In the Germanic languages, the conjugation of the weak verbs (q.v.).

weak declension: In German, and related languages, (1) the declension of the *weak nouns* (q.v.), (2) the inflection of an adjective when it is preceded by an indefinite article or by a pronoun of the same function or force.

weak noun: In Germanic languages, a noun which never undergoes an internal vowel change (*umlaut*).

weak phoneme: Cf. *strong (2)*.

weak verb: In the grammar of various Indo-European languages (notably the Germanic group), the designation of those verbs which form the various tenses, especially the past or imperfect tense, by the addition of regular, uniform suffixes, without internal vowel change.

Welsh: A language of the Brythonic branch of the Celtic group of the Indo-European family, spoken in Wales by about 1,000,000 people. (Also called *Cymric* or *Cymraeg*.)

Wend: See *Lusatian*.

Wen-li: The traditional standardized literary language of China; its written symbols have no phonetic values, but are mere ideographs and are pronounced differently by the speakers of different Chinese vernaculars. (The new "National Tongue" of China, called *Kuo-yü*, uses the *Wen-li* symbols with definite, uniform spoken values assigned to each.)

West Germanic: A branch of the Germanic group of the Indo-European family of languages, consisting of the Anglo-Frisian subdivision (Anglo-Saxon, its modern descendant, English, and Frisian), the German and Dutch (including Flemish) languages, with their numerous dialects and variants.

West Romance: A collective name for those Romance languages and dialects (Portuguese, Spanish, French, Provençal, Sardinian, Rumansch, North Italian) which are characterized by retention of the Latin final *-s* and by the tendency to voice or drop Latin intervocalic plosives (cf. *East Romance*). This division of Romance is rejected by some Romanists.

West Saxon: That Anglo-Saxon (Old English) dialect, from which the Southern division of Middle English was derived.

West Semitic: A branch of the Semitic group of the Semito-Hamitic family of languages, divided into Northern West Semitic (Aramaic and Canaanite) and Southern West Semitic (North Arabic, or Arabic proper, South Arabic, and Ethiopic).

West Slavic: A branch of the Slavic group of the Indo-European family of languages, comprising Polish, Czech, Slovak, Lusatian (also called Wend or Sorbian), Kaszub and the now extinct Polabian.

West Tokharian: The designation (*Westtocharisch*) applied by W. Krause to *Tokharian B* (see *Tokharian*).

Western Aramaic: A branch of Aramaic, a Northern West Semitic language, used as a *lingua franca* in the Near East from the fourth century B.C. till the middle of the seventh century A.D. The known variants of Western Aramaic were: Old Aramaic, Biblical Aramaic, Palestinian Aramaic (including Palestinian Judaeo-Aramaic and Christian Palestinian Aramaic) and Samaritan. Western Aramaic survives as the spoken language of a small speech-community in the Ante-Lebanon.

Western Caucasian: A branch (also called *Abasgo-Kerketian*) of the North Caucasian family of languages. It consists of the Adyghe, Abkaz and Ubyk groups.

Western (Standard) Hindi: An Indic language; the number of its native speakers is estimated at 38,000,000.

Western Laotian: Thai Yüan (q.v.).

Western Mongol: See *Kalmuk*.

Western Turkic: A language-group, a subdivision of the Turkic branch of the Altaic (or Turco-Tartaric) sub-family of the Ural-Altaic family of languages; it comprises Bashkir, Chuvash, Irtysh and Kirghiz.

whisper: In phonetical terminology, the sound-waves produced by the vocal cords in contact, while the space between the arytenoids remains open.

White Russian: An East Slavic language, the native tongue of about 10,000,000 persons in Western Russia, eastern Poland and Lithuania. (Also called *Byelorussian*.)

widened meaning: The use of a word with a specific meaning in an extended or more general sense (e.g., when a lion or a tiger is referred to as a "cat"). (Cf. *narrowed meaning*.)

Wisa: See *Bisa*.

Wolof: An African Negro language, member of the Sudanese-Guinean family of languages.

word: A spoken or written symbol of an idea, usually regarded as the smallest independent sense-unit. Variously defined as "the smallest significant unit of speech and language" (*Ullman*), "a minimum free form" (*Bloomfield*), "the smallest speech-unit capable of functioning as a complete utterance" (*Palmer*), etc.

word group: Two or more words used in close combination, but without forming a compound word.

word order: The sequence or relative position of words in a sentence.

word stress: The stress (q.v.) within a word.

word writing: Logography (q.v.).

world-auxiliary: A generic term for artificial languages.

wrenched accent: Incorrectly placed vocal stress.

writing: The act of representing, or the representation, of thoughts, ideas and speech by conventional material signs.

Wu: A Chinese vernacular, spoken by about 40,000,000 persons around the Yang-tse Delta (Shanghai, Soochow).

Wyandot: See *Huron*.

Xhosa: An alternative name of the *Kafir* language.
Xosa: An alternative name of the *Kafir* language.

Y

Yakut: A language spoken in northeastern Asia; while generally considered a member of the Altaic sub-family of the Ural-Altaic family of languages, some linguists classify it as a member of the Turkic branch, and some others regard it as a member of the Mongol group.

Yao: (1) A Man (q.v.) language, spoken by about 30,000 persons in Upper Burma and southwestern China.—(2) An East African Negro language, member of the Bantu family of languages.

Yärava: A Little Andamanese language, spoken on South Andaman Island.

Yarkand: An Asiatic language, member of the Central Turkic group of the Altaic sub-family of the Ural-Altaic family of languages.

Yenisei-Ostyak: A language spoken in the Yenisei River region, in eastern Siberia, by about 1,000 persons; considered by some linguists to constitute, with the extinct Cottian (or Kottish) a branch of the Sino-Tibetan family, while others hold the view that Yenisei-Ostyak and Cottian form an isolated linguistic family. (Not identical with *Ostyak*, which is a Finno-Ugric language.)

Yeru: A Great Andamanese language.

Yiddish: A language spoken by Jews in Eastern Europe and America; it is based on fourteenth-century German with admixtures of Hebrew, Slavic and Romance (recently also English) words, and is written with a modified Hebrew alphabet. The number of the native speakers of Yiddish was estimated, prior to World War II, at 7,500,000.

yodization: The changing of a pure vowel (usually *e* or *i*) in hiatus (q.v.) into the semivowel which in English orthography is usually written *y*, and called *yod* after a letter of the Hebrew alphabet. (E.g., the Latin *vinea*, which was pronounced as three syllables, changed into the Vulgar Latin *vinya*, sounded as a two-syllable word.)

yo-he-ho theory: Noiré's theory, according to which human speech originated in the sounds produced by the strong expulsion of breath by primitive men when performing any work requiring strong muscular effort, i.e., sounds produced spontaneously, without any conscious effort to imitate natural sounds.

Yoruba: An African Negro language, spoken by about 2,500,000 persons in western Nigeria; a member of the Sudanese-Guinean family of languages.

Young Grammarians: See *Junggrammatiker*.

Yüeh: See *Cantonese*.

Yurak: A member of the Samoyedic group of the Finno-Ugric (or Uralic) sub-family of the Ural-Altaic family of languages; spoken by a few thousand persons.

Z

Zande: One of the Ubangi (q.v.) dialects.

Zapotec: A family of Central American Indian languages, consisting of Zapotec proper, Chatino, Papabuko and Soltec, spoken in southern Mexico.

Zenaga: A language, of the Berber group of the Hamitic subfamily of the Semito-Hamitic family of languages, spoken in Mauritania.

Zend: An alternative name for *Avestan* (q.v.).

Zenete: A group of Berber dialects spoken in North and North-East Africa.

zero: This word is used to express *lack* or *absence of*. (E.g., *zero tonality, zero ending*, etc.)

zero ending: In morphology, the bare stem of a word when used as such in discourse is said to have zero ending.

zeugma: A construction in which one word is made to serve a double purpose in the same sentence, by relating to two different words—to one of these expressly, to the other one in a supplementary sense.

Zulu: An African Negro language, spoken in Zululand, Natal, Cape Colony and the South-East African Coast; a member of the Bantu family of languages.

Zyrien: A language, also called Syryen, member of the Permian branch of the Finno-Ugric (or Uralic) sub-family of the Ural-Altaic family of languages; the native tongue of about 260,000 persons in Asiatic Russia.